THE FIGHTING
ISRAELI
AIR FORCE

THE FIGHTING
ISRAELI AIR FORCE

Brig. Gen. Stanley M. Ulanoff, USAR
Lt. Col. David Eshel, IDF, Ret.

ARCO PUBLISHING, INC.
NEW YORK

Published by Arco Publishing, Inc.
215 Park Avenue South, New York, N.Y. 10003

Library of Congress Cataloging in Publication Data

Ulanoff, Stanley M.
   The fighting Israeli Air Force.

   Includes index.
   1. Israel. Hel ha-avir. I. Eshel, David. II. Title.
UG635.I75U43   1985   358.4'0095694   84-16871
ISBN 0-668-05578-2 (Cloth Edition)

Printed in the United States of America

10 9 8 7 6 5 4 3 2 1

Dedication

To the heroes of the Israel Air Force and their comrades in the Israel Defence Force. May their bravery be rewarded with peace.

Contents

Acknowledgments

Eshel-Dramit Ltd., Israel. Text and photos excerpted from a number of Eshel-Dramit periodic publications, including *Born in Battle* (now titled *Defence Update International*), copyright 1978 through 1983 by Eshel-Dramit, Ltd.

Israel Defence Force Spokesman. *The Israeli Air Force in the Yom Kippur War,* published by the Historical Division, Israel Air Force, Ministry of Defence, Tel Aviv, Israel.

Official U.S. Government Publications. Excerpts from DOD PG-10A and *MATS Flyer.*

Maj. Charles E. Mayo, "Lebanon: An Air Defense Analysis," *Air Defense Artillery,* Winter 1983.

The authors gratefully acknowledge the cooperation of the Israel Defence Force, which has given its permission to reprint excerpts from various official documents in this book.

THE FIGHTING
ISRAELI AIR FORCE

Chapter 1

Thunder in the Sky—
An Overview

Knifing across the Lebanese border like giant juggernauts, four massive columns of Israeli tanks, armored personnel carriers, and self-propelled artillery—each miles long—raced north, past United Nations Force checkpoints, in pursuit of Palestine Liberation Organization (PLO) terrorists. Above them roared the Israeli Air Force's (IAF) F-16 Fighting Falcons and F-15 Eagles, prepared to do battle with the MiG-21s and MiG-23s of the Syrian Air Force, if the Syrians chose to oppose them in the skies over Lebanon. The Israelis called it Operation Peace for Galilee; it was the sixth Arab–Israeli war since Israel declared its independence in 1948.

Gray wings flashing in the sunlight, the Israeli F-15 dropped its fuel tanks as it wheeled and turned in a long, graceful, descending arc to pounce upon a desert-camouflaged Syrian MiG-21 above Lebanon's Bekaa Valley. His head constantly turning to the right and to the left and his eyes darting to the mirror (to make certain that no enemy fighter was approaching from either side or from the rear), the Israeli fighter pilot fixed the MiG in his sights. Closing the gap between them, he could see clearly the green, white, and black cockade with three tiny red stars in the white ring on its fuselage. He fired a Shafrir air-to-air missile that flew unerringly at the tailpipe of the enemy aircraft ahead of him. It struck with an explosive flash of flame and smoke. This was the young Israeli lieutenant's first victory on his first combat mission, but he had no time to think about it. As he broke sharply to the right to avoid the

cloud of debris that had been the MiG he was pursuing, his wingman flashed by to finish off a MiG-23. The neophyte, now a veteran, wagged the wings of his American-built fighter plane as a sign of victory. The blue, six-pointed Star of David in the white circle shone brightly as he dived after another Syrian MiG. Ironically, he dreaded returning to base more than facing the enemy in combat, for traditionally an IAF pilot is dunked in a big tank of water by his ground crew following his first air-to-air victory. Darting in and out, diving, climbing, he plunged into the fray once more. Other Soviet-made MiG-21s and 23s fell from the sky around him, trailing smoke and flame as triumphant Israeli F-16s and F-15s roared by. Hundreds of fighter aircraft were engaged over Lebanon in the greatest of all air battles since World War II. Neither the Korean nor the Vietnam wars, nor any other preceding Arab–Israeli conflicts had seen such a scrap in the sky—a dogfight most reminiscent of World War I.

On two fateful days in early June 1982, Syrian fighters tore at the Israeli machines with a vengeance, despite the fact that the government of Israel had informed Syria and had announced publicly that its quarrel was not with them and that Israelis would only fire if fired upon. Unfortunately, this was not to be. Both air forces wer equipped with the latest, most up-to-date aircraft and weapons—the best that U.S. and Soviet technology could produce. When the smoke of battle had cleared, close to 90 Soviet-built MiGs littered the Bekaa Valley below, and

The world's hottest jet fighter—the McDonnell Douglas F-15A Eagle—in IAF colors. This newest addition to the air force was delivered in December 1976. Each plane cost some 16 million dollars—without spare engines or parts, or any other ancillary equipment.

not one IAF plane had fallen in air-to-air combat.

In the first of these great air battles, the IAF tangled with 60 enemy MiGs and destroyed 35 of them. The remaining Syrian aircraft withdrew to lick their wounds. The following day 50 MiGs rose to challenge the Israeli Air Force, but not a solitary enemy jet returned to base. The battle score was an astounding 85 to 0. From that moment on, the Syrian high command kept its fighters on the ground, leaving IAF in undisputed control of the skies over Lebanon—a protective cover for the advancing Israeli ground forces.

At the end of August 1982, the prestigious London-based Institute for Strategic Studies announced that the tiny nation of Israel was the fourth strongest military power in the world, following immediately behind the United States, the Soviet Union, and China. However, it also stated unequivocally that *the Israeli Air*

Force is second to none! In the words of the Institute, the IAF is "without doubt the best in the world."

Earlier that same month Gen. Wilbur L. Creech, commander of the USAF Tactical Air Command, had stated that, up to that time in the conflict, the IAF had destroyed 92 Syrian Soviet-built MiG-23s and MiG-21s, 85 of them in air-to-air combat. The Israelis had accomplished this without the loss of a single fighter of their own. According to Gen. Creech, approximately half of the Syrian aircraft losses were of the advanced MiG-23 model and the balance were MiG-21s. The U.S.-built Israeli F-15 Eagles had shot down 40 of the enemy MiGs; 18 additional MiGs had been brought down prior to the onset of the conflict in Lebanon. Forty-four Syrian MiGs fell to Israeli Shafrir and U.S.-made Sidewinder air-to-air missiles fired by IAF F-16 Fighting Falcons, and one of the MiGs was shot down by an older F-4 Phan-

An IAF F-16 Fighting Falcon armed with Sidewinder air-to-air missiles.

tom. Another USAF general, America's top soldier, Gen. David C. Jones, Chairman of the Joint Chiefs of Staff, had only one word for the stunning performance of the IAF in battle: "Fabulous!"

In addition to the crushing victory over the Syrian Air Force, U.S. intelligence confirmed that the IAF had wiped out 23 Syrian Soviet-made anti-aircraft missile sites in Lebanon's Bekaa Valley, again without the loss of a single Israeli jet fighter. The missile battalion, which had been brought in from Syria to reinforce their existing batteries in the valley *after* the Israelis had moved into Lebanon, was the IAF's primary target when its pilots were opposed by the MiGs in that classic dogfight. The destroyed SAM missiles consisted of 19 mobile SA-6s, ten of which were destroyed in one brief ten-minute attack. The remaining missile batteries were the far superior mobile SA-8s, SA-2s, and SA-3s. In the following days, the Syrians brought in more SAMs, but they too were systematically destroyed by the IAF.

One of the reasons given by Gen. Creech for the brilliant performance of the Israeli Air Force was their astounding rate of readiness. For example, the IAF reported all of its 72 F-16s ready for battle each morning. By comparison, the USAF can field only 60 percent of its force. (This, however, is a peacetime rate and the general predicted that the Americans could match it in wartime. However, he added, "I don't mean to suggest that we (the U.S.) can get an 85-to-0 kill ratio" against the Soviets, "but I think we can do very, very well.") Another reason for the unequaled performance of the IAF in combat is its superior equipment, including the American-built Grumman E-2C Hawkeye battle-control aircraft—a junior-size AWAC with the capability to provide its fighters with the element of surprise. Yet another reason is the superior quality of IAF personnel (pilots and ground crews), their training, their high morale, and their reason for fighting. Israeli ground crews repair, rearm, and refuel their aircraft in an extremely short time. Their turn-around rate is unequaled anywhere. However, their "reason for fighting" is probably the most important for the success of the Israeli Air Force: They are the air force of a free democratic nation, the only one in the entire Middle East, and *they are fighting for their very survival!*

To sum up, IAF personnel have high morale and spirit, superior skill, a willingness to die for their freedom and independence, the tenacity to hold on to and fight for what they believe in, dogged determination not to be "pushed around," and sheer military effectiveness. When asked by CBS Network News commentator Mike Wallace about the strength of the Israeli military forces, the late Gen. S.L.A. Marshall, AUS ret., a distinguished military authority, replied that "they took desperate chances, and they are superb marksmen, probably the best the world has ever seen, both in the air and on land."

Attesting to that statement is the fact that the IAF did not, as was commonly believed, use "secret weapons" ("smart" bombs or other electronic weapons) to wipe out the enemy air forces during the Six-Day War. They simply employed extremely accurate airborne cannon fire and conventional "iron" bombs. In fact, the Israelis had insisted on keeping these "obsolete" weapons in lieu of more modern ones that Dassault, the French aircraft manufacturer, wanted to install on the IAF's new Mirages and Mystères.

At some time before the Israeli drive into Lebanon in the spring of 1982, Menachem Begin, at that time the peppery, outspoken prime minister of the tiny Jewish state, paid a glowing tribute to the IAF. Never at a loss for words himelf, in this case he chose to repeat the historic accolade given to the British Royal Air Force, under similar circumstances, by then Prime Minister Winston Churchill during the grim, dark days of World War II: "Never in the field of human conflict was so much owed by so many to so few." This glowing, heartfelt tribute was Churchill's expression of undying gratitude to the fighter pilots of the RAF, that handful of men who had saved their island nation from annihilation by the powerful Nazi war machine during the critical Battle of Britain. Prime Minister Begin's parallel tribute to the IAF was also fully justified, fitting, and proper.

The Israeli Air Force is the air arm of the Israeli Defense Force (IDF), as the Israeli Navy is its sea arm. Like the USAF and the RAF, it is simultaneously an integral part of the overall defense force and an independent arm. (The USAF became an independent force in 1947, shortly after the end of World War II, in which it had served as the Army Air Force. The RAF changed its status from the British Army's Royal Flying Corps in the middle of World War I.) The IAF is known in Israel as Cheyl Ha Avir (the "Ch" is pronounced with a guttural sound, as it would be in German). It literally means "corps of the air."

Respected by friend and foe alike as a superior fighting unit, the Israeli Air Force is one of the most formidable military organizations in the world—not in number of aircraft or pilots but as an experienced, professional fighting group. As for professionalism, it is interesting to note that a good part of the strength of the Cheyl Ha Avir comes from reservists or part-time soldiers—both officers and enlisted ranks, pilots and mechanics—who in most armies are considered "weekend warriors." But the Israeli reservists are most definitely first-class professionals. Usually outnumbered but never outfought, IAF aircrews have seen action on a continuous basis from the inception of their nation to the present. They have seen more combat and fought in more wars than any other air force in the world (with the possible exception of the opposing Arab air forces). In all, they have fought six major wars and have been engaged in a constant series of battles with one or more of the hostile neighboring Arab states. Not only has the IAF been victorious in air-to-air combat over its Arab adversaries, but the fighter aircraft of the vaunted British Royal Air Force and of the Red Air Force of the USSR have fallen before their guns, as well.

Born in battle, in 1948, the Cheyl Ha Avir was blooded at that time and has continued to play a major role in keeping Israel free from those who would destroy her. It was in mid-May 1948 that the British mandate over Palestine was ending and the State of Israel was about to emerge. Poised on the borders of this tiny new nation (112 kilometers at its widest point and 10 at its narrowest) were the regular armies of six Arab nations, outnumbering the fledgling

Israeli Defense Force ten to one in arms, men, and equipment. As the British convoys pulled out, the Arab hordes poured in. The State of Israel was born. The War of Independence had begun!

History clearly shows that the Jewish people have always lived with the threat of annihilation hanging over their heads. The Promised Land and Jerusalem, its capital and site of the Temple, had the ill fortune of being at the crossroads of the great trade routes of Europe, Asia, and Africa, putting the Hebrews at the mercy of the great powers for more than a thousand years. From biblical times their land—the same land the Israelis are fighting to hold today—has been coveted and invaded by other peoples. These have included the Philistines, Assyrians, Babylonians, Persians, Greeks, Romans, Crusaders, Turks, British, and Arabs, to name a few. And, historically, once the Jewish people were scattered to the "four corners of the earth" (the Diaspora) by the Romans, they lived in and became citizens of many other countries. There, as minorities, they have been the scapegoats whenever these countries suffered economic, religious, political, military, or other reverses. Typical of such periods of persecution were the Spanish Inquisition, the pogroms or massacres in Poland and Russia, and the more recent Nazi holocaust of World War II. Fearsome as was the Arab boast to "push them into the sea," history had proven that they could survive, and the new nation was determined to prevail. The world's newest fighting force was in a struggle for its very life.

BIRTH OF THE IAF

The IAF began in the Jewish Settlement in the British Mandate of Palestine with the creation of the Sherut Avir, or Air Service, by the Haganah on November 10, 1947. The new service immediately acquired 11 light planes from Aviron, a civilian aviation company. (Most of these aircraft were manufactured in Poland.) Its pilots were recruited from among the flying clubs that existed in Palestine at that time and from the few Palestinian Jews who were trained by, and flew with, the RAF in World War II.

Three of these RAF veterans later served as commanders of the IAF.

The first commander of the Air Service was Yehoshua Eshel. His original command consisted of a "squadron" that flew out of Lydda Airport, and later from Sde Dov Airfield in Tel Aviv. This force, formerly commanded by Eli Feingras, was immediately expanded into two units—the Galil Squadron and the Negev Squadron. Early in 1948 the Sherut Avir acquired 21 British Auster aircraft as surplus equipment from RAF bases in Palestine. This was the tiny force that served the Jewish population in Palestine at the outbreak of the War of Independence.

THE WAR OF INDEPENDENCE

At this time the Air Service undertook reconnaissance missions, and maintained communications with isolated settlements (including beleaguered Jerusalem and the isolated settlements of the Ezion bloc, the Negev, and the Galil). The Air Service flew mail, supplies, weapons, and ammunition to the besieged settlements, relieved commanders, evacuated casualties, and protected the Negev water pipelines. Its planes accompanied marching columns and even engaged in small-scale combat missions. In Operation Nachshon (whose mission was to clear the roads and break through to Jerusalem) Israeli planes attacked Arab troops and armor concentrations and guided relief columns making their way to Jerusalem.

On May 14, 1948, the State of Israel declared its independence. At the end of May, Zahal, or the Israel Defense Force, was established, and along with it the Israeli Air Force. On the day after the declaration of independence, regular Arab armies invaded Israel; the Egyptian Air Force, the largest of the Arab air forces, bombed Tel Aviv and Egyptian Spitfires strafed Sde Dov airfield. With the armed forces of four neighboring nations—Egypt, Lebanon, Syria, and Jordan—plus contingents from Iraq, the Sudan, Saudi Arabia, and Morocco roaring across their border, the neophyte IAF, armed

An Israeli Messerschmitt Bf-109. This fighter had been the pride of the Nazi Luftwaffe in World War II.

with only a handful of light planes and facing an onslaught of squadrons of Hurricanes, Spitfires, Furies, Fiat G-55s, and other first-class fighter aircraft, was truly born in battle.

On May 18, the Central Bus Station in Tel Aviv was bombed. Protection against air attack amounted to a few rifles and machine guns. An effort was underway to procure transport and fighter planes abroad, and Operation Balack brought Messerschmitt fighters from Czechoslovakia in the bellies of surplus C-47 Dakotas bought in the United States.

The acquisition of the Messerschmitts presented a strange situation. Paradoxically, young Israeli pilots who had flown British Spitfires for the RAF two years earlier were now flying BF-109s, the great German fighters that had flown against them in World War II. The plane was also a symbol of the Nazi oppression that had ruthlessly murdered six million of their fellow Jews. On May 29, four Messerschmitts (the first ones in the country) attacked and stopped an Egyptian armored column that had

reached Ashdod, 20 miles south of Tel Aviv. The following day, Israeli aircraft foiled an Iraqi and Jordanian assault from Tulkarm on Kfar Yona. On June 3, two Egyptian Dakotas again attempted to bomb Tel Aviv but were shot down by Modi Allon flying the only available Messerschmitt.

Meanwhile, by various unconventional methods, the procurement campaign was bringing in B-17s, Spitfires, Beaufighters, Mustangs, and other aircraft, which were immediately thrown into action. Israeli planes bombed Cairo, Gaza, El-Arish, Damascus, Kuneitra, and Amman, though these and other missions required considerable effort and improvisation in the maintenance and arming of aircraft and fighting methods.

The initiative of the air was slowly swinging in favor of the Israeli Air Force. Fighters and bombers began to play an active part in the IDF's large-scale operations in the Negev, center and north of the country, while transport planes moved troops to the Negev and kept up

Spitfire Mk-IXE being revved up in its hardstand on an air base in southern Israel.

the flow of supplies and ammunition from abroad. The air force was also beefed up by the arrival of "Machal" and "Gachal," volunteer pilots from abroad with experience gained in World War II, who contributed greatly to the IAF effort. Meanwhile, in the thick of battle, the IAF continued to train new pilots. In spite of its small size, the young air force coped successfully with the Egyptian Air Force in air combat and inflicted heavy losses upon it. Toward the end of the war, the IAF led attacks on enemy forces on all fronts. During the "Ten Days" battle, the IAF supported ground forces in different operations, and its airplanes bombed Cairo.

During the late operations of the war, the IAF continued its intensive activity, shooting down enemy planes in aerial combat, carrying troops, leading tactical attacks, and supporting ground forces. The logistic potential of the IAF was demonstrated during the War of Independence in Operations Balack and Avack, in which cargo planes of the air cargo wing transported equipment, armament, and ammunition from abroad and brought reinforcements and supplies to the fronts. As a result, the mobility of the army was increased. These operations emphasized the superiority of the IAF. On January 7, 1949—at the end of Operation Horev—this superiority was further demonstrated by the shooting down of four Spitfires and one Tempest of the RAF, which were flying patrols in support of Egyptian forces, over the battlefields of the south. Aerial combat in the War of Independence resulted in the destruction of 15 Egyptian and two Syrian planes. The two principal Arab air forces virtually ceded the skies over Israel to the Israeli Air Force.

FROM THE WAR OF INDEPENDENCE TO THE SINAI CAMPAIGN

At the end of the war, most of the Machal, the foreign volunteers, returned to their homes, and the IAF Command began to shape and organize the Israeli Air Force as a permanent arm of the IDF. The first task was to create a structure for training pilots and mechanics. A most important milestone in this development of the IAF was the formation of the Flight School. Its first four graduates received their wings in 1950. That same year, the Air Force Technical School was also founded, with the purpose of preparing ground crews and maintenance personnel. The beginning of 1950 was also marked by the establishment of tactical conceptions. These concepts were at the base of the air combat doctrine in the following order of priority:

- protection of Israeli skies
- achievement of aerial superiority by destruction of enemy airpower
- participation in the ground war, transport, and casualty evacuation

Organizationally, the IAF was structured on the principle of centralized control, with three main branches: Air (Operations), Equipment, and Manpower. Following prolonged discussion in the IDF General Staff, it was decided that the IAF was to be an independent arm, oriented to combat in the air and from the air. Because of budgetary limitations and the severe economic straits of Israel, aircraft procurement abroad was directed to World War II-vintage piston-engine planes: Mosquitoes and Mustangs began to replace Messerschmitts and Spitfires in the order of battle.

The Arab states had not reconciled themselves to the existence of Israel, and the armistice agreements were not considered as any more than a temporary "time-out" in the war to destroy the new state. The Arabs began to rearm with modern weapons that included jet aircraft from Britain. Then, in 1955, Egypt signed an arms deal with Czechoslovakia under which 200 Soviet jet fighters and bombers, 530 armored vehicles, 500 artillery pieces, naval vessels, etc., began to arrive on the Middle Eastern scene. The balance of power was decidedly tilting against Israel.

In 1952, the IAF acquired the last of its propeller-driven fighters, the Mosquito. Israel could not afford to lag behind the Arabs, and so, in 1953, the first Meteor jets were purchased in England. Strengthened political ties with France led to the procurement, in 1955, of Ouragans and, in 1956, of swept-wing Mystère IVs. However, the Israeli Air Force did not succeed in closing the quantitative gap and therefore did not withdraw piston-engine aircraft from its tables of organization and equipment or order of battle. Consequently, all systems had to be capable of operating and maintaining both modern and obsolete craft.

The IAF kept a constant vigil. Egyptian Air Force jets flew reconnaissance sorties near the border and attempted to penetrate Israeli airspace. One result was an aerial battle over Yad Mordechai in which two Egyptian Vampire jets were shot down, followed by another skirmish in April 1956. These clashes proved the superiority of IAF pilots, closing the quantitative gap by means of quality.

THE SINAI CAMPAIGN

In this campaign, Israel fought alongside its British and French allies. When the IDF entered the Sinai campaign on October 29, 1956, the IAF employed jet formations for the first time. The operation included approximately 50 jet fighters and an equal number of piston-engine fighters. Before it began, eight pairs of Mustangs severed telephone lines in the Sinai with their propeller blades after special equipment designed for the purpose failed to function. The campaign opened when 16 IAF C-47 Dakotas dropped 395 paratroopers of the 890th Battalion in the Mitla Pass. The planes, escorted by 12 Ouragans, flew at low altitude to avoid Egyptian radar. With the parachute drops in the Mitla and later at At-Tur, the Israeli Air Force demonstrated its striking attributes: mobility, speed, operational range, and payload capability. The Mitla drop added new dimensions to IDF strategic doctrine: the

A Dassault Mystère IVA jet fighter-bomber. First seen in action with the IAF during the 1956 Sinai campaign as an interceptor, it remained in service as a ground-support aircraft to the beginning of the 1970s. Note the M4A3E8 Sherman (M50) tank mounting a 75-mm gun with a searchlight on the turret.

transfer of battle to the enemy's rear, surprise, and the indirect approach. During the campaign, the air force was called on to support ground forces by strafing roads and attacking enemy positions. The transport wing flew men, equipment, and supplies. In every air battle, the IAF demonstrated its superiority. Israeli pilots shot down seven Egyptian jets and scored hits on two others. No Israeli fighters were lost. On October 31, 1956, IAF planes joined naval craft in attacking and capturing the Egyptian destroyer *Ibrahim el-Awal.* Piper Cubs of the IAF did great work in facilitating effective control and coordination of ground forces by transferring senior officers from unit to unit, maintaining communications and reconnaissance flights, and evacuating the wounded. The campaign ended with a cease-fire on November 6.

BETWEEN THE SINAI CAMPAIGN AND THE SIX-DAY WAR

Following the Sinai campaign, the General Staff formulated the concept—already accepted by the air force—that the key to victory in war lies in the achievement of superiority in the air over the battlefield. The criteria for the distribution of defense resources were fixed accordingly, and priority was given to air power. At the same time the IAF was formulating its own concept: Victory should be achieved by an air attack on, and the destruction of, enemy air forces in the first stage of war. The freedom of the airspace over the battlefield that would thus

Fitting 127-mm rockets to P-51D Mustang.

be acquired would allow fast and efficient support to the IDF ground forces. In a parallel cushion, the air force also opted for the principle that multipurpose aircraft, both interceptor and attack planes, should form part of the order of battle.

Organization of the force was determined by the procurement of aircraft. First, all of the piston-engine planes were withdrawn and replaced by additional Mystères, Super Mystères, and Vautours. In 1962 the IAF acquired the French Dassault Mirage, one of the most modern warplanes in the world at the time. The Arab countries, meanwhile, were receiving MiG-17s, 19s, and 21s, Sukhoi-7s, and TU-16 bombers from the Soviet Union.

The period was characterized by tranquility on the Egyptian border. After the Sinai campaign, the waterway to Eilat was open, UN forces were on the Sinai border separating Israel from Egypt, and Egypt was busy with a remote war in Yemen. The Israeli Air Force continued to train with its new aircraft and to develop tactics and modern weapons systems. Exercises were held, lessons were learned, and contingency plans were prepared. Beginning in the mid-1960s, Israel developed a large-scale program, the National Water Carrier, which was intended to be a major factor in the economy of the country. The Arab countries, led by Syria, made considerable efforts to prevent implementation of the project and, following failure of those efforts, began to dig a canal on the Golan Heights to divert water sources from Israel. Border incidents were frequent. In November 1964 the IAF was activated to attack Syrian heavy equipment on the Golan. Tensions grew, and in July 1966 the Israeli Air Force

Mystère pilots receiving a final briefing before a mission.

struck at the heavy excavation equipment. There were also dogfights that claimed a number of Syrian MiGs.

At the end of 1966, two Egyptian MiG-19s were shot down on the southern frontier as they attempted to shoot down a light IAF Piper flying over Israeli territory. April 1967 saw more violent incidents on the Syrian border and on April 7, following a Syrian artillery bombardment of targets inside Israel, the IAF was called upon to silence the source of the gunfire. In the course of the attack, two aerial battles were fought in which six Syrian MiG-21s were brought down.

Israeli leaders warned the Syrians against a recurrence of the attacks on Israel's northern settlements. The Syrians spread rumors of concentrations of Israeli forces preparing for an assault on Syria. The Soviets and Eastern Bloc countries "confirmed" the concentrations, and the Russians recommended that the Egyptians mass forces on the southern border in order to compel Israel to thin out troop concentrations

in the north. Egypt publicly complied with the Soviet request and sounded fanfares of martial trumpets. Israel, with no interest in increased tension, repeated that it was not preparing for war and denied the Syrian allegations. The Israeli denials were taken by the Arabs, and primarily by President Nasser of Egypt, as a sign of weakness. The tension was further aggravated by the removal, upon Nasser's demand, of UN troops from the Sinai and by the closing of the straits leading to the port of Eilat. Israel did everything possible to prevent war but could not accept Egyptian forces massed on the border and, above all, could not accept the blockade of Eilat.

THE SIX-DAY WAR

At the start, it should be noted that the Six-Day War was the greatest feat of the IAF with the possible exception of the aforementioned

Mirage fighter pilots in G-suits carrying dome-type helmets. Over six days IAF pilots destroyed over 450 Arab combat planes on the ground or in the air, opening the way for ground troops to complete the victory.

victory over the Syrian Air Force, above Lebanon, 15 years later. The war began, on Israel's initiative, on June 5, 1967. The opening move was an Israeli Air Force strike on the Egyptian airfields. Within the first three hours, most of Egypt's air power was destroyed. The IAF followed up with attacks on all air forces of Syria, Jordan, and Iraq, with similar results. By noon of the first day, the Israeli Air Force held unchallenged superiority on the fronts and

began to provide support to the ground forces, primarily by flying sorties against enemy columns on the move toward Israeli lines in the Sinai, on both sides of the Jordan, and on the Golan Heights. The transports flew men, dropped supplies by parachute, and evacuated casualties, while the light planes flew reconnaissance missions and operated as artillery spotters. In the IAF strikes against enemy airfields, 391 planes were destroyed and 26 airfields were made completely unusable. Another 60 Egyptian, Syrian, Jordanian, and Iraqi aircraft were shot down in aerial combat. On the ground IAF planes destroyed some 500 tanks, other vehicles, gun batteries, dugouts, camps, supply bases, and many radar stations.

The Israeli Air Force conception of air superiority as the key to victory was confirmed irrefutably, as was the wisdom of coping with hostile air power on the ground in preemptive strikes as a means of achieving that superiority. The IAF's capability—the result of years of planning and training—was brought into play in the first three hours of the war. Israeli armor was free to move under skies free of hostile aircraft and, even more important, could receive massive air support to facilitate rapid mobility.

Within six days, four Arab armies had been routed, their dispositions smashed, their armor destroyed, and their forces dispersed. The IAF's share in this was decisive, and the airplane proved to be a versatile tool for a multitude of battlefield tasks. The IAF itself listed five reasons for the decisive victory:

1. Simplicity of planning and faith in success.
2. Almost total compatibility of planning and implementation.
3. Precise execution of orders by pilots.
4. Centralized control.
5. Precise intelligence.

WAR OF ATTRITION AND AFTER

Immediately after the Six-Day War, the Israeli Air Force participated in a new kind of warfare—against terrorists. At the end of 1967 IAF planes bombed terrorist concentrations in Jordan and silenced Jordanian artillery that had been shelling the Jordan River Valley settlements in Israel. Simultaneously, IAF helicopters played an important role in pursuing terrorists who had penetrated Israeli territory, enabling ground forces to find and destroy them. Meanwhile, the IAF continued to build up its strength in planes and manpower. However, Gen. Charles de Gaulle's political switch

in support of the Arabs and the resultant French embargo on the supply of planes and parts forced Israel to seek alternative sources. The era of American acquisitions was heralded by the A-4 Skyhawk, an excellent little fighter-bomber that contributed greatly to the air force's power. These were followed by the F-4 Phantom II, the American "top-of-the-line" fighter. In addition, the Israeli-built Kfir was added to the IAF inventory.

To the IDF, the War of Attrition on the Egyptian front posed the problem of Israeli artillery inferiority along the Suez Canal. Israeli Air Force Skyhawk and Phantom jets attacked and silenced Egyptian missile, anti-aircraft, and artillery batteries, thereby closing the "artillery gap." In addition, the Israeli Air Force took part in the IDF's daring raids behind enemy lines, some of which were well within Egyptian territory. In one such assault a complete Soviet radar station was transported by air to Israel. In January 1970 the IAF undertook strategic bombing missions deep in the heart of Egypt, which were to hit hard at Egypt's combat capability and expose her weaknesses, weaknesses that forced Egypt to demand Soviet military involvement in the form of an anti-aircraft defense system, built, regulated, and controlled by Soviet personnel.

The significant increase in Soviet involvement did not force the IAF to discontinue attacks on Egyptian positions along the Canal. On one such patrol, on July 30, 1970, *Israeli pilots, flying Phantoms and Mirages, found themselves doing battle with Soviet MiG-21s flown by Soviet pilots, and shot down five of them—without the loss of a single Israeli fighter.* Continuing air operations, in conjunction with Zahal ground activity and the resistance of the troops in forward strongholds, brought the Egyptians to a cease-fire agreement that took effect on August 7, 1970. In the last stage of the War of Attrition the principal problem facing IAF pilots was missile batteries supplied by the USSR to the Egyptian and Syrian armies. The Israeli Air Force developed various technological means and combat techniques to cope with the enemy's new anti-aircraft weapons (as will be discussed later).

After the cease-fire agreements with Egypt took effect, IAF pilots continued the effort of training for all types of attack and evasive maneuvers in air combat, ground support, night fighting, and, particularly, the attack on and evasion of missile batteries. Following the cease-fire, the main operational activities were in the northern sector, where the air force took part in battles with the Syrian Army and in attacking terrorist bases under Syrian protection. However, the Egyptian front was not absolutely calm, and IAF planes occasionally had to respond to provocations and penetrations of Israeli airspace.

THE YOM KIPPUR WAR

At the start of the Yom Kippur War, the Israeli Defense Force was effectively deprived of its strategic arm—the great IAF. Now Israeli pilots had to face the greatest density and mix of air defense systems ever deployed. More than 10,000 systems—including conventional anti-aircraft guns and the latest mobile SA-6 and SA-8 missiles, in addition to SA-2s and others—were physically arranged to provide a devastating cross fire and to cover both high- and low-altitude attacks. Clearly, it was a practical example of how the power of air superiority can be substantially diminished by massive air defense. With the Israeli Air Force practically immobilized, Egyptian forces were able to cross the Suez Canal and establish a beachhead. Although the Egyptian advantage was short-lived, it was a costly operation in terms of loss of life and equipment to both the IAF and the IDF.

The war began on October 6, 1973, as a surprise attack initiated by Egypt and Syria, with a heavy artillery bombardment and air attacks on IDF targets on the Golan Heights and in the Suez Canal area. Close on the heels of the bombardment, Egyptian troops crossed the Canal and Syrian forces broke through the IDF lines on the Golan. The few regular IDF units on both fronts were unable to prevent the breakthrough. The IAF went into action against the Canal crossings in the south and the advancing Syrians in the north in order to block their advance long enough for the reserve army to report for duty and move forward. Due to the efforts of the IAF, the entire reserve complex

was able to mobilize in its emergency bases, move up to the lines, and go into battle without fear of attack from the air. Not a single enemy plane penetrated Israeli airspace to attack mobile columns or other targets—though not for want of trying.

Once the IDF had deployed its reserves and had begun to repel the invaders, the air force turned to attack Syrian and Egyptian positions, bridges, and armor. Sorties were also flown against enemy airfields and missile batteries. The Syrians, having failed to attack targets in the north, began to launch ground-to-ground Frog missiles against civilian objectives in Israel. The Israeli Air Force responded by attacking economic and strategic targets in Syria, including the General Staff, air force and navy headquarters, power stations, fuel storage tanks, bridges, radar stations, and military installations.

The Syrians were pushed back from the Golan by October 10 with the help of massive air support. On the next day the IDF Northern Command opened a large-scale offensive on the Kuneitra–Damascus road. The IAF took part by bombing positions, gun batteries, and armored columns as ground forces moved through the "Bulge" to within 32 kilometers of Damascus. At this point the Israeli Air Force attacked airfields, forcing the Syrian Air Force into aerial combat in which they lost scores of MiGs and Sukhois. In the last stage of the war in the north, infantrymen were landed from the air on Mount Hermon and were supported throughout their assault on the Hermon positions by air strikes. The IAF also attacked Iraqi columns on the Golan Heights.

On the Egyptian front, the enemy succeeded in capturing all the Suez Canal line positions apart from the "Budapest" strongpoint in the extreme north, but could not transfer massed armor to the Sinai because of constant harassment from the air. A brigade-strength column from the Egyptian Third Army attempted to advance southward to Abu-Rodeis and At-Tur, but was attacked constantly by Israeli aircraft. For five days the brigade tried to move south, but to no avail. The Egyptians finally gave up after sustaining heavy losses. On October 14, it seemed to the Egyptians that they had amassed sufficient armor to attempt a breakthrough toward the central Sinai. In the tank

IAF F-4 Phantoms taking off for action over Syria.

battles that ensued, the Egyptians were pushed back with heavy losses.

The IAF hit airfields in Egypt, disrupted Egyptian Air Force attempts to support their ground forces, strafed convoys, and prevented reinforcements from reaching the front. IDF troops encircled the Egyptian Third Army on the east bank of the Canal, and the IAF pushed back all Egyptian attempts to reach the trapped units.

Under pressure from the United States and other powers, Egypt agreed to a cease-fire. With Israel's agreement, the cease-fire took effect on October 24. During the war, Arab losses amounted to 450 aircraft. Egypt lost 300, 180 in air-to-air dogfights and others to anti-aircraft missiles and guns. The Syrians lost 150 planes, 100 of them in aerial combat. Israeli losses were 100 planes (nearly 25 percent of its strength) of which six were lost in dogfights; and the remainder were hit by missiles and anti-aircraft guns.

As a result of the Yom Kippur War, the IAF was able to accomplish the following:

1. Though the enemy achieved initial surprise, their air forces were unable to penetrate Israeli airspace and disrupt reserve mobilization.
2. The Israeli Air Force played a major role in the blocking actions on the Golan and in the Sinai.
3. Effective and comprehensive air support was supplied on both fronts as Israeli ground forces turned to the offensive.
4. The enemy was prevented from bringing up reinforcements at the critical stage of the war.
5. The IAF paralyzed Egyptian and Syrian airfields and thus prevented air assaults on Israeli forces.
6. The Syrian missile system was hit hard, while the Egyptian missiles were completely destroyed.
7. Severe damage was done to the Syrian economic infrastructure. The IAF effectively destroyed its strategic and national resources: electric power stations, water and gasoline systems, Syrian Air Force and Naval Command headquarters, and the GHQ. This apparently convinced Jordan not to join the war for fear of similar treatment.
8. Hundreds of Syrian and Egyptian aircraft were destroyed.

The results of the war convinced the leaders of Egypt and Syria to accept the cease-fire and the later separation of forces. The Syrians, in an attempt to achieve better terms, kept up a war of attrition until April 1974 (in which they were the losers).

Together with the artillery duels, the IAF fought aerial battles and hit targets inside Syria. However, both sides depended very heavily on foreign sources for resupply of major weapons and equipment. The Arab forces received their replacement material by airlift from the Soviet Union, and the Israelis were resupplied by a massive airlift from the United States. Giant C-5As and C-141s of the USAF's Military Airlift Command (MAC) delivered replacement Phantoms and Skyhawks, in addition to tanks and other weapons.

Following the war, the IAF continued to train its personnel and to update its aircraft and equipment, including the design of its new fighter, the Lavi. During this time, it was called upon to perform a number of major missions. Among these were the unprecedented rescue at Entebbe, Operation Litani and other retaliatory actions against PLO terrorists, resultant air battles with the Syrians, the amazing attack on the Iraqi nuclear reactor, and Operation Peace for Galilee.

RESCUE AT ENTEBBE

On June 27, 1976, a French commercial airliner was hijacked en route from Israel to Europe and forced to land at Entebbe in Uganda, 3,600 kilometers from Israel. There were 245 passengers, but the terrorists released the non-Israelis and non-Jews and held the Israeli and Jewish passengers against demands for the release of terrorists from prisons in Israel and elsewhere. The government of Israel first resorted to diplomatic efforts. Meanwhile, Operation Jonathan, a military operation to release the hostages, was planned. At the heart of the plan was the airlifting of a task force to Entebbe in order to gain control of the airport and release the prisoners. Once it became clear that diplomatic efforts were not going to resolve the crisis, it was decided to go ahead with the military action. On the night of July 3, 1976, four IAF C-130 Hercules aircraft, escorted much of the way by Phantoms, landed at Entebbe with the task force. In the ensuing action seven terrorists and 20 opposing Ugandan soldiers were killed. The Israelis also destroyed 11 Ugandan MiG-17s and MiG-21s. The element of surprise was the key factor. The hostages were released and brought home, receiving medical care on the planes on the way.

OPERATION LITANI

On March 11, 1978, a PLO terrorist unit landed by sea and moved onto the Tel Aviv–Haifa highway. Gaining control over a busload of daytrippers, they tried to enter Tel Aviv while firing indiscriminately at traffic on the road. In a rescue operation 34 people were killed and many more injured. In response to this raid it was decided to occupy southern Lebanon and clean out the terrorist nests. In a combined operation, between March 15 and 21, armor, airborne, and other units moved north while IAF planes attacked terrorist targets, artillery batteries, etc., and interceptor aircraft patrolled the area, protecting both their comrades on strafing and bombing missions and the ground forces from enemy aircraft. The air force also provided aerial photography and reconnaissance. Transport planes and helicopters took part in the operation, moving men and supplies, maintaining communications, evacuating wounded, and so forth. Some 300 terrorists were killed in this operation. The Israeli Air Force sustained no losses; two planes were slightly damaged but returned safely to base.

AIR ATTACKS IN LEBANON

After Operation Litani, Israeli forces withdrew from southern Lebanon, and UN forces moved in to prevent terrorist action against Israel; but terrorist activity continued, encouraged by Syria. The Baghdad Summit, in November 1978, aimed at torpedoing the Camp David Agreement between Israel and Egypt, added fuel to flames. In response to the continuing terrorism, and particularly after the Nahariya raid in which Israeli children were killed, the IAF was called in to strike at terrorist targets in Lebanon. The Israeli Air Force played a part in the military policy of combined activity, both in response to terrorist raids and as a preventive measure.

SUBSEQUENT AERIAL BATTLES

Motivated by interests in Lebanon, opposition to the peace treaty with Egypt, and internal problems, Syria took measures likely to hamper IAF freedom of action in Lebanon. The Syrian objective was to prevent IAF activity in Lebanon, even at the cost of losing Syrian aircraft. On five occasions, aerial battles took place and resulted in the following Syrian losses:

1. June 27, 1979: five MiG-21s were shot down.
2. September 24, 1979: four MiG-21s were downed.
3. October 24, 1980: two MiGs were shot down.
4. February 13, 1981: one MiG was brought down.

All of these actions underlined the IAF's aerial superiority.

HONORING THE CAMP DAVID AGREEMENT WITH EGYPT

In conformity with the peace treaty with Egypt, by which it was agreed that Israel would evacuate the Sinai with American help, the construction of alternative airfields in the Negev began, at Nevetim, Mashabim, Ramon, and Ovda. During 1979–80, IAF airfields at Refidim, Atour, Santa-Katherina, and elsewhere were evacuated from the Sinai. In total approximately 600 structures were moved, with 200 left behind because of an inability to displace them.

THE IRAQI NUCLEAR REACTOR

On June 7, 1981, IAF American-built F-15 and F-16 fighters, bearing the blue Israeli six-pointed star, flew over three hostile nations to attack the atomic reactor under construction near Baghdad in Iraq. Precision bombing placed accurate hits directly into the reactor core and delayed its completion date by three to five years. All IAF planes returned safely to base.

The next major milestone in the relatively short history of the IAF was Operation Peace for Galilee in Lebanon, which began this overview. This and all the operations sketched here will be covered in greater detail in the pages that follow: the exciting saga of the IAF.

Chapter 2
The War of Independence, 1948

The true origin of the IAF can be traced back to World War II. Under neither Turkish nor later British rule did the Jews develop air training to any really significant extent. Although some Palestinian Jews were flying light planes and gliders during the 1920s and 1930s, the British refused to train them as members of combat aircrews—even during World War II. When the war broke out thousands of Jews flocked to local recruiting offices, but all the volunteers to the RAF were shuffled to ground crew and support services, and only the most persistent later made it to flight school. Of the 30 or so who did receive flight training from the RAF or one of the Commonwealth air forces, three later became IAF commanders—Aharon Remez, Dan Tolkovsky, and Ezer Weizman. Remez and Tolkovsky served in RAF fighter squadrons, but Weizman got his wings too late to see combat.

During the war, the Jewish underground in Palestine created a small contingent of flyers who secretly photographed almost the entire country from the air. Concentrating on prospective landing grounds near isolated Jewish settlements, especially in the Negev Desert, this aerial survey was of great use in airlifting troops and supplies during the War of Liberation in 1948.

As the end of the British Mandate loomed and with it the evacuation of the British troops, the Jewish leadership was forced to prepare to defend the Yishuv (the Jewish population in Palestine) against the threat of invading Arab regular armies. With no suitable aircraft available, the multitude of complex problems inherent in attempting to build an air force from scratch were of utmost concern to the Jewish leaders. They began a frantic worldwide search for combat and transport planes and for trained men to fly them.

While the victorious Allies were scrapping, burning, and junking war-surplus arms and munitions by the millions of tons all over the world, the British blockade on arms supplies to Jewish Palestine made the purchase of any sort of aircraft extremely difficult and hazardous. Although American public opinion sided with the Jewish cause, the U.S government observed a very strict embargo on arms exports to the Middle East, and anyone caught smuggling arms out of the country faced being charged with committing a major federal offense. European countries also observed this rule, mainly as a result of British pressure. Meanwhile, parked on airfields throughout the United States were thousands of surplus aircraft of all kinds and sizes, some of which had never actually seen active service. The U.S. government, anxious to help war veterans and also wishing to expand the civilian aircraft industry and services, sold these planes at a small fraction of their original cost to pilots wanting to set up their own charter air companies.

One of these ambitious American veterans willing to try his luck was Al Schwimmer. A placid flight engineer with much experience in the World War II Transport Command,

Schwimmer approached the Haganah (as the IDF was called before the State of Israel was proclaimed) purchasing mission in New York with the idea of buying surplus transports and bombers and flying them out to Israel immediately after its declaration of independence in 1948. His first acquisitions on behalf of the budding air force were three Lockheed Constellation four-engine transports at $5,000 each. He then set about recruiting experienced aircrews and technicians to recondition the planes. (Schwimmer's aircraft-renovating operation continued and expanded in Israel, eventually developing into the Israel Aircraft Industries).

The Western powers' embargo on vital arms supplies for the new country forced the Jewish leaders to look for other sources. Ironically, the saviors of that period were the Eastern Bloc countries, such as Czechoslovakia and Yugoslavia, who, with Russian endorsement and for payment in much-sought-after American dollars, sold arms and services to the hard-pressed Jews (and to the Arabs as well). In March 1948, the underground purchasing mission in Czechoslovakia bought some surplus Messerschmitt Bf-109s that the Czech factory at Prag-Cakovice had manufactured for the Germans during the war. With the rise of the Communist government, the Czechoslovakian Air Force was equipped with more modern Russian planes, and the dollar-hungry Czechs welcomed the opportunity for a lucrative deal. Thus, the Jews who had served with the Allied forces and flown British Spitfires against German Messerschmitts would now be flying Messerschmitts against Spitfires in the hands of their enemies. But first these precious aircraft had somehow to reach Israel—and fast. To dismantle, crate, and transport them by sea was out of the question, the earliest they could arrive would be three months after packing, much too late to be effective in the forthcoming battles. The only possible solution was to transport the Messerschmitts by air.

The first Bf-109 to leave for Israel in May 1948 was dismantled and transported in a chartered American Skymaster in the airlift code-named Operation Balak. A number of volunteer pilots and Czech technicians accompanied the dismantled planes to reassemble them in Israel, and by the end of May a number of fighters were ready for action. To step up the momentum of the Balak airlift, additional transport aircraft were urgently needed, and the airworthy C-46s bought by Schwimmer were flown to Europe as soon as possible.

From Independence Day, May 15, 1948, to May 29 when the first Bf-109s were put into service, Israeli airspace was completely controlled by enemy Arab air forces. The north and center of the country were dominated by the Syrians and Iraqis, and the region from Tel Aviv to the south became the hunting ground of the Egyptians. While the Syrian and Iraqi air forces were still rather backward—flying mainly Harvard fighters—the Egyptian Air Force contained all the elements required for a modern force. Founded in the early 1930s with the help of the RAF, some of its pilots had seen combat during World War II and were qualified to form the staff, command, and training nucleus of its force. On the eve of the invasion of Israel the Egyptian Air Force consisted of two fighter squadrons (about 40 Spitfires) and two transport squadrons (C-46s and C-47s), some of which had been equipped as medium bombers. The El Arish air base became the operational headquarters for the attacks on the Jewish state.

To oppose the attacking Arabs, the Israelis could muster only three flights of light planes, mainly Auster army liaison aircraft. Though these were useful for transporting supplies and casualties and supporting isolated settlements while the RAF still ruled the skies, they were now at the mercy of the Arab pilots.

The Arabs wasted no time in taking advantage of their position. Early on Independence Day, Egyptian Spitfires attacked the main IAF base at Sde Dov just north of Tel Aviv, damaging the field and three planes. The Egyptian Air Force pilots flew low over Tel Aviv, bombing and strafing the nearly defenseless city. Their self-confidence proved exaggerated, however, when in an attack later in the day a Spitfire was shot down by anti-aircraft fire and the pilot captured. In general, however, during the first weeks of the war the Arab pilots roamed freely all over Israel, attacking targets at will, unopposed from the air.

During this time, the IAF was also stepping up its activity, though operating mainly at night to avoid the Arab fighters. The lightly armed Israeli planes flew close-support missions in aid of hard-pressed troops and settlers in all

Messerschmitt Bf-109s purchased by Israel from Czechoslovakia.

parts of the country. For many settlements, especially in the Negev, which was cut off from the north by the invading Egyptian army, the planes of the IAF were the sole means of support and supply.

With all restrictions to immigration now removed, the IAF was quickly undergoing important changes with the influx of highly experienced volunteers from abroad. Coming mainly from English-speaking countries, these fliers rapidly occupied key positions on the staff and as flying personnel in the force, and English soon became almost exclusively the operational language of the air force. Along with these

changes in personnel came dramatic developments in equipment as well as in its fighting capabilities.

By the end of May 1948, the Czech technicians at Ekron airfield had completed the assembly of four Messerschmitts, and an attack was planned on the Egyptian Air Force field at El-Arish in the north Sinai, from which the Egyptian attacks on Tel Aviv originated. As the Israeli planes were preparing to take off on their mission, an urgent call was received for help in stopping Egyptian armored columns that had advanced to a point along the coastal road only 32 kilometers south of Tel Aviv.

Loading jeeps into a Curtiss C-46 commando transport during Operation Dustbowl, autumn 1948. This airlift brought in some 1500 men and 2500 tons of matériel to the beleaguered Negev settlements in 417 sorties—preparing the way for the offensive that liberated the whole of southern Israel and entrapped an Egyptian brigade in the Faluga Pocket (including Maj. Gamal Abdel Nasser).

The four aircraft took off, flown by two Israeli pilots (one of them Ezer Weizman), and two volunteers. They dived on the surprised Egyptians coming in from the direction of the sea and bombed the column. Little actual damage was caused, but the resulting confusion succeeded in stopping the advance. During this sortie one plane, flown by a South African volunteer, was brought down by anti-aircraft fire, and another crash-landed at the base. The Israeli Air Force had lost 50 percent of its strength on its first mission. It was soon down to one serviceable plane after losing yet another near Natanya in an attack on an Iraqi armored column approaching the coast from Tulkarem. When his aircraft was hit by anti-aircraft fire, the pilot bailed out over a Jewish settlement on the coast, shouting down frantically in Yiddish to save his life from the angry settlers who took him for an Arab. At that time the Jewish farmers did not even know that they had fighter aircraft!

But the Messerschmitts continued to enter service at the rate of one or two a day. On June 3, the Israelis won the first of their aerial victories. In time, such victories began to indicate a measure of air superiority as yet not seriously threatened. That evening two Egyptian Air Force Dakotas began what had become routine bombing runs over Tel Aviv, when an IAF Messerschmitt flown by Mody Allon suddenly dived on them, shooting down one immediate-

A bomb attack by IAF B-17 on Egyptian positions near Faluga during the 1948–49 war. The hardstands, lower left, indicate that this was a former British air base constructed during World War II.

ly. The other fled but did not get far and was downed by the same Bf-109. From that time the Egyptian Air Force ceased bombing Tel Aviv almost completely and confined itself to attacks on remote and defenseless settlements.

The next day three Egyptian ships approaching the Tel Aviv shore with their guns blazing were counterattacked by an assortment of IAF light planes. While scoring only one bomb hit, the aircraft drove off the Egyptian vessels, suffering the loss of one plane and its crew. After these victories, in the air and against naval units, the IAF rapidly gained confidence and its makeshift bombers attacked Ramallah, Amman, and Damascus. By the onset of the first truce on June 10, 1948, the IAF had become a full-fledged air force. Though usually engaged in tactical "fire-fighting" missions without an overall strategic objective, the

IAF had emerged as a factor with which the Arab air forces had to reckon.

The IAF took great advantage of that first month-long truce for an extensive reorganization, establishing an Air Transport Command to coordinate airlift capabilities, and sending a group of pilots abroad for advanced training, among other things. When the truce broke down on July 8, the IAF sent its meager forces on attacks reaching from Faluga in the Negev to Mishmar Hayarden in the north. Approximately one month earlier, Al Schwimmer had acquired four B-17 heavy bombers as well as some A-20 medium bombers at surplus dumps in Oklahoma and Florida. Though stripped of their military equipment, they were in relatively good flying condition. Because of the urgency of the situation, it was decided to smuggle the planes out of the United States as fast as pos-

The first IAF fighter pilots of the first fighter squadron, stationed at Herzlia Airfield, discussing tactics prior to takeoff on a combat mission. Ezer Weizman, later Israel's defense minister, then a young fighter pilot, makes his point.

sible, without even attempting to receive permission from the authorities. On June 12, 1948, three of the four B-17s were ready at Miami International Airport. The fourth was delayed by technical problems. The planes did not attract undue attention among the numerous flights of ex-military aircraft at that time, and the formation took off for Milville, New Jersey, the first leg in the long flight which ran north through Greenland, then southeast to Zatec, Czechoslovakia.

Volunteer technicians at Zatec, working on the Messerschmitts acquired in Czechoslovakia, set about rearming the arriving bombers with jerry-rigged guns. Ray Kurtz, a former USAAF bomber squadron commander in the European theater of operations, was flown in from Israel

to take charge. In July orders were received to fly the bombers out to Israel, bombing Cairo en route, but the planes were far from ready to fly a combat mission. Of the three planes, only one had a makeshift oxygen system put together from welder's oxygen tanks. This was also the only aircraft with a bombsight. Rudimentary bomb releases were installed, together with a motley collection of instruments, making the whole project precarious and unreliable. But urgency threw caution to the winds, and Kurtz decided to fly the mission despite the difficulties.

After a briefing at the Stalingrad Hotel in Zatec and last-minute instructions for the long flight ahead, the three bombers took off, loaded to maximum with fuel and bombs. Trouble hit

Three of the first IAF-trained fighter pilots in the spring of 1949. These flyers began flight training on light civilian planes before the establishment of the State. They continued their training during the War of Independence, but received their wings only after the fighting ended.

them almost as soon as they were airborne. Immediately after takeoff, Kurtz lost one engine, and the artificial horizon gave out. Then the air pressure fell, rocking the aircraft in the sky. As if this were not enough, the bombers ran into bad weather over the Alps and lost each other in heavy cloud turbulence. Skirting the Albanian coast, they were fired upon by anti-aircraft batteries of the ever suspicious Albanians. Fighting to bring their rocking planes through the stormy skies, the exhausted pilots finally emerged into clear weather over the Mediterranean and, to their relief, located each other again. Reaching the Greek islands, the formation parted company. Only Kurtz was flying to Cairo; the other two pilots were making bombing runs over Egyptian bases located in the northern Sinai on their way to Israel.

As he put his aircraft into a steady climb to use the commercial airliner flight paths to Egypt, trouble struck Kurtz again. At 7,500 meters the navigator suddenly fell unconscious over his chart table. Other crew members fainted soon after. Beginning to feel queasy himself, Kurtz realized that the pressure and concentration of the welder's oxygen were apparently inadequate. He then brought the ship down to 4,500 meters until all the crew recovered. In order not to lose precious time, he ordered everyone onto emergency oxygen and then regained altitude, but there was no way of knowing if the supply would last, expended at that rate, through the run over Cairo.

When they reached the African coastline 160

A B-17G over the Mediterranean. The midsection upper gun turret is missing and the direction-finder aerial seen here was not standard on USAAF B-17s.

kilometers west of the Nile Delta, the crew took action stations, some still faint from lack of oxygen. Homing in on the RAF Fayid radio beacon in the Canal Zone, they saw Cairo below them, fully lit and unaware of the impending danger. Making his run over the Royal Palace, the bombardier directed the plane on target and released the bombs. Although some 2.5 tons of high explosives were dropped, mainly around the Abadin Palace, physical damage was not heavy. However, the psychological impact of surprising the Egyptian defenses was immense, and public pressure forced the army to devote much more of its combat resources to defending Cairo.

As the bombs fell Pilot Kurtz felt a sharp lurch as the suddenly lighter bomber gathered speed. Pushing the nose down he set course for Israel and landed at the Ekron airfield in the south at 2245 local time.

On that day, July 14, the Israeli Air Force received a major reinforcement when the three B-17 Flying Fortresses landed. Now flying "real" bombers, the IAF carried out numerous strikes against objectives from Cairo to Damascus. However, the Arab pilots avoided air encounters and concentrated on hit-and-run attacks against isolated settlements in Israel. This pattern of air warfare continued until the end of the war, the IAF steadily becoming more powerful and aggressive and the Arabs restricting themselves to isolated bombing attacks and engaging only in unavoidable dogfights.

One IAF effort worthy of special note was the airlift of soldiers and munitions to the Negev in preparation for the final offensive against the Egyptian Army positioned in the Gaza Strip and El Arish. During two months of intensive flying, Air Transport Command made over 400 flights, delivering 5,000 tons of equipment and carrying more than 10,000 passengers.

As the war was coming to a close, a strange series of events took place. Early in 1949, the road to the Suez Canal seemed unobstructed as the Israeli troops advanced swiftly into the Sinai, pushing the remnants of the Egyptian Army back through their last defenses. However, the British still maintained large forces in the Canal Zone and, acting under the 12-year-old Anglo-Egyptian Treaty, they deliv-

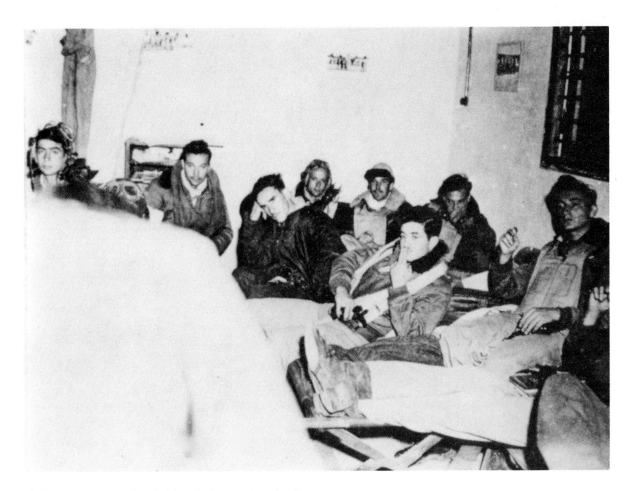

A B-17 crew being briefed by their squadron leader.

ered an ultimatum demanding immediate Israeli withdrawal from Egyptian territory. (This was in sharp contrast, to say the least, to their apathy toward the Arab invasion of Israel in May 1948—even though the British still retained military control of the northern area!) Faced with the British ultimatum and numerous political threats, especially from the United States, the Israelis halted their advance near El Arish.

To verify Israeli compliance with the ultimatum, the RAF flew several photo reconnaissance missions close to the Israeli border on the morning of January 7, 1949. Flying undisturbed, they carried out their mission and returned to their base in the Canal Zone. But a more extensive mission was flown later the same day. Six Mk-XVIII Spitfires of the 208th Middle East Tactical Squadron roared low over the desert and entered Israeli airspace over the

El Auga–Beersheva road and then turned north to fly in the direction of the Gaza–Rafah area. Mistaking them for Egyptian planes, Israeli ground troops opened fire, but missed. However, one Spitfire was hit over Rafah, perhaps by Egyptian fire, and the pilot bailed out, landing near Israeli troops.

Circling overhead, watching their comrade descend, the remaining British Spitfires were suddenly pounced upon by Israeli Spitfires. Two RAF aircraft were downed at once. One crashed, its pilot dead at the controls. Another crash-landed in the dunes, its pilot survived and returned to his base with the help of Bedouins. The dogfight was short and sharp, as the Israelis quickly broke away with nearly empty fuel tanks.

Although taking an active part in the air war since the beginning, Ezer Weizman, the new operations officer of the fighter squadron (later

Maintenance crews reconditioning a Spitfire Mk-IX. The first of these entered service with the IAF early in 1948, when an Egyptian Spitfire crash-landed on the beach after being hit by a lucky shot from an alert Bren gunner on a roof in northern Tel Aviv. Using parts found in scrap heaps on abandoned RAF airfields, the fighter was refitted to fly again.

A Lockheed Hudson twin-engine medium bomber being serviced at the Ekron air base.

to become the IAF commander), had yet to shoot down an enemy plane, a feat many of his pilots had achieved both in World War II and in the air battles over Israel. From his office at the airfield at Hatzor, Weizman watched a flight of Spitfires return and land. One of the pilots, a Canadian volunteer, casually sauntered over to him and reported shooting down a Spitfire, adding just as casually and almost as an afterthought, "a *British* Spitfire." Catching his breath for several moments in astonishment, Weizman was amazed at the audacity of the pilots in striking at the mighty empire that only a few months earlier had ruled his country. But he agreed wholeheartedly with the pilot's reasoning for his action. To retain air sovereignty, a country must keep out *all* intruding foreign warplanes. Later in the day another pilot came in and reported that the British were trying to locate their missing aircraft, and

added that he too had brought down a British fighter.

Now that the cease-fire with the Egyptians was about to come into effect, Weizman saw his last chance for a personal victory in the war. Quickly convincing headquarters that a final "show the flag" patrol over El Arish would be valuable, Weizman took off immediately, closely followed by three other pilots. Climbing to 2,000 meters they reached the border area and saw eight unknown aircraft approaching from the west. They were soon identified as British Spitfires and Tempests crossing into Israeli airspace.

Attacking from above, the four Israeli Spitfires closed quickly onto the tails of the British aircraft. One immediately trailed smoke and crash-landed; the others scattered, with the Israelis in hot pursuit. The RAF pilots seemed inexperienced, whereas the Israelis, being old

An Egyptian Spitfire, brought down by ground fire at Ashod, being examined by Israeli technicians.

hands at the game, picked them off like sitting ducks. Finding himself alone, Weizman pursued a British Spitfire climbing away from the battle and opened fire with his two 20-mm guns. The British craft turned over and went down, crash-landing near El Arish. The pilot, uninjured but thoroughly shaken, walked away.

Soon afterwards the cease-fire put an end to hostilities. However, following the War of Independence the Israeli Air Force continued to enlarge and upgrade its inventory of aircraft. The remaining Mk-IX Spitfires purchased from the Czechs during the war were delivered early in 1949, bringing the total of IAF planes to 50. A number of additional Spitfires, of the more advanced model HF Mk-IX, were obtained from the Italian Air Force, enabling the IAF to phase out the unreliable Messerschmitts.

While looking for suitable aircraft to fill the various needs of an expanding air force, the purchasing mission came across a few hundred Mosquitos on a French Air Force base at Chateaudun, where they stood waiting to be sold for scrap. A group of technicians was flown over to prepare them for transfer to Israel. This time the French cooperated and the work progressed smoothly. The reconditioned aircraft were tested by the highly experienced British volunteer John Harvey, a gentile who held the rank of captain in the Israeli Air Force. On one of these test flights his Mosquito went down in a spin, killing this brave man. In this crash the young air force lost one of its most skillful pilots. Harvey had contributed immensely to the building of the IAF in its first years by flying a collection of motley aircraft to Israel from all over Europe and passing on his vast knowledge and experience to the young Israeli pilots.

An early commander of the air force was an RAF-trained pilot named Aharon Remez, who envisaged the growth of the air force to a size enabling it to perform missions beyond the per-

A pair of Spitfires taking off from a northern Israeli air base. The aircraft on the right is already "tucking-in" his undercarriage.

ception of his superiors at that time. The Israeli High Command's concept of the future air force was that of a medium-size air corps for use in supporting role in much the same way as they regarded the Armored Corps. But this was not Remez's view; his ideas went far beyond this. He foresaw the creation of an offensive weapon with the main objective of achieving air superiority before rendering offensive support to ground troops. Eventually these very objectives became the basic doctrine of the IAF, but the more pressing problems in the eyes of the High Command were organizational. With this in mind, GHQ appointed nonflying army officers as the next two air force commanders. Lack of agreement on the organization and shape of the air force and disputes over budget priorities severely complicated the development of the air force during the early 1950s. Two air force commanders, Aharon Remez (1948–50) and Haim

Laskov (1951–53) resigned over differences in budgetary concepts.

Though the IAF commanders were eager to equip their first-line squadrons with jets, 25 ex-Swedish Air Force P-51 Mustangs were purchased as interim replacements for some of the Spitfires. It was therefore around the Mustang and Mosquito, thoroughly proven and highly effective weapons in their time, that the early multirole fighter-bomber concept was conceived.

In 1954 Dan Tolkovsky, a former RAF pilot and one of the few Palestinian Jews to achieve officer status, became commander of the IAF. Under his leadership, the air force lost the temporary and makeshift atmosphere that had characterized it from the beginning and became a highly disciplined and professional fighting force. By then the veteran volunteers had gone back to their countries of origin, and young, enthusiastic Israelis joined the IAF. The early models of organization were on the lines of proven RAF procedures, but soon a completely new style was devised to suit the conditions prevailing in Israel and the Middle East. The best pilots and commanders were sent abroad for advanced courses, mainly to Britain.

It was under Tolkovsky that the IAF developed the concept of a force relying solely on multipurpose fighter planes to be operated in two successive stages: first, the seizure of air superiority and, second, tactical support of land and naval operations. In the Middle East, where most weapons were imported and the wars brief, the effects of "strategic" bombing were too slow. The heavy bomber was therefore not a priority item for the IAF.

The IAF started to phase out the last of the veteran Spitfires after it obtained its first jets, Gloster Meteors, from Belgium and Great Britain in 1954. Thirty of the Spitfires were sold to Burma, but the Israelis were faced with the problem of delivery. Since the Arabs would refuse overflight and refueling privileges to any plane that they knew originated in Israel, the Israeli aircraft were painted in Burmese colors and flown to Sicily. From there a British charter company was to fly them to Burma with false flight plans indicating that they came directly from Britain. However, several aircraft crash-landed on the way to Burma, and the story leaked out. The planes were then refitted with long-range fuel tanks and flown via an alternative route over Turkey, Iran, Pakistan, India, and East Pakistan, eventually reaching Burma.

The Israelis were now in the market for more modern and sophisticated jet aircraft. The acquisition of advanced jet aircraft presented political as well as financial problems that were not easy to solve. After the failure of negotiations for the purchase of Canadian-manufactured F-86 Sabre jets, the Israelis turned to France, whose problems with the Arabs in North Africa were expected to influence favorably the political consideration of the deal. Negotiations were completed successfully for the purchase of sturdy Dassault Ouragan fighter-bombers in 1955. This deal marked the beginning of the era of Franco-Israeli friendship and cooperation that was to last until the Six-

Day War, and from which both parties profited, militarily and politically.

On the "other side of the hill" things looked very different. The low-level guerrilla war that had been going on for years increased in intensity and volume with time. Early in 1955, after a series of Israeli retaliatory attacks on Egyptian army positions in the Gaza Strip and Khan Yunis that caused serious losses in men and prestige, President Nasser resolved to build an armed force capable of overcoming the Israelis in any future conflict. In August 1955 he concluded an arms deal with the Czechs, encouraged by the Soviets, that would completely modernize the Egyptian armed forces. Acquiring large numbers of MiG-15 fighters, the EAF was rebuilt into a modern all-jet force, stationed on air bases abandoned by the British in their recent evacuation of the Canal Zone.

The massive Egyptian modernization, backed by the Soviet bloc, presented a potential threat that had to be countered quickly if Israel wished to retain air superiority. As the French Ouragan was somewhat inferior to the MiG-15, the Israelis had to choose between the Dassault Mystère IIC, which could be supplied immediately, or wait for the newly designed Mystère IVA, which would not be available until early 1956. After intense deliberations and a visit to France by senior IAF officers to watch test flights of the Mystère IVA, the IAF commanders decided to wait; and as time showed, their patience was handsomely rewarded. The Mystère IVA proved to be more than a match for any Soviet fighter in the area at the time, and it was to stay in service for a long time, flying countless missions with great effectiveness.

The IDF now had its hands full. The threat of the Soviet buildup of Egypt's arsenal, increasing terrorist raids into Israel from both the Sinai and Jordan, Egyptian artillery shelling of Jewish settlements along the Gaza Strip, and Israel's repeated reprisal raids kept the IDF very busy maintaining a semblance of normal peacetime life. On April 12, 1956, the first clash between Egyptian and Israeli jets occurred, resulting in an Egyptian Vampire being shot down by Meteors and crashing on Israeli territory. The Sinai War loomed ahead.

Chapter 3

The Sinai Campaign, 1956

The Sinai campaign, which was intended to break the Egyptian blockade of the Tiran Straits leading to Eilat and to eliminate the terrorist attacks from the Gaza Strip, was coordinated with an Anglo-French operation to capture the recently nationalized Suez Canal. At the specific request of Prime Minister Ben Gurion, two French Mystère IV squadrons were brought to Israel to protect civilian targets from possible attack by Egyptian IL-28 jet bombers while the Israeli fighters were engaged in the offensive. As it turned out, the Egyptain Air Force was in no condition to pose a threat to towns in Israel, but the fear of a repeat performance of May 1948, when the Egyptians ruled the skies over Israel, was everpresent in the minds of the Jewish leaders and was to remain so even later, notwithstanding the arguments of the IAF commanders.

Identified by the code name Operation Kadesh,* the Sinai campaign opened with a daring mission deep behind enemy lines. Four propeller-driven P-51 Mustang fighters, retreads from World War II, had been given a strange assignment that would take them dangerously close to several enemy MiG bases. After days of grueling training and nerve-wracking waiting, the day finally arrived: October 29, 1956. The day before, the four pilots scheduled to take part in the operation were summoned to a briefing. There, they were informed that within 24 hours Israel would be at war with Egypt. The first stage would be the dispatch of

Dakotas, escorted by Mystères and Meteors, to the Mitla Pass, where paratroopers would be dropped. Prior to that the Mustangs would be assigned to cut the Egyptian telephone lines in and around the Mitla area, in order to preserve the atmosphere of total surprise. Following the detailed briefing Mustang crews were sent to Lod to pick up another seven Mustangs from storage at what was then known as the Aircraft Overhaul Facility—now headquarters for Israel Aircraft Industries. The Mustangs arrived at Ekron with neither armament nor sights, and squadron mechanics had to work furiously all night to ready them for combat.

The line-cutting teams had been selected on the morning of October 29. Two pairs of Mustangs would go out, headed by Zachik, the squadron CO, and Harry, his deputy. Zachik's Number Two was Rabbit; Harry's wingman was a young but widely experienced pilot nick-named Cheetah, a graduate of the first IAF Flight School pilot course. Harry, with his thick mustache and thicker English accent, was to earn the nickname "Harry the Cutter" as a result of his part in the operation.

The four pilots were carefully briefed. They were to approach the targets at 30 meters—high enough to avoid dragging their cutter cables, but low enough to avoid being spotted by Egyptian radar. One pair was assigned to a target 10 kilometers east of Suez City, and the other to a spot 30 kilometers east of the Mitla Pass. Navigation would be done by the configuration of desert hills and streambeds rather than by (nonexistent) roads. Takeoff was scheduled for 1400; at the last moment, this was delayed to

---

*IAF activities were specifically designated Operation Machbesh ("Press").

1415. Since a prerequisite for the operation's success was absolute radio silence, the four coordinated visual signals. A waggle of wings meant "Come closer"; a thumb pointed backward meant "How's my cable?" The last question was answered by either thumb up or thumb down—"Cable OK" or "Cable torn off."

Each pilot was issued what was then the standard IAF survival kit: a pistol, a knife, an overall, two ammunition clips, a Mae West life jacket, a heliograph, combat rations, first-aid kits including morphine, and—of course—the "lucky scarf," a vividly colored silk scarf worn loosely around the neck. All documents except their International Pilot's Certificates, recognized by the Geneva Convention, were left behind. As the pilots strode to their aircraft— one Swedish and three Italian Mustangs— ready for the first combat mission of the war, they were understandably tense. The tension dissolved into laughter soon afterward: Entering the aircraft, they were surprised to discover that the water-filled cushions designed to block the shock of cable impact had heated up in the sunlight and were nearly at the boiling point. Harry, the perpetual Englishman, did not waste a moment. "Anyone want a cup of tea?" he smiled, pointing to the steaming cushions.

The pilots started their engines and rolled to the last checkpoint. There they were met by a 6 × 6 truck bearing the cutter cables. Two teams jumped down from the truck and attached the cables to the first pair of Mustangs. Cheetah's aircraft, its motor roaring, raced down the runway and lifted off. Behind it, the cable tossed back and forth a moment on the runway, then climbed into the sky behind the Mustang. Now it was Harry's turn. Down the runway he roared, making a lovely takeoff, but, to his astonishment, the cable tore off and remained behind on the runway. Making as tight a turn as possible, Harry came back, landed and rolled back to the checkpoint, where a spare cable was attached. The second time, the takeoff went off without a hitch.

As the second pair readied for its takeoff 20 minutes later, the runway was lined with dozens of apprehensive paratroopers heading for the Dakotas that were to take them into the Sinai. Some, glancing at the Mustangs, apparently thought that these outmoded aircraft were all the IAF could offer in the way of an escort.

Their fears were to prove ungrounded: At 300 meters they could clearly see the then brand-new Mystère jets escorting them into battle. Of course, the Mustangs, too, were intended to protect the paratroopers, but not by their physical presence. Rather, they would prevent the news of their landing from reaching the Egyptian rear lines during the 48 hours to come, hours critical for the success of the entire campaign.

At 1435 hours Zachik and Rabbit took off without trouble and headed for the Sinai. Before them lay a 150-minute flight to their target, near Temed, east of the Mitla Pass. Harry and Cheetah's target—near Suez City on the Canal—was even farther away, necessitating a full three hours in the air. As they raced toward their targets at 30 meters, the ground poured out beneath them at an amazing rate.

Near the Ramon Crater, Harry and Cheetah executed their first scheduled turn, from south to west-southwest, and flew 16 kilometers south to the main road into the Sinai. Once they crossed this road, their entire navigational procedure would be based on streambeds and hills, with no other roads in sight.

The ground streams under the Mustangs at a staggering rate. Harry flashes the thumbs-up signal at Cheetah, who responds in kind: Both cables are still intact. The pair is cruising at 320 Km/h, slowed by their cables to 80 Km/h below the Mustang's usual cruising speed, but fast enough for Harry and Cheetah. The aircraft are armed with 12.7-mm machine guns (MGs) and are full of ammunition. True, HQ hasn't authorized opening fire, but sometimes you have to fire anyway. . . .

Suddenly Harry waggles his wings. Cheetah closes in, astounded to see that his Number One's thumb is pointed down. Cheetah's cable has snapped. Chances of success are now 50 percent at best, but the pair has already reached the Mitla area and it is pointless even to think of going back at this stage. Nearing the target, they climb to 900 meters, skimming along the streambeds between the hilltops. Suddenly, the landscape opens up as if by magic and the Suez Canal plain spreads out before them, with the Gulf of Suez gleaming 20 kilometers away.

The pair drops lower and lower, to a bare 30 meters. Within minutes, their target is below them—in the heart of enemy territory, hundreds of kilometers from home, and only minutes away from three Egyptian air bases well stocked with MiGs. On the outskirts of Suez City, the telephone cables stretch out below the Mustangs, almost inviting them to come down and "have a go."

Harry continues the story:

> We approached the target from the northeast. It was nearly sunset, and we were headed right into the sun and nearly blinded by the glare. I raised my fist to the back of my neck, signalling my Number Two to fly behind me, and went into an identifying run. Spotting the easiest point to attack, I made a full turn and entered the attack pass. The telephone lines rushed up at me, but I couldn't see them because of the strong sunlight; I therefore selected a promising-looking gap between two poles and headed into it. I thought I'd torn the lines, but I couldn't be sure—I hadn't felt the impact. What I did know, however, is that my cable had torn off.

In other words, the pair was not sure they had completed their mission, but even if they had not, doing so looked hopeless at first glance. Neither Harry nor Cheetah still had their line-cutter cables.

The pair, however, was not inclined to give up easily. Glancing at each other, each seemed to read his partner's thought. They were recalling an incident that had happened several years previously, with a Stearman from the IAF Flight School. One of the instructors had inadvertently passed too close to some high-tension electric cables, cutting through them with his propeller. The Stearman landed safely, with no damage whatsoever, but the entire area was blacked out for hours.

"I thought to myself, 'If that old junk heap of a Stearman could do that to a high-tension cable, I'll bet my Mustang can cut its way through a miserable telephone line!' " recalls Harry. His and Cheetah's decision to cut the cables with their propellers—a feat totally against pilot instinct—has remained throughout the years a shining example of determination and perseverance in the history of the IAF.

"We made a tight turn and came back to the first attack point. We tried to identify the cables, but couldn't see them." Another identifying pass would have endangered the pair,

scant kilometers from Suez City and its defending MiGs. Revving his engine up to 3,000 rpm, Harry went in for the kill.

On the first pass, with Cheetah following, Harry rushed toward the cables at 320 Km/h. However, at the last second, pilot instinct took over; instead of tearing through the telephone lines, the Mustangs sailed over them. Refusing to give up, Harry went into yet another pass. This time he managed to overcome his natural reluctance to use his aircraft as pliers. Staying low, he headed into the wires—which sprayed his windshield with a fine fog of metal—feeling a light jolt as the aircraft sped through: He had cut through the cables. Cheetah picked two other poles, also fogged in, and proceeded to duplicate Harry's feat. As they turned and headed for their next target, the pair could clearly see the cut lines lying on the yellow ground below. This encouraged them to repeat the process at the second target, several kilometers to the north. Within minutes, those lines were also cut to ribbons. Any fears the pair might have had as to possible engine damage proved ungrounded; even after the most unorthodox mission, the Mustangs functioned perfectly, as detailed examinations back at Ekron were to point out. Jubilantly, Harry and Cheetah headed home. On their way back their path crossed that of the Dakotas, bringing the IDF paratroopers to the Mitla. Knowing that they had helped to keep those young men safe, the pair smiled at each other and sped for home.

Meanwhile Zachik and Rabbit were also receiving moral support from the ground forces—in their case, the armor of the famous Seventh Brigade, deployed near Abu Agheila. Passing over the armor, they continued in flight for another 45 minutes, to the eastern end of the Mitla Pass. Spotting the target, they dropped below 30 meters, a maneuver fatal to both their line-cutter cables. First Zachik, then Rabbit, felt the shock of impact as their cables hit the ground and tore away. However, they too remembered the incident with the Stearman and decided to take a chance on their propellers. On their first pass, as had been the case with Harry and Cheetah, Zachik's pair climbed above the cables instinctively at the last moment. This, they realized, would never do. Accordngly, on the next pass, they utilized "flight psychology"—each took turns forcing the other lower and lower, until they were nearly touching the desert sand. This time they tore through the cables with no difficulty; Rabbit later admitted not even having felt the jolt. Another three passes totally destroyed the telephone lines in the area, and the pair moved on to its second target.

Passing northwest of Temed, they reached another concentration of telephone lines. This time Rabbit had decided to try something new. His instinctive dislike for things that got tangled in his propeller made him decide to take on this lot of lines with *his wing*. On the first pass Rabbit came in low, too low. Realizing that he could not pull up in time, he flew under the cables like a crop duster, then came around for another try. This time, as he approached the telephone lines, he dipped his wings and cut through the cables with no effort. (Back at Ekron, the IAF engineers were shocked to hear of Rabbit's feat, commenting rightly that this was much more dangerous than attempting to use the propeller.) Fifteen minutes over this target were enough to tear through anything remotely resembling a telephone cable. Smiling as they looked down on the useless strands of wire scattered over the sand, the pair turned and headed back to base, also passing on their way the Dakotas headed for the Mitla.

The flight back to Ekron was uneventful, and all the Mustangs landed safely with ample fuel and untouched ammunition. Following the debriefing, a similar mission was scheduled in the northern Sinai the next afternoon, with Cheetah and Rabbit as leaders; their Number Twos were two pilots hurriedly trained for the mission. This, too, was a success, earning the squadron the unofficial nickname of "The Cutters." These missions had completely disrupted the Egyptian military communication systems, based as they were on land-line telephones. Moreover, as the IDF ground forces took over the Sinai, they endeavored without success to use the existing telephone system, not realizing that the IAF had cut the lines.

Later that afternoon the Israeli airborne assault began when 395 paratroopers were dropped from 16 C-47 Dakotas near the Mitla Pass in the western Sinai. Flying close escort for the transports were ten Gloster Meteor jets. A few miles to the west at a higher altitude 12 Mystères kept the Egyptian air bases on the

Suez Canal under observation. But all remained quiet, and the only Egyptian reaction to the appearance of the Israeli planes was to disperse their aircraft from their neat lines on the tarmac. This airborne attack was the first of its kind in the Middle East.

That evening another force from the same brigade crossed the Israeli–Egyptian border north of Eilat to link up with the Mitla force. Spearheaded by the First Battalion, which used armored personnel carriers, the remaining soldiers and equipment were loaded into conscripted civilian trucks. But some 242 kilometers of partly fortified desert lay in the way, and the paratroopers at Mitla had to rely on air support until their comrades joined them—quite a risk, with the Egyptian Air Force bases along the Canal only 2½ minutes of flying time away. The IAF commanders had their own ideas on how best to deal with this danger. However, political considerations ruled out preventive air strikes on the enemy fields prior to the drop. Thus the IAF was in the very precarious position of having to wait for the Egyptians to make their move before planning its counter-strategy.

Two hours after the drop, the transports made another run, parachuting anti-tank weapons, jeeps, and supplies; and still the Egyptians did not react. But the next morning, as the reinforcing column of paratroopers in half-tracks and trucks was moving toward the pass, it was attacked by two EAF MiG-15s sweeping in low from the west and strafing the column with cannon fire. A few vehicles were set on fire and a number of casualties sustained.

Having spent a quiet night deep in enemy territory, at sunrise the Mitla force received another supply drop from French Nord-Atlases flying out of Haifa. The first serious attack on Mitla was made on October 30 at 0745, some 14 hours after the force set down. A pair of MiG-15s raked the pass with cannon fire, knocking out the Piper Club liaison plane on the ground. Fortunately, the pilot was not in it at the time. A second attack, an hour later, this time by Vampires flown from Fayid, did little damage, but neither of these attacks was intercepted by the Israeli patrols. The battalion commander called for immediate air cover and the force dug in deeper, waiting for the inevitable counterattack that it would have to face. Later, however, air patrols were kept up almost with-

A flight of Gloster Meteors over Israel. The first combat of jet planes in the Middle East took place on August 31, 1955, when five intruding Egyptian D.H. Vampires were shot down over the Negev by IAF Meteors.

out a break. In a battle that developed in the afternoon over the Kabrit airfield between 12 Egyptian MiGs and eight Israeli Mystéres, two MiGs were shot down and two more were "probables"; one of the Mystéres was hit but managed to return to base and land safely.

Though air activity at this time was limited largely to close support and cover for the paratrooper forces at the Mitla Pass, there were many attacks against Egyptian ground targets, mostly convoys of vehicles and artillery moving from the Canal Zone into the Sinai. Following their telephone line-cutting gambit, the propeller-driven P-51 Mustangs had been breaking up enemy motor columns east of the Suez Canal whenever they could spot them.

For the hundreds of sorties flown by the IAF on the first day, the Egyptians flew only 40. The following day the Arabs were more enterprising and dogfights developed all over the Sinai, as the Egyptians finally realized the magnitude of the Israeli operation. By this time, IDF forces had also entered the Sinai along the central axis,

moving towards Jebel Libni, halfway to the Canal, and the mechanized column of the Airborne Brigade had linked up with the Mitla Pass force, beating off enemy counterattacks as heavy fighting developed.

Patrolling the sky above the Mitla, two pairs of Israeli Mystères spotted a flight of Egyptian Vampires strafing the pass. Diving on the fighter-bombers, the Mystères shot down three of them in seconds, leaving their burning wreckage scattered over the hills. The Egyptian pilots had been so engrossed in their attack that they had not spotted the oncoming danger.

Unhampered by any intervention from Egyptian reinforcements, which had been successfully stopped by the IAF attacks on the roads to the west, the Israeli advance was picking up momentum. In the northern sector, they now mounted another attack on the Egyptian-held Gaza Strip, with the objective of taking El Arish and the northern coastal road to the Suez Canal. One Israeli light-plane pilot on a reconnaissance patrol spotted a glittering object just

De Havilland DH-98 Mk-VI Mosquitos gracefully banking over Israel's coastal plain. Mostly assembled from scrapped parts purchased throughout Europe, these planes entered service with the RAF after the War of Independence and were used as interceptors, bombers, and photo reconnaissance craft until just after the Sinai campaign.

off the coast of the Bardawil Lagoon west of El Arish. He circled lower and identified it as an apparently intact MiG-15 that had crash-landed in the shallow waters. Navy salvage experts who were called in raised the aircraft, placed it on a makeshift raft, and towed it to an Israeli port. Air force technicians restored the MiG-15 to flying condition, and it was subjected to thorough flight and technical tests to discover the secrets of the first Soviet jet interceptor captured.

On October 31 the air force and navy again combined forces in a successful mission. In the pre-dawn darkness an Egyptian destroyer, the *Ibrahim-el-Awal*, bombarded Haifa with 220 100-mm high-explosive shells. The destroyer was spotted and attacked by the French cruiser *Crescent* patrolling off Haifa, but contact was lost in the dark. Israeli destroyers patrolling farther out at sea were ordered to intercept the Egyptian attackers. Shortly after dawn they sighted, identified, and opened fire at her from a range of 8,200 meters. Answering a request for air support, two Ouragans dived on the ship and caused heavy damage with salvos of armor-piercing rockets. The Egyptian captain ordered the crew to abandon and scuttle the ship, but the seacocks were rusty and could not be

turned. The Israelis boarded quickly and towed the destroyer into Haifa port. The vessel, renamed *Haifa*, was later put into the service of the Israeli Navy.

As Operation Kadesh moved rapidly to a successful climax, the Anglo-French Operation Musketeer to capture the Canal Zone got underway. The general plan, disregarding the Israeli operations in the Sinai, was to capture the Canal Zone beginning with an amphibious landing and parachute drop at Port Said, at the northern end of the Canal. The assembled force, which consisted of some five French and British divisions, was supported by an armada of warships and over 450 combat aircraft. It turned out to be a classic overestimation of enemy potential.

A massive preparative aerial bombardment was to destroy the Egyptian Air Force on the ground prior to the landing. By this time the Egyptian Air Force was already heavily engaged with the Israelis and, as a result of constant dogfights in which it had lost several aircraft, had become extremely discouraged. Though the RAF attack on the airfield was not very effective materially, as it took place at night and from high altitude, it was lethal to Egyptian morale. When followed up the next day by a low-level Anglo-French air attack, the

Egyptians, fearing complete destruction, flew their remaining aircraft to bases in Syria and Saudi Arabia. Their IL-28 bombers were flown to faraway Luxor for protection, but they were eventually destroyed by French F-84 Thunderstreaks modified for the long-range flight from Lydda, in Israel.

After the unnecessary four-day-long air preparation, the Anglo-French attack finally began with a paratrooper drop and a heliported group flown in from aircraft carriers in the area of the northern end of the Canal. But the whole operation ended in a great fiasco and gave the Egyptians every reason to be jubilant and arrogant, even though they had lost the Sinai to the Israelis. The vast number of troops and supporting arms contributed by the British and French failed to achieve their objectives due to slow implementation, weak political leadership, and intervention by the United States and the UN.

There remained one more objective for the Israelis to attain, in fact the primary objective of the campaign—in opening of the Tiran Straits. Sharm el-Sheikh, guarding the outlet to the Red Sea from the Gulf of Eilat, was a fortified position held by a strong force supported by naval guns. On November 2 the Ninth Infantry Brigade set out from Eilat towards the southern tip of the peninsula, making its way along the coast by a track that had been secretly reconnoitered in 1955. The attack was well supported by air. An Egyptian officer of the Sharm el-Sheikh garrison has been quoted as saying, "I learned about close air support . . . in England, or so I thought until I stood at Sharm el-Sheikh."

With the capture of Sharm el-Sheikh, the Sinai campaign was brought to an end. The Israelis had achieved all of their objectives in a lightning war of only 100 hours. The IAF had gone into action facing an air force equipped with more and better aircraft, and under severe strategic limitations that prohibited a preemptive strike and raids against bases across the Canal. Four days later, the air force had emerged from the Sinai campaign with a clearcut victory over its opponent. The air battles during the Sinai campaign showed clearly that piston-engine planes could no longer cope with modern combat conditions. The Mustang fighter bombers had proved to be quite vulnerable to ground fire, and though they had done an outstanding job, they needed to be replaced. The same applied to the Mosquitos and the B-17s, both of which had taken only a limited part in the fighting.

The question was, what aircraft would best suit the needs of the air force and, more important, be available to the Israelis? France was still the only country that was willing to sell them modern jets. The French aircraft had proven their worth in the fighting, especially the Ouragan, which had played a leading part in ground support as it was able to carry heavy combat loads. A new order for 45 of these aircraft was immediately placed. A jet-powered replacement for the Mosquitos was found in Sud Aviation's Vautour, a rugged twin-engine fighter-bomber that fulfilled the air force's requirements for a true multipurpose aircraft. The Israelis were now better equipped to strike at the enemy's hinterland, countering the Arab capacity to attack Israeli population centers and rear-area installations with their IL-28 bomber force.

The IAF was now in the process of becoming an all-jet force. The newly created Israel Aircraft Industries—or Bedek, as it was then called—signed a contract with the French Air-Fouga Company for rights to assemble the Fouga-Magister jet trainer in Israel. The first aircraft left the new plant in June 1960 and started a production line that by 1974 was to produce the modern Kfir fighter-bomber.

By the beginning of the 1960s, the Israelis were again seriously worried about the extent of a new Arab arms buildup. Russian weapons were being supplied in great quantities, and the Egyptian armed forces, especially the air force, were receiving, by Middle East standards, ultramodern combat equipment such as the latest MiG-19 interceptors. To strengthen Israel's defenses against the increased Arab air warfare capabilities, 24 Super Mystère B-2s were ordered. This advanced Mystère model was able to reach the speed of sound in level flight, but it was only an interim solution to the problem.

The answer was found in the Dassault Mirage III. Theoretically it possessed a speed of Mach 2.2 at 12,000 meters and, with the help of a rocket booster-motor, could climb to 15,000 meters in six minutes flat. At subsonic speeds it had a combat radius of 1,200 kilometers,

Sud Aviation SA-4050 Vautour single-seat light bomber landing on a northern Israeli air base. The braking chute is out, helping to stop the airplane. Later versions were painted with camouflage colors. These aircraft flew long-range bombing missions as far apart as the upper Nile Valley in Egypt and Iraqi airfields during the Six-Day War.

enabling it to reach far into Egypt or any other Middle Eastern country. Redesigned to Israeli specifications, the extremely powerful and versatile weapons system could also carry a significant load of outside hardware for fighter-bomber missions. The outstanding qualities of this aircraft were evaluated by Israeli experts, and, after the Egyptians received the Mach 2+ MiG-21, the initial order for 24 was increased to 72.

In July 1958, General Ezer Weizman was appointed commander of the air force. Trained as a pilot in the RAF during World War II, he had served with the first Israeli fighter squadron in the War of Independence and was among the pilots whose attack stopped the Egyptian advance toward Tel Aviv. Having been General Tolkovsky's deputy after commanding two of

the air force's combat wings, General Weizman now took charge and set out to hone the air force into the formidable weapon that under his successor, Motti Hod, would reach its zenith with the lightning destruction of the Arab air forces on June 5, 1967.

The special emphasis in Weizman's doctrine was on the creation of a highly motivated, exceptionally well-trained professional pilot who would overcome the Arab advantage of quantity by higher quality. Constantly stressing this point, he set out to achieve his aim by placing very stringent qualifications on trainee advancement, standards so high that a pilot's course in 1960 ended with only one graduate receiving his wings, the rest having "washed out." But his persistence paid off, and the pilots that graduated from the courses were the very es-

A formation of Mirage IIICs, still in the original silver paint, over the Jezreel Valley before the Six-Day War. The IAF basic combat formation was a flight of four aircraft.

sence of Israeli military enterprise—or, as they chose to call themselves with no undue pride, "the best of the best."

Several air battles took place, especially with the Syrians, prior to the Six-Day War. Constantly gaining the upper hand, the Israelis were convinced of their technical as well as professional superiority. This aerial ascendancy was the basic premise for the dynamic planning of the preemptive strike concept with which the Israeli High Command prepared for war.

General Mordechai Hod was appointed commander of the air force in the spring of 1967, replacing General Weizman, who was appointed head of the General Staff Division. Weizman was the first air force officer to be named to this post, which is second only to the chief of the General Staff.

The air force was now* an impressive fighting force equipped with modern combat equipment. Flying mainly French aircraft, it operated 72 Mirage IIICJ fighter-bombers in three squadrons, one 18-plane-strong Super Mystère squadron, and one squadron each of Mystère and Ouragan fighter-bombers. Including the obsolete Vautour light bombers and transport planes, total IAF strength amounted to some 350 aircraft, as opposed to some 800 first-line combat aircraft of the combined enemy air forces, now equipped almost solely with Soviet-made planes. The MiG-21s were the backbone of the Arab fighter force and, with the bomber force of Tupolev-16 medium jet bombers, posed the main challenges to the IAF.

---

*According to foreign military analysts.

Chapter 4
The Six-Day War, 1967

It was a frightening time for the people of Israel. The neighboring countries had been arming themselves at a rapid rate, and some had their armies massed on the borders of the tiny state. To the south the Egyptian dictator, Gamal Abdel Nasser, was shouting provocative threats and rattling his saber. To wait for their enemies to engulf them would have been a folly tantamount to suicide for the Israelis.

By the night of June 3, D day and H hour had already been chosen: 0745 hours on June 5. This hour was ideally suited for the kind of preemptive air strike Israel would have to take. In the first place, it was an unusual hour for attacking; most air attacks were carried out at dawn. Accordingly, Egypt had gotten into the habit of sending up MiG-21s to patrol Egyptian skies at first light. By 0745 (0845 Cairo time), these patrols would have landed. In addition, the mist that covers the Nile, the Delta, and the Suez Canal in the early morning usually disperses by 8:00 A.M., leaving excellent visibility and still air. Another important consideration (according to Israeli intelligence) was that Egyptian military personnel get to their offices at 9:00 A.M. Striking 15 minutes before that time would catch much of the Egyptian Air Force between home and base.

Early in the morning of June 5, 1967, Maj. Gen. Mordechai Hod, commander of the IAF, issued a battle order to his troops. That order might well have come directly from the Old Testament:

Soldiers of the air force, the blustering and swash-buckling Egyptian Army is moving against us to annihilate our people. . . . Fly on, attack the enemy, pursue him to ruination, draw his fangs, scatter him in the wilderness, so that the people of Israel may live in peace in our land, and the future generations be secured.

In a flash Israeli Mirages, Mystères, Super Mystères, Vautours, Ouragans, and Fouga-Magisters roared into action, clawing for the sky. Operation Focus—the air strike—was underway.

The first wave of IAF aircraft, flying in double-pair formation, reached Egypt exactly on schedule. Flying close to the ground at first, to avoid Egyptian (and perhaps Soviet) radar, the aircraft climbed into detection range a few minutes before reaching their targets. Thus they succeeded in catching Egyptian fighter aircraft, alerted too late, on the runways.

In the IAF command and control center in Tel Aviv, Gen. Hod, affectionately known as "Motti," sat calmly, watching and listening. As the first reports began to come in, the excitement was unbearable; but Motti Hod remained cool, almost detached. The one sign of the terrible strain the IAF commander felt was the prodigious quantities of water he consumed. While others clenched their fists and held their breaths, Hod picked up jug after jug of water and drained them dry. IDF Head of General Staff Division Ezer Weizman, seated beside Hod in the IAF bunker, recalls: "I relieved my tension with a momentary thought: 'What will happen first—will a couple of hundred Egyptian planes go up in flames—or will (Hod's) radiator burst?'"

The radiator did not burst. By 0855 hours 11 Egyptian airfields had been attacked. Some 197

A last-minute check before takeoff at dawn.

enemy aircraft had been destroyed—189 on the ground and two MiG-21 foursomes in air combat. Six airfields had been rendered inoperable and 16 radar stations disabled. All this had been accomplished by 185 aircraft, nearly all of Israel's first-line planes. The IAF High Command, playing for high stakes, had left only three foursomes to guard the whole of Israel, eight flying top cover and four on standby at the end of the runway.

All but 19 of the IAF strike force made it home undamaged and set out immediately on a second wave. ("Immediately," by the way, meant just that: In those crucial first hours of the war, air turnaround time had been reduced to an incredible 7½ minutes!) The second wave attacked 14 air bases, destroying an additional 107 Egyptian aircraft. After destroying the aircraft, the IAF strike force attacked the runways with "dibber" bombs. These included a retro-

0630 hours, June 5, 1967, at an IAF air base. The fuel tanker is filling up the Mirage IIIC on which the ground crew has worked all night, readying it for the mission. Matra R-530 air-to-air missile and drop tanks indicate that this plane is assigned an interceptor, high cover, or air superiority role.

rocket to stop the bomb's forward impetus, a booster rocket to drive the bomb deep into the concrete runway, and a time fuse. Some of the bombs exploded instantaneously, others only after the original damage had been repaired. (At one airfield, El Arish near the Gaza Strip, specific orders had been given not to use bombs on the runaway. As the fighting progressed the reason for this became obvious. Forty-eight hours after the start of the war El Arish was already being used by the IAF as a forward base!)

At the time of the initial attack a single Egyptian plane was airborne: a twin-engine Illyushin heading westward over the Sinai and carrying three of the highest-ranking Egyptian commanders, including Chief of Staff Gen. Amer. Listening in on the Israeli frequencies, the commanders could not make out any unusual traffic, and flying west, the Illyushin headed for Kabrit air base. At that precise moment, the control tower informed the pilot that it was under air attack. Confused by chatter which covered all frequencies with excited announcements that all air bases were being attacked, the

commanders, in complete frustration, vainly tried to find a base where they could land. As they searched, they watched the bases along the whole length of the Canal going up in flames. They finally landed at Cairo International Airport and rushed to the Command Room, only to be informed that for all practical purposes the Egyptian Air Force no longer existed.

For two hours, the IAF ravaged the Egyptian airfields; as each flight of four fighter-bombers completed its attack, the next formation of four took over. The results of the precise air strikes far surpassed the expectations of the Israeli commanders and stunned the world.

So accurate was the marksmanship that the pilots rarely missed. The enemy aircraft were knocked out by unerring aerial cannon* fire, and the runways were destroyed with bombs: conventional "iron" bombs that were right on target, not the new radar- and TV-guided "smart" bombs.

At Cairo West Airfield the Israeli Mirages caught all 30 of the Egyptian Tu-16 bombers

---

*Israeli-manufactured 30-mm DEFA cannon.

A Dassault Super Mystère B-2 jet fighter-bomber pilot strapped into his seat. The hood is already closed for takeoff—target: Egypt. Along the top canopy brace can be seen two rear-view mirrors. The transparent rectangle below the left mirror is the gun sight.

parked in their hardstands and blew them to pieces, eliminating the danger to the Israeli cities posed by the Egyptian Air Force. Twin-engine Vautours crossed the Red Sea and streaked deep into Upper Egypt to destroy the planes at Luxor and Ras Banas, where the Egyptians had dispersed their aircraft in search of safety.

Though most of the Arab planes were destroyed on the ground, some dogfights nevertheless did develop. The largest one took place over Abu Suweir, near Ismailia, where 16 Mirages and 20 MiG-21s clashed high over the battle zone. The Egyptians courageously hurled themselves at the Israelis, but four of them were shot down within a few seconds and the remainder scattered; trying to land on the bomb-pitted runways of their airfields, many crashed in the attempt.

Influenced by Egyptian boasts of their ascendancy over the Jewish state, Jordanian, Syrian, and Iraqi aircraft attacked targets in Israel. Twelve Syrian MiG-17s took off from Damascus at 1250 hours. Of these, only three attacked a military target, an airfield in the Jezreel Valley; the others bombed, strafed, and rocketed civilian kibbutzim, a dam on the Jordan River (which they missed), and a convalescent home near Nazareth. Jordanian Hawker Hunter aircraft took off at noon, attacking one airfield and destroying a Noratlas transport aircraft on the ground, as well as bombing the coastal resort of Natanya in the mistaken belief that they had reached Tel Aviv. At 1400 hours three Iraqi Hawker Hunters rocketed the Israeli settlement of Nahalal (coincidentally, Moshe Dayan's home), causing no damage.

This was enough to convince Motti Hod to

A MiG-21 destroyed on the runway—the pilot hastily abandoned the aircraft before it went up in flames.

use the IAF to attack Syria, Jordan, and Iraq as well. Minutes after the first reports of Syrian aircraft over Israeli territory, eight flight formations were diverted in midair toward air bases in Syria and Jordan. That same day Israeli jets destroyed the entire Royal Jordanian Air Force, as well as its two main air bases at Mafraq and Amman. Syria lost 53 aircraft—out of a total of 112—in attacks on five airfields: Damascus, Dmeir, Seikal, Marj Rial, and T-4. And a single three-sortie attack on H-3 airfield in Iraq destroyed ten Iraqi aircraft.

By the evening of June 5 the skies above the Golan Heights, the West Bank, and the entire Sinai Desert were the exclusive province of the Israeli Air Force. Total Israeli losses on that day were 19 planes—nine in Egypt and ten in Syria—and ten pilots. An additional four pilots were taken prisoner. The air forces of Egypt, Syria, Jordan, and Iraq were effectively put out of action.

The Israeli ground war could now pursue its objectives, supported by a victorious air force that could operate at will over the battlefield. Battles were raging on all three borders. In the west the Israeli armored divisions advanced into the Sinai with the objective of reaching the Suez Canal.

During and after the strikes on the Arab airfields the IAF was also used against the enemy ground forces. In fact, some two thirds of the total IAF sorties flown during those six days were directed against ground forces. These operations were carried out by every kind of

Morning, June 6, 1967—Cairo West Airfield under IAF attack. Note the neatly lined-up transport on the far side of the runway. Many were destroyed in the first surprise attack.

warplane in commission in the Israeli Air Force, from the supersonic Mirage IIICs, through the Super Mystères, Mystères, and Ouragans, down to the Fouga-Magisters, training aircraft outfitted with machine guns and rockets for use on armored and mechanized troops.

On the first day of the war IAF aircraft flew missions against artillery batteries protecting the Rafah and Umm Katef fortifications, winning a respite for the attacking IDF armored and parachute units. Fouga-Magisters also shot up a munitions train in El Arish, with what one IAF correspondent described as "spectacular effects." Toward evening Israeli warplanes attacked Jordanian tank reinforcements moving up the Jordan Valley toward Jerusalem; by morning almost all of the Jordanian tanks had been destroyed.

On June 6, the IAF was used against the ground forces of Egypt, Jordan, Syria, and Iraq. The principal area of activity, however, was in the Sinai; IAF aircraft smashed everything that moved along the desert roads all the way to the Suez Canal, as well as the railroad line to El Arish. That same day IAF planes carried out strikes against Jordanian Pattons engaged in a tank battle in the Jenin area, and knocked out several artillery batteries in Qalqilya farther south. The Iraqi mechanized brigade sent to Jordan's assistance never reached the West Bank of the Jordan: A devastating air strike forced the brigade back across the Damiya Bridge, which it had just begun to cross, and it took no part in the fighting. On the Syrian front the IAF took out artillery on the Golan Heights as well as reinforcements being moved

Entrance to Mitla Pass, June 1967. Egyptian military convoys destroyed by IAF fighter-bombers.

up to the front lines. Syrian infantry and armor that had tried to break through the defenses of two Israeli border settlements were quickly routed in an air strike.

On the second day of the fighting Algerian MiG-21s that had been rushed to the battle area made several surprise attacks, mainly on the coastal sector in the northern Sinai. Though effective, they could not replace the strength of the shattered Egyptian force. The third day of fighting was marked by mass destruction of Egyptian convoys in retreat. Air strikes at the Mitla and Gidi passes trapped thousands of Egyptian vehicles jammed at their approaches. From the air the pilots could see the Egyptians abandoning their immobilized, burned-out equipment and setting out on foot for the Suez Canal, 60 kilometers to the west. On the Jordanian front the IAF softened up Arab Legion positions at Augusta Victoria in East Jerusalem and helped attack Jordanian tanks west of Nablus prior to taking the city.

On the eastern front the Israeli attack on the West Bank gained momentum with the capture of Jerusalem and the hills of Samaria, thus bringing to an end Jordanian rule over the territories annexed in 1948. In the heavy fighting for the Old City of Jerusalem, the Israeli fighter-bombers strafed Jordanian army positions on Mount Scopus, enabling the Israeli paratroopers to capture their objectives.

After June 7 Jordan was no longer in the war, and the IAF concentrated its efforts on Egypt and Syria. In the Sinai the aircraft kept the roads blocked to retreating Egyptians while systematically destroying those enemy units still at large. In Syria the air force attacked the Golan Heights on June 8 and ran long-range missions deep into Syria on the last two days of the war. The most intense bombing and strafing of the war was directed against the Syrian-fortified Golan Heights. This major obstacle was subjected to heavy bombing, which was ineffective because the well-dug-in fortifications were almost impenetrable. This necessitated hand-to-hand fighting, with the air force holding off enemy reinforcements and attacking concentrations of artillery inside Syrian territory. It was during this fighting that the Russian SA-2 surface-to-air missile was first en-

An Israeli Mirage III on its way to the target.

Gun camera sequence of downing of Syrian MiG-21 during Six-Day War. The Syrians lost eight MiG-21s and three MiG-17s in aerial combat during that war. At the beginning the Syrians had about 40 MiG-21s, 40 MiG-17s, and a few bombers.

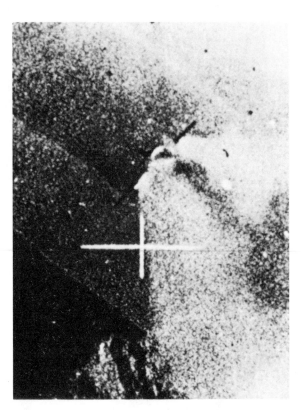

Tracking   *Destruction*

Samoa, Jordan, 1967. A Royal Jordanian Air Force Hunter Mk-IX shot down by IAF jets in a dogfight during an Israeli retaliatory raid prior to the Six-Day War. The rocky heights on the left are the hills of Judea near the Dead Sea. The Jordanian pilots showed a high standard of training and fighting spirit in these air battles.

countered. (This was the same deadly missile the USAF encountered later over Vietnam.) Though the SAMs did not succeed in downing an Israeli plane, they were to have an immense impact on the combat environment of future wars.

When the cease-fire came into force on Saturday, June 10, the IAF had lost a total of 46 aircraft, all but three of which had been brought down by ground fire. Some badly damaged planes had crashed on return to their base, and a few pilots had bailed out over enemy territory and were taken prisoner. For an air force that had started the war with fewer than 200 combat aircraft, this was a serious loss. However, a crushing blow had been dealt to the enemy in the destruction of 452 of their aircraft, 79 of them in air combat. Eight SA-2 missile batteries had been destroyed and a ninth taken intact by ground forces with air support. A total of 18 radar stations had been put out of action in Jordan, Syria, and Egypt. The Egyptian and

Syrian Air Forces lost all effectiveness as fighting units; the Royal Jordanian Air Force, in effect, ceased to exist. Moreover, the IAF had protected Israeli airspace, shooting down every plane that crossed Israel's borders. All this does not take into account the destruction of hundreds of Arab tanks and vehicles, nor the absolute air superiority that played a decisive role in breaking enemy resistance on every front. Without a doubt, this gave the elated IAF aircrews an overwhelming sense of victory. On the other hand, they were under no illusions that the fighting was over and the final battle won.

It is fascinating to study the background of a war and the steps that led to it. The Six-Day War is a classic case. Most military analysts agree—and with good reason—that the Six-Day War was Israel's finest hour. It is certainly true that the events of June 5 through 10, 1967 are without parallel in modern military history. In six short days the armed forces of Israel, mostly made up of reservists, vanquished three

IAF Mirage IIIs.

regular enemy armies, each of which was equipped with matériel as good as or better than that of the IDF. The incredible valor and persistence of Israel's army, navy, and air force brought about the conquest of territories three times the size of prewar Israel.

The usual description of the war's beginning—the Israeli Air Force suddenly swooping down on more than two dozen enemy airfields—is incomplete and inaccurate for two reasons. First of all, although the IAF was indeed the spearhead of the striking force, the role played by Israel's ground forces was no less important. And second, to those who had followed Middle Eastern developments in the months prior to June 1967, the Israeli preemptive strike was not at all "sudden."

For nearly three years before the Six-Day War Israel's northern border had been the scene of escalating hostilities, nearly all of which were carrried out by Syrian armed forces against Israeli civilian agricultural settlements in the Galilee. They stemmed from a long-standing dispute over Israel's plan to operate a National Water Carrier from Lake Kinneret to the parched Negev Desert in the south. Syria (wrongly, according to the UN) felt that Israel would be stealing water from the Arabs. Accordingly, a two-pronged plan was devised. The Syrians developed a blueprint for a water carrier of their own that would divert the Jordan sources even before they got as far south as Lake Kinneret. At the same time they began to disrupt the construction and operation of Israel's water carrier with massive artillery and rocket attacks on Israeli tractors and engineering machinery, as well as on Israeli fields near the Syrian border. When IDF patrols began protecting the civilian border settlements, the Arabs fired on them, too. On several occasions IDF armored and mechanized troops were sent in, putting a rapid end to the Syrian water carrier project. But the harassment continued, and grew in intensity. In the early months of 1967 Prince Minister Levi Eshkol gave permission for the Israeli Air Force to enter the scene. Several air clashes took place in March and April 1967; one of these, on April 7, resulted in the downing of six Syrian MiGs over the Syrian capital.

It was not only the Syrian Army that used Israel's northern border as a springboard for

Israeli jet fighter pilots returning from a combat mission. The officer on the left—a lieutenant—is wearing G-suit trousers and a light khaki shirt over which he is wearing an inflatable life jacket. The boxes contain gun camera film.

Super Mystère B-2 in power takeoff. The first true supersonic aircraft in the IAF, it served as the front-line fighter from 1958 until the arrival of the Mirage in 1963.

Ground-support bombing of Egyptian positions at last light in the Sinai.

A Sud Aviation Potez-Air Fouga CM 170 Magister jet trainer during the 1967 war. These aircraft were armed with 7.5-mm machine guns, 12 to 16 80-mm rockets or four 100-pound bombs, and, flown by reserve pilots, carried out ground-attack missions during the Six-Day War on the Eygptian and Jordanian fronts. On the first day the Fougas destroyed three radar stations, 40 tanks, an ammunition train, and many light vehicles. Lacking an ejection seat and too slow to evade anti-aircraft fire or enemy fighters, the Fougas were dangerous aircraft to fly. Note stencils on fuselage—this plane has already taken out two trucks and a tank.

hostilities. The Palestine Liberation Organization, a terrorist group dedicated to the annihilation of the State of Israel, was founded in 1958. Six years later its leaders obtained Syrian permission to stage raids into Israel from inside Syria. In addition—although without the official sanction of the governments involved—terrorist cells operated from within Jordan and Lebanon, striking at undefended civilian targets inside Israel. In 1965 and 1966 the IDF carried out several reprisal raids into Arab villages known to be harboring terrorist activists. These reprisals, however, had two unfortunate effects: They tended to escalate terrorism instead of repressing it, and they provided an excuse for the Arab nations to turn UN and world sympathy against Israel.

Through all this time Egypt had not carried out any overtly hostile acts against Israel. Admittedly, the Egyptian government tended to sympathize with Syria and the PLO; however, they neither sent assistance to Syria nor permitted terrorist activity against Israel from within Egypt. As it happened, Egypt had very good reason for not wishing to get involved. First of all, since 1962 the Egyptian Army had been conducting a long, arduous campaign in Yemen. In 1967 some 50,000 Egyptian troops were committed in Yemen; almost daily, Egyptian Air Force missions bombed and strafed hundreds of Yemeni villages. Further, President Gamal Abdel Nasser had no desire to see his villages razed by IDF commandos or his new MiGs shot down over Cairo, as the Syrian MiGs had been downed over Damascus. Accordingly, Egypt confined itself to promises of aid to any

Arab countries attacked by Israel—promises that seemed empty to Syria's rulers.

In May 1967, however, the situation shifted. Following the April 7 incident Syria decided to force Nasser's hand. A few weeks after the battle Syria began to convey deliberately falsified intelligence reports to Egypt, reports that claimed an Israeli military presence of up to 11 brigades on the Syrian border. Echoes of these reports were amplified by the Soviet Embassy in Tel Aviv, despite efforts by Israel to disqualify them. Actually, at the time Israel had no more than a single company in the area, a fact that was confirmed by UN observers. But Nasser chose to listen to his allies, Syria and the Soviet Union. The Egyptian president realized that caution on his part could mean the loss of Soviet support—and possibly that of the "hawks", among his own people as well. Accordingly, on May 14, 1967, Nasser decided on a demonstration of strength: He dispatched two divisions into the Sinai, tripling the number of troops committed east of the Suez Canal. This move was calculated to fulfill a dual purpose: Not only would it convince Syria of Egypt's sincerity and loyalty, but Israel, in the face of an Egyptian troop concentration in the Sinai, would be deterred from attacking Syria. Thus Nasser would be spared having to rush troops and matériel to the assistance of her northern ally. Israel, which had never intended to attack Syria, was not unduly distressed by the Egyptian move at this stage. Apart from the mobilization of one IDF reserve brigade, life in Israel on May 15 was normal.

Nasser's next move, however, was escalatory rather than deterrent. On May 16, following the transfer of the Egyptian divisions into the Sinai, he asked his chief of staff, Gen. Fawzy, to cable Gen. Rikhye, commander of the United Nations Emergency Forces (UNEF) in the Sinai. In the telegram, Fawzy instructed Rikhye to withdraw his troops from the Sinai, concentrating them inside the Gaza Strip. The reason given ("The complete secure [sic] of all UN troops . . . along our borders") convinced neither Rikhye nor UN Secretary-General U Thant. Thant's reply, the following day, stated that the UNEF troops could not in conscience perform such a partial withdrawal. Nasser would either have to allow the UN troops to remain in their existing positions or request the complete withdrawal of the UNEF from Egyptian territory. However, by the time this reply was received, Egyptian troops had already begun the forcible eviction of the UN forces from the Sinai. Taking this as Nasser's answer, U Thant ordered his forces home. This, in effect, left the Sinai clear for action.

The next steps were rapid. On May 20, both Israel and Egypt ordered partial mobilizations of reservists. Two days later Nasser announced that the Straits of Tiran—and hence the Gulf of Aqaba—were closed to Israeli ships. The Egyptian president was fully aware that this was tantamount to a military challenge; ten years earlier, UN Ambassador Golda Meir had stated that Israel would regard interference with her shipping in the Straits of Tiran "as entitling her to exercise her inherent rights of self-defense." Had United States President Lyndon Johnson not promised international assistance in clearing the straits for Israel, Levi Eshkol might well have sent the IDF into the Sinai as early as May 24. In the face of such an American promise—which never materialized—Eshkol decided not to take immediate action. Israel's reserves were fully mobilized, a move that seriously affected the country's economy. But the troops sat on the border, teeth clenched, and waited.

Meanwhile surprising things were happening on Israel's eastern front. On May 24 Radio Amman had announced King Hussein's permission for Saudi Arabia and Iraq to send expeditionary forces to Jordan. At the time, these countries ignored the "little king's" invitation. But six days later, on May 30, to the surprise of all and the great dismay of Israel, Hussein suddenly turned up in Cairo. His mission: the signing of a defense pact between Jordan and Egypt. The following day Iraq's President Aref agreed to send troops and armored units into Jordan. And when PLO spokesman Ahmed Shukairy announced in Amman that it was "possible and even most likely" that his organization would fire the first shot, none of the Arab rulers even bothered to protest.

These developments convinced Levi Eskhol, who was then both prime minister and minister of defense, of two things. First of all, he realized his country was definitely headed for all-out war on at least two fronts. This led to the realization that Eshkol himself, a gifted statesman but one with no real military experience to speak of, could not hope to continue holding both his portfolios if he wanted Israel to end that war with victory. A senior military man, an "old fox" at the art of fighting the Arabs would have to be appointed as minister of defense. At first, Eshkol considered giving the post to the former chief of staff, Yigael Yadin; the Israeli public, however, demanded that it be assigned to Moshe Dayan, who as chief of staff had led the IDF to victory in the Sinai campaign. Dayan himself, as it happened, had thought he would be appointed GOC (General Officer Commanding) Southern Front. The possibility of a ministry had not occurred to him, as he had resigned the Ministry of Agriculture on leaving Israel's ruling Mapai party two years previously. As Dayan whimsically remarked in an interview the day after his appointment, "It took 80,000 Egyptian troops to get me back into the government!"

As May gave way to June, it became more and more evident that the only way for Israel to win the impending war would be by preemptive strike. The willing Soviet assistance given to Egypt and Syria had brought the Arab arsenals to such power that they could easily wipe the Israeli nation out of existence if allowed to attack first. The Egyptian forces, now six divisions strong in the Sinai, were an imposing threat indeed—and not the only one. Syria had already shown over the years what it could do to Israel's northern settlements without even moving troops over the border. Should the Syrian and Jordanian armies decide to adopt a more concentrated version of this harassment, they would be able to control the Jerusalem–Tel Aviv and Jerusalem–Haifa highways, all of Israel's airfields, and many of its cities. But the main danger lay with the Arab air power. By this time Israel's three closest neighbors had more than 800 first-line combat aircraft between them, massed in dozens of ultramodern air bases in Egypt, Syria, and Jordan, as well as two Iraqi squadrons brought forward from Habaniya Air Force Base near Baghdad to H-3, Iraq's westernmost military airfield—only minutes away from Israel. This fearsome strength, ranged against 350 Israeli aircraft (of which only 197 were first-line), meant that, if preemptive action were not taken, Arab aircraft could saturate Israel's defenses minutes after

the start of the war. Israel could not hope for air support from the United States or any other friendly nation. It would have to take preemptive action and destroy the Arab air forces alone.

This requirement, obvious as it may seem, represented a tall order for the existing Israeli Air Force. The many targets which would have to be destroyed in order to knock out Arab air power on the first run would make it necessary to carry more than 1,000 tons of armament. This was an obvious impossibility: Most of the aircraft in Israel's possession prior to June 1967 could carry less than 500 kilograms of armament apiece, and some only 250 kilograms. The 48 A-4 Skyhawk jets on order from the United States had a considerably higher payload; these, however, would not be delivered until some months later.

Accordingly, a plan was devised which met the IAF limitations and still rendered a decisive blow to the Arab air forces. A strict timetable of flight schedules, approach routes, and high-priority targets was worked out. All IAF air bases received standing orders to cut turn-around time below the minimum known anywhere else in the world. Highly efficient, up-to-date air intelligence was obtained for dozens of targets Israel would have to destroy. All this considered, Israel had reason to be optimistic. Even so, former IAF commander Ezer Weizman—who had handed over his command to Motti Hod ten months previously and was now serving as IDF head of General Staff Division—was regarded as overconfident following his public statement that Israel could wipe out the Arab air forces in a matter of hours.

Meanwhile, the situation on the ground had become extremely grave. The IDF High Command watched with awe the daily reports of Arab troop buildups on all of Israel's borders. More and more forces poured in from nations farther away: Kuwait, Saudi Arabia, Algeria, Iraq, and many more sent contingents to the aid of their brothers in Egypt, Syria, and Jordan. All this was accompanied by a "saber-rattling" mass-hate campaign on Arab radio and television, calling for an all-out *Jihad*—a holy war—that would eliminate, by driving the Jews into the sea, the "pestilence" that had infested the Middle East. And what was most frightening was that the Arabs seemed to believe this Nazi-style propaganda. Inciting to violence were the radio messages from Damascus, Cairo, and Baghdad:

The time has come! Silence the enemy! Destroy him! Liberate Palestine! O ye Arabs! Soon we shall return to the captive homeland! Yes, yes! See you in Tel Aviv!

The echo of this threat had a sobering effect throughout the world: Once again the Jewish people faced annihilation.

Israel's defense plans on the ground were, like those in the air, basically offensive in nature. The main effort would be directed at the destruction of the most numerous and potentially dangerous enemy, Egypt. To this end, the majority of Israel's ground forces were concentrated in the Negev. Three "divisions" were deployed (not regular divisions but the Ugda, unique to the IDF; an Ugda is a division-sized formation that allows much more freedom of action for its individual brigades). The regular armored division led by Maj. Gen. Israel Tal was stationed along the southern Gaza Strip near Rafah, facing the Egyptian Seventh Infantry Division and the Twentieth Palestinian Division. A second Ugda led by Maj. Gen. Ariel Sharon was deployed against the strongly held Second Infantry Division sector, which controlled the Abu Ageila–Kusseima axis through the Sinai to the Suez. A third division, under the command of Maj. Gen. Avraham Yoffe, was kept in reserve between the two, to ward off possible intervention by the Egyptian Fourth Armored Division (concentrated at Bir Gafgafa) and the division-size force commanded by Gen. Shazali (headed east from El Arish to the Negev). To stem off any offensive efforts to the Negev itself, a mechanized brigade commanded by then Brig. Gen. Albert Mendler (later to reach the rank of major general and to be killed commanding the Sinai in the Yom Kippur War) was operating as an independent force near Kuntilla.

Against an Egyptian force of seven divisions and 900 tanks, the IDF deployed three divisions and one independent brigade. The strongest division, that commanded by Tal, included some 205 tanks—mostly Patton M48s and Centurions with some AMX13s. Sharon's division had about 150 tanks—mostly Sherman M50s with one battalion of Centurions and one of AMX13s. With Yoffe's two undersized Centurion brigades and some 50 tanks in the southern Negev, Israel had under 600 tanks deployed in the south against an enemy with 50 percent greater numerical strength. Even this comparison did not take into account the fact that many of the Egyptian tanks were modern Soviet T54/5s and Stalin IIIs.

In the north and east Israel's situation was no less grave. The Jordanians had seven tank-supported infantry brigades strung out along Israel's border. Two armored brigades were deployed in the Jordan Valley: the Fortieth (Jordan's elite tank formation, later to be sent to Syria in the Yom Kippur War) in the north and the Sixtieth in the south. In addition to these 270 tanks, an Iraqi mechanized brigade had already assumed position at Mafraq, a military complex serving ground and air forces in the north of Jordan. The Syrians had some 300 tanks ready to fight. Against all these, Israel could deploy only two undersized mechanized brigades, one west of Jerusalem and the other in the Jezreel Valley. An armored brigade, equipped with obsolescent Sherman M50/51s and light AMX13s, was held at GHQ reserve near Haifa. In all, Israel had only 180 mostly inferior tanks available to head off two Arab armies.

The following serves as an effective summary of how the IAF accomplished its mission:

In those devastating attacks on June 5, 1967, the Israeli Air Force knocked out, on the ground, most of the Egyptian, Syrian, and Jordanian Air Forces. These missions were carried out according to specifications set up in an operational plan called Moked ("Focus"), a result of an air warfare study made by the IAF from 1962 to 1965. The purpose of this mission was, in case of emergency, to destroy the enemy air forces on the ground in one surprise, preemptive attack.

Surprise was the key. Aircraft were to take off and ingress in complete radio silence, at a very low level, and on precise schedule. Routes chosen were not the shortest to the target, thus not disclosing their objectives The major objective was to cripple enemy bomber and interceptor forces (Tu-16, I1-28, and MiG-21). In order to achieve this goal, the IAF tested all

Egyptian aircraft caught napping on the ground.

possible solutions—high-level penetration using accurate dive bombing, and low-level approach under enemy radar coverage, providing total surprise and relative freedom from SAM threat. Various runway attacks were tested on dummy targets constructed in the Negev Desert. Attacks were practiced on centerlines, crossed runways, parallel runways, taxiways, installations, etc.

One of the lessons gleaned from these tests was the need for special weapons for runway destruction where, on low-level attacks, bombs would not have time to arm before hitting the runway and would bounce back from the runway surface. The Israel Military Industry constructed a special device to solve this problem, the Runway Destruction Bomb (RDB)—a new concept (now widely known and manufactured in various countries) consisting of a retarding mechanism to slow the bomb, thus protecting the aircraft from the blast. The mechanism, a small parachute, also aims the weapon at a 60° angle to the ground and activates a rocket motor that pushes the warhead to penetrate

IL-28 parking complex at Abu Sueir. The location, although designed to ease maintenance and reduce taxiway construction, enabled single-pass multiple hits on the bombers.

through the runway's thick concrete layer. Then the bomb explodes, creating a 5-meter-diameter crater, about 1.60 meters deep. Tests were concluded in 1966, and the IAF received about 250 bombs just before June 1967.

When the Gulf of Aqaba was blocked on June 5, 1967 (two years after planning for Operation Moked had been terminated), the order was given to implement it and the IAF took off. The first missions that day were carried out by Fouga-Magister trainers (turned combat air-

craft) against four radar sites and communication facilities in the eastern Sinai, to ensure total surprise. The first wave of 95 aircraft was already en route to its targets—and just in time!

The attacks went off like clockwork. Each formation reached its target on time and most of the runways were hit by the RDBs on the first pass. Mystère IVs and Mirage IIIs carried the RDBs. Each plane carried two bombs (70 or 100-kilograms each), fuel tanks, and guns. Vautours, the heaviest IAF bombers, carried 500–1000 kilogram bombs and four 30-mm guns; Super Mystères, two 250-kilogram bombs or rockets and fuel tanks with two guns; and Ouragans, either 16 rockets or four 100-kilogram bombs with four 20-mm guns.

The formations flew very low, about 10 meters or lower, their exhausts trailing steam and spray over the sea. They hardly had time to locate themselves over the dense and homogeneous Delta topography, where navigation proved very difficult. Hazards presented by electric lines and trees were no less formidable than those of possible anti-aircraft artillery. Attacking the Sinai bases, the IAF formations concentrated over the Bardawil area, and coordinated their timing, which was crucial due to the relatively clustered positions of the enemy bases: Escaping enemy aircraft could endanger the IAF aircraft attacking other bases.

In the Sinai most airfields proved to be easy targets, except Bir Gafgafa. Being the Egyptian Air Force's main forward interceptor base, it was heavily defended with anti-aircraft artillery (AAA) and SA-2 surface-to-air missiles. Five MiGs were scrambled to intercept—but too late. Four were hit on the runway, with only one managing to escape.

Less lucky were the aircraft attacking Abu Sueir. This air base, one of Egypt's biggest, received the alert call on time. MiGs were already taking off when IAF Mirages started diving at the runways. Escaping the craters caused by the RDBs, the MiGs took off quickly, shooting down one of the oncoming Vautours. A long time passed before an IAF Mirage CAP was able to reach this area and shot down three of the MiGs.

However, most of the missions carried out in this first wave were successful. Egyptian aircraft, set in lines exposed and unprotected on the parking area, were destroyed. Airfield infrastructure was damaged, including control towers, maintenance hangars, and ammunition and fuel dumps. In less than an hour about 200 planes were left burning on the runway: half of the Egyptian Air Force strength. The IAF lost eight aircraft, a relatively small loss that was due mainly to the surprise factor.

To complete its mission the IAF launched a second attack wave at 0934, making a total of 115 sorties against Egyptian bases. The already hard-hit bases did not pose much of a threat. Attacks launched in this wave swept deeper into the Delta and Nile Valley, where they hit the Egyptian Tu-16 bombers that had escaped from their bases in Cairo West and Bnei Sueif. These missions were carried out successfully and some formations were diverted to other targets after their primary objectives had been destroyed.

Each attack consisted of one bomb pass and three to six strafing passes—a total of five to seven minutes over the target depending on range and type of aircraft. Runways were destroyed with RDBs, installations with general-purpose 100–1000-kilogram bombs and aircraft by gunfire. Of the 16 airfields attacked, three of four Sinai bases were closed on the first wave, and seven others were closed on the second. Only two were able to stay open throughout the day (Inshas and Abu Sueir). The key to the overwhelming success of this operation was again the surprise factor.

This successful series of attacks highlighted some important points. Using the low-low-high profile enabled the IAF to stage a complete surprise in the first wave, while a low-high-high profile on the second wave gave them more time over their targets. Each wave, with about 100–150 sorties attacking from altitudes of 30–1800 meters, was capable of knocking out 50 percent of the force available at the time, leaving the enemy with only 25 percent of the force it had had only three hours previously!

Later that same day, at 1300 hours, the IAF commenced the same kind of operation in Syria. In one continuous wave all the Syrian Air Force bases capable of threatening Israel were attacked. Five of the Syrian airfields were devastated. RDBs were not used in these strikes, so general-purpose bombs, rockets, and gunfire demonstrated their powers. However, runways were operational, MiGs were airborne, and the cost the IAF paid for the lack of surprise was high. In all, six Israeli aircraft were shot down (an attrition rate of 7.32 percent, almost twice that of the average at the Egyptian front). However, a total of 61 Syrian aircraft were destroyed on the ground, and seven MiG-21s and three MiG-17s were shot down in dogfights. Due to the availability of fighter aircraft cover and more time to engage in dogfights, the IAF managed to keep its loss rate down.

After destroying the Egyptian, Jordanian, and Syrian air forces, the IAF had no trouble offering close air support to ground troops, and flying counter air missions throughout the war.

Many lessons were learned from this war, both by the Israeli and the Arab forces. For instance, where fighters were scrambled with advance notice, capable of taking off or being on runway in time, they could hamper the Israeli attack, but not prevent it. The pilots' readiness and determination to fight were crucial factors. An air base's runway layout and repair capability largely determined its chances for survival, because air bases capable of being repaired in order to meet the second-wave attack stood a better chance than those crippled throughout the whole war. A fast and thorough hardening program was commenced after June 1967 and has since been implemented. In Egypt and Syria all aircraft in parking areas are now protected in concrete shelters capable of maintenance operations, refueling, and arming. Taxiways have been reconstructed to act as emergency runways. In Egypt secondary runways have been paved, reinforced with concrete, and, where crossed runways had previously been used, third runways have been built. Installation hardening was also carried out, and the Egyptians instigated a weapons research program to acquire more effective runway-destruction weapons. All these programs, innovations, and renovations were put to their greatest test in the Yom Kippur War.

Chapter 5
The War of Attrition, 1967–70

The War of Attrition is the one Mideast war about which the rest of the world knows very little. It was, by far, the longest of the Arab–Israeli conflicts, and it probably came closer to erupting into a world war than any of the others. (Despite its length and all of the armed confrontation, some historians do not consider it to be one of the Arab–Israeli wars.) More interesting, however, in the War of Attrition *the Soviet Air Force took an actual part in air-to-air combat—and lost to the Israelis!* Needless to say, the Russians never reported the battle to the press, and, like the Soviet participation in the Korean War, it has been a closely guarded secret . . . until now.

The protracted series of raids, shellings, and bombings on both sides of the Suez Canal between the Six-Day War and the cease-fire on August 7, 1970, is generally termed the War of Attrition. This usage, though customary, is not quite correct. It is erroneous to speak of *the* War of Attrition: There was not one but several military efforts directed against Israel during that period. Responsible for those sporadic flare-ups—no two of which were coordinated to any great extent—were the various nations defeated by Israel in the 1967 conflict, as well as the then-fledgling group known as the Palestine Liberation Organization. However, the most serious of these, both from the standpoint of IDF casualties (367 killed, 999 wounded) and that of Israel's continued strategic security, was the ongoing struggle between Israel and Egypt—or, rather, between Israel and the joint forces of Egypt and the Soviet Union.

The unusual—indeed, unparalleled—degree of cooperation between the Nasser/Sadat regime and the Politburo resulted, as do most international alliances, from highly disparate motives. Egypt's main reason for requesting what amounted to a Soviet takeover of Egyptian air defense was, simply, the need to build up an effective counterforce to what even Nasser recognized as Israel's air superiority. This, reasoned the Egyptian president, was the only way in which the Sinai might be taken; once this was accomplished, the Russians could be (and, in fact, eventually were) sent home.

Russia, however, did not see matters quite this way. Obviously, the Politburo would never have agreed to send thousands of experts, hundreds of aircraft, and an entire air defense division into Egypt for purely altruistic reasons, no matter what their opinion might be of "Israeli imperialism" versus "the struggle of the Egyptian masses." Had Brezhnev not believed Egypt would reward his efforts by allowing a permanent Soviet presence in the Middle East—and especially on the Mediterranean Sea—he would never have committed himself to such an extent. However, he knew that failure to do so would almost definitely result in the rapid downfall of the Nasser regime; to prevent such a development—which would have seriously endangered Soviet strategic as well as political aims—he called in the Soviet air defense.

Immediately after the cease-fire of June 1967 the Russians again rebuilt shattered Arab forces. A vast Soviet airlift replenished the Arab arsenals so quickly that by the end of June 1967, only two weeks after the defeat, the Egyptians had almost 200 aircraft, mainly MiG-21s and Sukhoi-7s—an air force more modern and formidable than the one annihilated by the

Against the guerrillas. A Bell 205 giving support to an anti-guerrilla search in the Hebron hills. Operating in a tightly integrated force with crack paratroopers, the helicopter pilots flew countless missions helping to break the back of PLO guerrilla activities, which made life difficult on the frontiers.

Israelis. The Arabs, who had learned their lesson from the air strike that destroyed their air forces on the ground, now dispersed their planes widely in underground hangars with thick concrete roofs. Since most of their aircraft had been destroyed on the ground, the Egyptians had lost only a few aircrews in the fighting, and thus were at no loss for trained personnel to man the new planes. Furthermore, the Soviets agreed to train hundreds more pilots in their flying schools in Russia.

Israel, however, found it difficult to acquire replacement aircraft. The loss of some 40 planes in the war, with a few others damaged, seriously diminished the IAF's inventory. The one-sided French embargo imposed before the war was holding up delivery of *50 custom-designed and paid-for Mirage Vs.* The Americans also became evasive about fulfilling their commitment to supply Skyhawks, which they finally honored toward the latter part of the year.

The Egyptians, gaining confidence with the growing stream of arms and not wanting the status quo to solidify, began shelling Israeli positions along the Suez Canal intermittently. The Israelis, unable to match the massive Egyptian artillery force, dug in and prepared to absorb the blows, hitting back here and there with deep-penetration commando raids.

Although the War of Attrition is generally considered to have started in the summer of 1969, in actual fact it began only a few short weeks after the end of the Six-Day War. On July 1, 1967, an IDF armored patrol moving north toward Port Fuad on the eastern bank of the Suez Canal was cut off by an Egyptian infiltrating force that had crossed the Canal under cover of darkness the previous night. The resulting battle continued for several days until—with the help of the Israeli Air Force—the Egyptians were finally defeated.

Egypt, however, did not give up easily. Three days later two events occurred, both confirming what was then the Egyptian policy of continued harassment. On July 4, a MiG-17—the first of many Egyptian aircraft to attempt flights over the Sinai—was shot down; that same day Egyptian artillery opened fire on Israeli positions across the Canal. Another Egyptian aircraft, this time an SU-7, was downed over the Sinai a week later; on July 14, six Egyptian MiGs were downed and one IAF aircraft lost in a combined air/ground battle in the Suez area, which also claimed the lives of many Israeli soldiers.

Such skirmishes as these continued until October, when a more serious exchange of incidents occurred. On October 21, 1967, the Israeli destroyer *Eilat*, on a routine patrol mission along the Sinai coasts, was hit and sunk by a Soviet-made Styx sea-to-sea missile fired from within Port Said harbor, itself protected from Israeli reprisal by the presence of several Russian warships. Israel, however, chose to respond to the loss of its flagship and 47 Israeli Navy officers and men by striking at a target far away from Port Said. On October 24, the Egyptian oil refineries at Suez were shelled and set ablaze by IDF gunfire.

Despite Nasser's late November declaration of intent to renew the war, the October incidents were the last in the Canal area for nearly a year (during most of which time the IDF was busily fighting off terrorists on the Jordanian and Syrian fronts). It was not until September 8, 1968, that the Egyptian Army renewed hostilities with a thunderous artillery barrage along 100 kilometers of the Canal. Ten Israeli soldiers, taken by surprise in the midst of a football game, were killed instantly, 18 more were wounded, some of them seriously. Seven weeks later, on October 26, another barrage killed 15 Israelis and wounded 30. This barrage resulted in two distinct actions: The first, immediate reprisal consisted of heavy Israeli shelling of the cities of Suez and Ismailia, as well as of the now rebuilt refineries, followed five days later by a daring heliborne commando raid on two bridges spanning the Nile and a new power transformer at Nag Hammadi, hundreds of kilometers west of Suez. The second reaction—which made itself felt in the four months' respite Egypt granted Israel following the October 31 raid—involved the construction of a series of reinforced concrete strongholds from Ras el Eish in the north to Port Tewfik in the south; this was later named the Bar-Lev Line.

Aside from the downing of a single Egyptian aircraft south of Sharm-el-Sheikh in December 1968, there were no serious clashes between Egypt and Israel until the beginning of March 1969. The first move was made by the Egyptians: The fierce bombardment of the Israeli positions was resumed. Days later, on March 8, 1969, the first major battle (excluding IAF reactions to Egyptian Air Force incursions) took place. Four Egyptian MiGs, their pilots trained by the Soviet Union, attempted to penetrate the airspace over the Sinai. Almost at once, a pair of IAF Mirages challenged them. Two of the MiGs fled westward at once; a third, less cautious, opened fire on the Mirages and was immediately blown out of the sky. The fourth MiG tried to flee, but was hit by IAF cannon fire; its pilot bailed out over the Sinai and was taken prisoner.

This incident caused no small amount of concern in Soviet circles. Despite the incredible amounts of money, matériel, time, and human resources expended by Soviet Air Force instructors and logistics experts on the Egyptian Air Force, Russia did not feel the Egyptians were ready to challenge the IAF on a large scale, and hundreds of Egyptian pilots were trained at Krasnodar and Saratov operational training establishments in the USSR. Nevertheless, something had to be done to keep up the pressure on Israel. Accordingly, the Soviets accelerated deliveries of artillery and ammunition to Egypt's ground forces, making it possible to keep up the deadly shelling of Israeli positions on the Canal. (Ironically, they also invited Israeli artillery reprisals, one of which—on March 9—was responsible for the death of the Egyptian chief of staff, Gen. Abdel Muneim Riad, who was visiting a forward command post on the west bank of the Canal.) At the same time, they reduced shipments to the Egyptian Air Force.

The following weeks were marked by escalation of both artillery and commando raids on both sides; in all of April only one Egyptian MiG was downed. However, on May 21, several formations of Egyptian aircraft tried to fly over the Sinai. In the Port Said sector a formation of MiGs was scattered and its leader's aircraft shot down by an IAF Hawk missile, the first downing of a Soviet-made aircraft by a Hawk missile anywhere in the world. Farther south, three out of a formation of eight MiGs were downed by air-to-air missiles.

From the middle of June to July 7 no fewer than nine Egyptian aircraft were shot down by the IAF. However, the IAF action that had the most decisive effect on Egyptian air policy was a sortie in which no bombs were dropped, no Egyptian aircraft appeared to challenge, and no damage, other than smashed windows and wounded dignity, was inflicted on any target anywhere in Egypt. On June 17, 1969, a pair of IAF Mirages set out from an air base "somewhere in Israel" with a very special mission: scaring the president of Egypt out of his wits. This was accomplished, quite simply, by flying in low over the prestigious Cairo suburbs of Heliopolis and Manshieh el Bakri at speeds high enough to produce the loudest sonic boom Nasser had ever heard. Windows were shattered throughout the area. Nasser's immediate reaction was to dismiss both his air force chief, Air Marshal Hinawi, and O/C (Officer Commanding) Air Defense Hassan Kamal, both of whom had been on duty at the time and neither of whom had been able to warn him of the impending "attack." However, the daring IAF action produced another, more significant result: For the first time, the Egyptian president began to think seriously about improving his country's air defense.

The first step in the implementation of Nasser's decision involved improving both the number and quality of Egypt's early warning systems. In addition, the SA-2 surface-to-air missile systems (which Egypt had begun receiving from the Soviet Union even before the Six-Day War, but which were made operational only later) were moved to sites south of Suez, only 100 kilometers from Cairo. It did not, however, take long before the IAF had shown that these changes were largely ineffectual—witness the downing, mentioned earlier, of nine Egyptian planes. The first three of these were shot down on June 24, in a dogfight over the Gulf of Suez; the remaining six, in July, on two separate occasions over Suez City.

By now not only Nasser, but his Soviet advisors as well, were extremely perturbed by the trend of events. Having no possibility of matching the Israelis in the air, Egypt continued pounding the Bar-Lev strongpoints with withering artillery fire. The effect of the continued barrages was to create a vicious cycle: (1) Egyptian aircraft downed, (2) Egyptian artillery shells IDF posts, (3) Israel, incensed at the shelling, increases its aerial efforts. Finally, on July 20, the IAF High Command gave the long-

awaited permission for Israeli pilots to launch an all-out attack along the Suez Canal.

The aerial attack was preceded by an extremely audacious commando raid on a potentially threatening Egyptian position, Green Island, the day before. Green Island, located in the Gulf of Suez, was used by the Egyptians as part of their anti-aircraft system; in addition to a radar station, it housed AAA gun emplacements of several kinds—all deadly. At dawn on July 19, a composite force made up of naval commando and elite Special Forces units landed on Green Island. The force, led by Col. Ze'ev Almog (now a major general and O/C Israeli Navy), stormed the radar and gun nests, putting them out of action and neutralizing the Egyptian troops stationed there. Within hours Green Island no longer presented any kind of threat to the flying force to come.

At noon on the next day the skies over the Sinai were suddenly filled with wave after wave of IAF aircraft. Missile sites, radar installations, conventional and AAA emplacements, everything west of the waterline was fair game to the attackers. On they came, discharging their deadly payload of bombs, napalm, rockets, and cannon fire; then they quickly returned to IAF bases, where the unbelievably rapid turn-around techniques the IAF had used in the Six-Day War once more came into play. By last light hundreds of sorties had been flown, wreaking havoc up and down the west bank of the Canal. Not many missile batteries or gun emplacements remained intact.

The stunned Egyptians hardly reacted to this onslaught. Only three hours later, while the Israeli pilots were still harassing the Egyptian positions, did the Egyptian Air Force finally show its hand. A flight of Sukhoi-7s and MiG-17s struck in a low-level hit-and-run attack into the Sinai, causing little damage. However, the Israeli high-cover interceptors fell on the attackers and shot down five Egyptian aircraft for one Israeli plane hit.

It was at this point that certain Egyptian General Staff officers began entertaining thoughts of a Canal crossing. However, this plan did not meet with Nasser's approval, nor that of his Soviet advisors—far from it. Nasser knew—and, in fact, had stated as early as March of that year—that he could not hope to succeed in an invasion of the Sinai. Accordingly, he instructed his General Staff to keep up the shelling; at the same time he instituted an intensive training program for Egypt's armor and infantry, thereby giving these forces the illusion of doing something useful. Meanwhile, the Russians simply made it impossible for the Egyptian armed forces to organize any attempt to cross the Suez Canal and invade the Sinai. Crucial supply orders were "lost" or mixed up; shipments of spare parts were "unaccountably" delayed. Eventually, even the most obdurate officers of Egypt's General Staff were forced to accept Nasser's plan for a protracted war of attrition as being—at least for the present—the most viable.

In the interim the IDF High Command began to plan a series of joint armor/air strikes deep into Egypt, in retaliation for the constant shelling that had by then cost Israel hundreds of casualties and tremendous economic damage. The first of these, a deep-thrusting raid on Egyptian territory southwest of the Gulf of Suez, was planned for September 9. However, it would first be necessary to knock out an SA-2 missile battery some 30 kilometers from Suez City, in order to ensure freedom of movement for the IAF air cover. There was no way to launch a commando raid against this battery; it had to be taken out from the air. Accordingly, at dawn on September 9, shortly after Israeli armor had landed on the west bank of the Gulf, several pairs of IAF aircraft swooped in low over the battery. The first bombs shattered the SA-2 command and control center; another pair of fighter-bombers knocked out the launchers; while still others attacked additional targets further inland, including an important Egyptian radar station in the Ras Zafrani area. One IAF aircraft was lost in this action. The aircraft was hit by Egyptian anti-aircraft artillery fire near Ras Zafrani; the pilot, despite efforts to bring his aircraft back to base, was forced to eject over the Gulf of Suez and drowned in the swirling water. Israel's naval commandos also played their part in the preparations for this strike: The day before, commandos penetrated the harbor of Ras Sadat on the Gulf of Suez, sinking two torpedo boats and damaging harbor facilities. The subsequent armored strike was very successful, killing many Egyptian military personnel, among them Soviet advisors, and causing extensive damage to a number of priority military targets. Once again Nasser was not informed of the raid, nor of the fact that neither aircraft nor armor had challenged the raiders, until the Israelis had already left Egypt eastward across the Gulf. Nasser's response was typical: He dismissed his chief of staff.

September 11, 1969, was a red-letter day in the annals of the Israeli Air Force. On that day the IAF's pilots and air defense crews downed 11 Egyptian aircraft, seven of them MiG-21s—the largest number of enemy aircraft to be shot down in one day since the Six-Day War. On that day, the Egyptian Air Force had attempted to retaliate for the IDF armored raid of the ninth. At least 40 Egyptian aircraft were slated to fly attack sorties on IDF targets; dozens of others were scrambled for intercept and cover missions. The assault began at 0900 hours; it was met by a "welcoming committee" of Israeli Hawk missiles and anti-aircraft artillery downing two of the potential attackers before they had had a chance to reach their targets. Three hours later, the Egyptian Air Force launched a second wave; it, too, was repulsed, pushing the attacking Egyptians back into their own airspace and downing several more. The third wave, later that afternoon, never even crossed the Canal. IAF formations engaged them 15 kilometers west of the waterline, chasing them 65 kilometers into Egyptian territory and downing three MiG-21s.

Israeli aircraft began attacking the western shore of the Gulf almost daily. As the weeks passed, the Port Said sector became another routine target. Although the IDF spokesman made it clear that the Israeli offensive would cease the moment the Egyptians silenced their artillery, Egypt showed no sign of wanting to do so, and so the raids continued. Eventually, the IAF began flying night bombing missions as well. This had an understandably destructive effect on the Egyptian Army's morale, which began to founder seriously as the IAF again proved its ability to dominate the skies.

While the fighting continued along and over the Canal, the air force also had its role to play in the fight against the guerillas and their Arab regular army backing on the Jordanian front. By this time the Iraqis had also entered Jordan with a strong force concentrated around Irbid in the north, opposite the Israeli side of the Jordan River Valley. The PLO guerillas were not making much headway in their efforts to infiltrate into Israel. To support them, the Iraqis and Jordanians began shelling Jewish settlements in the valley. The air force was again called in to stop the artillery harassment. On December 12, the IAF subjected the Iraqis to a smashing blow, bombing their installations and artillery concentrations and causing heavy losses of men and matériel.

Then the Syrians joined in the fighting. Shelling started all along the Golan Heights and the Israelis retaliated by bombing El Fatah camps near Damascus. In one dogfight between Syrian and Israeli planes over Damascus, a MiG-17 was shot down by a Skyhawk still carrying its full load—an unprecedented feat. It became clear that the Israeli pilots still retained an unquestionable superiority over their Arab counterparts, however modern their aircraft and however advanced their training in Russia.

In December 1969 the Israelis executed another spectacular operation. Reconnaissance units had located a newly erected Egyptian radar station on the western shores of the Gulf of Suez. From aerial photos, experts identified the installation as a new Soviet type. Because of its threat to future air operations, it was essential to determine its technical characteristics. This was a classic mission for the paratroopers, and a raid was mounted to "lift" the complete station.

Landing silently by boat at night on the western shore of the Gulf of Suez, the raiding party overcame the guards and dismantled the radar station. Helicopters then arrived in the dark, and, hovering over the base, they lifted off the entire secret tracking station. While the troopers fought off Egyptian reinforcements, helicopters flew the equipment over the Gulf to the Israeli side. This operation was a severe blow to Egyptian use of Russian electronic techniques and hardware.

By the end of October the IAF had destroyed the last two missile batteries on the Canal, leaving its entire length clear of any effective air defense. Now there was no way Egypt could halt the raids. Intercept missions were strongly discouraged both by Egyptian Air Force Command and its Soviet advisors; the Israelis found it easy to avoid what few AAA guns remained in the Canal area. The Egyptian Air Force tried "copycat" tactics—sending assault aircraft to bomb IDF targets along the east bank of the Canal. These attempts, however, were few and far between; in addition, the great majority of them were wildly inaccurate.

New Year's Day 1970 showed a definite edge in favor of the Israelis. They had already managed to knock out most of the hundreds of artillery pieces the Egyptians had concentrated along the Canal, making it nearly impossible for Egypt to continue shelling IDF positions. Other matériel lost included AAA guns, ammunition dumps, and three Soviet-made P-12 radar stations. (Two of these, located in Jordan and manned by an Egyptian expeditionary force, were bombed in an IAF raid on November 17, 1969. The third, at Ras Gharib on the Gulf of Suez, was captured intact and transported back to Israel in an IDF/IAF heliborne commando raid.) An attempt to move more missile batteries to the Canal Zone in mid-December had been discovered by Israeli intelligence within a matter of days. The IAF struck on December 25, smashing every battery from Kantara to Suez City in one continuous eight-hour wave of bombings. In addition, concentrated IDF armor and artillery assaults had become more or less the order of the day. Four major Egyptian cities along the Canal—Port Said, Ismailia, Kantara, and Suez City—had been evacuated, and the west bank of the Canal was rapidly turning into a sort of no-man's-land.

And then, on January 7, 1970, the long-range bombings began.

Several senior IAF officers had been advocating long-range bombing months beforehand, claiming that this was the only way to maintain the advantage Israel had so painstakingly built up in the War of Attrition. One of these, Defense Minister Ezer Weizman, also stressed that this tactic would be the only way to convince Egypt to halt the war—which was, after all, what Israel was most interested in doing. The arrival of the first Phantom fighter-bombers—aircraft whose range, payload, strength, and instrumentation greatly exceeded anything previously held in the IAF inventory—allayed the fears of the more conservative officers in IAF Command. At the beginning of January, then O/C Air Force Motti Hod concluded that the IAF could now successfully bomb targets in the heart of Egypt.

Against the Egyptians. McDonnell Douglas A-4 Skyhawk fighter-bomber—the workhorse of the IAF—over the Sinai hills. These were the first American-manufactured combat aircraft officially supplied to the IAF.

The success of the first such mission proved unqualifiedly that Hod had been right. On January 7, while IAF A-4 Skyhawk formations pounded targets along the Canal, Israeli F-4 Phantoms were speeding farther west, toward three military sites in central Egypt. These were evenly spaced at some 40 to 50 kilometers from Cairo: one at Inshas to the northeast, another at Dahshur in the Nile Valley south of the capital, and the third at Tel el Kebir, on the Cairo-Ismailia road. The Egyptians were, amazingly, taken completely by surprise; Egyptian Air Force Command did not even manage to order the air force base near Inshas to scramble aircraft in pursuit until the Israelis had already re-crossed the Canal.

The following day the Egyptian Air Force attempted a reprisal, raiding the Israeli-operated oil fields of Ras Sudar on the eastern shore of the Gulf of Suez. While they did succeed in penetrating Sinai airspace and causing damage, two of their SU-7 bombers were downed over the Sinai.

On January 13, the IAF struck again, this time even closer to the capital. IAF aircraft bombed the Egyptian supply depot at El Hanka, only 25 kilometers northeast of the capital, near Cairo International Airport. On the 16th, during a deep-penetration raid in the Tel el Kebir area, the IAF lost one aircraft to AAA fire. This, however, did not deter them from bombing the military camps of Huckstep, some

18 kilometers from Cairo International Airport, and the fuel and ammunitions depot of Wadi Hof, 20 kilometers southeast of Cairo itself.

Meanwhile, the IDF ground forces had not been idle. On January 21, an armored raiding party smashed into the west bank of the Gulf of Suez, destroying, among other targets, radar and early-warning installations. The following day a combined IAF/IDF operation resulted in the capture of Shadwan Island in the Red Sea and the sinking of two Egyptian MTBs about 18 kilometers south of the island. Although the Israelis withdrew from Shadwan after only 36 hours of occupation, they took with them a complete British-made radar unit, as well as quantities of arms, ammunitions, and Egyptian prisoners.

That was the day Nasser finally admitted that Egypt could no longer hope to defend its own airspace. On January 22, while the Israelis were busy taking Shadwan Island, Gamal Abdel Nasser was en route to Russia. Despite his failing health and the bitter Moscow cold, the Egyptian president flew to the Soviet capital for four days of intensive, secret meetings. During the course of these talks, the ailing leader stressed that Israel had achieved definite air superiority—a fact the Soviets had already known for some time—and that Egypt would have to receive massive Soviet assistance in the field of air defense.

To Leonid Brezhnev and the Politburo, Nasser's request posed a definite problem. The Soviet Union did indeed have the weapons Egypt needed, including sophisticated SA-3 surface-to-air missiles. However, they were understandably quite reluctant to let these out of the Communist bloc, and especially into Egypt. Their reasons for this position were twofold: First, they feared the new matériel would be too complex for Egypt to maintain and operate effectively (as had been the case with the SA-2s the Soviets had deployed in North Vietnam). Second, and more pressing, was the danger that Israel might manage to capture one or more of the new SA-3 batteries, as it had done with the P-12 radar installation the previous month. Nevertheless, Brezhnev was well aware that, should he refuse to grant his ally Nasser the aid his country so desperately needed, the Nasser regime might well topple. In such a case, it was doubtful whether the next Egyptian president would be such a close friend of the Soviet Union.

In the end the Politburo (whose meetings were attended by a full complement of 12 Soviet marshals for the first time since World War II!) decided on a solution that would meet Egypt's needs while protecting the Soviet matériel. Not only would Russia provide Egypt with all the interceptors, missiles, AAA guns, and radar it could possibly use, but it would also send in Soviet military personnel to man them. It was decided that the Soviets would take over Egypt's air defense by stages; in addition, Soviet instructors would continue to train Egyptian Air Force personnel, and the Soviet Navy would establish at least one base in Egyptian waters. A complete, detailed battle order was devised by the Soviet High Command, alerting Air Defense, Frontal Aviation, and Transport commands for a massive effort without delay.

The first massive Soviet airlift of new weapons and matériel began in late January. By that time the Israelis had made several more in-depth raids in both the Cairo and northern Delta areas, including the bombing of the El Maadi camps in what was practically a residential suburb of Cairo on January 28. For the first time the Egyptian civilian population began showing signs of concern. Civil defense preparations became the order of the day. Even some Egyptian Air Force base commanders in the Cairo area, as yet unaware of the help to come, appealed to Nasser to order their bases moved farther west; some Egyptian aircraft were actually dispatched to Sudan and Libya, to prevent their being destroyed on the ground by the IAF (as had happened on June 5, 1967, in the opening move of the Six-Day War).

Meanwhile, however, the Soviet transports had begun to arrive. The first of these landed at the airfield known as Cairo West; however, after the bombing of the El Maadi installations, the Russians apparently felt it more prudent to move their airlift to the Alexandria area. Thus the first of the new SA-3s were set up by Soviet air defense crews near Alexandria; there they protected the airspace of the western Delta, which was usually full of Soviet AN-22 transport aircraft, sometimes as many as five per hour!

Following the transports came the interceptors flown in from the Soviet Frontal Aviation Air Army based in Tokol, Hungary. These were Soviet-made MiG-21J aircraft, a considerable improvement over the basic MiG-21s that Egypt had been operating for some time. The new interceptors had better radar, more effective fire control, and were capable of carrying detachable fuel tanks, increasing their range to the point where air strikes within Israel could become not only possible, but practical. As opposed to the SA-3s, the interceptor aircraft were based in the Cairo area; by mid-May a total of some 150 Soviet-piloted MiG-21Js would be operating in ten combat squadrons on five Egyptian air bases. However, for the time being, the Soviets refrained from active encounters with Israeli aircraft.

Shortly after the beginning of the Soviet airlift the IAF nearly plunged the area into all-out war—according to Israel, totally by mistake. On February 12, IAF aircraft set out to bomb three targets inside Egypt, including the Hanka encampment already attacked the previous month. Less than three kilometers from Hanka, at Abu Zaabal, lay a huge civilian smelting plant, which, however, bore an astonishing similarity to a military complex when viewed from the air. One of the Israeli aircraft had a technical malfunction; its pilot was forced to choose between identifying his target visually or aborting his mission. He chose the former course and, mistaking the plant at Abu Zaabal for the Hanka encampment, leveled it with five tons of bombs. This would have been bad enough; but even worse was the realization that one of the bombs dropped on Abu Zaabal was of the delayed-action type, set to explode the following day, when, in all probability, diplomats and foreign press would be visiting the site. Bearing this possibility in mind, Israel's defense minister and O/C air force agreed to ask the Red Cross and the UN to inform the Egyptians of the delayed-action bomb. By this move, which in effect amounted to an IAF apology, Israel hoped—rightly, as it turned out—that Nasser would be sufficiently placated to avoid escalating the conflict into full-scale war. In addition, the IAF Command ordered the in-depth bombings halted for three days and a comprehensive inquiry carried out.

Meanwhile, the arrival of the Soviet regular troops and matériel had begun to bolster the confidence of the Egyptian Air Force. In late February it began attempting to engage IAF aircraft in aerial combat, while Soviet pilots flew high cover. Although this proved rather less of a success than the Egyptians had hoped for—13 Egyptian-piloted MiGs were downed by the IAF between February 26 and the end of March—the fact remains that now the Egyptian Air Force was at least trying to interfere with the Israeli bombings.

By the end of March 1970 the Soviet presence in Egypt was considerable. A complete air defense division had been flown out of the Odessa air defense district and posted throughout the western Delta region, with its headquarters at Alexandria. A special forward Air Transport Command had been installed at Cairo West, with direct links to the air transport communications network. Also included were the squadrons of MiG-21J and SU-15 (*Flagon A*) aircraft, with their maintenance and ground facilities that had been flown out of Russia and Hungary into the Cairo and Delta areas. And more arms were coming all the time.

That same month the IDF spokesman announced that Israel was aware of the presence of Soviet-manned SA-3 missiles in Egypt. In addition, the Israeli ground forces along the Canal were dismayed to discover that the Egyptians, their confidence restored along with their artillery, had begun to renew the deadly shellings of IDF positions, which had slowed to a near halt in the previous months. The IAF now had to play a dual role: In addition to the in-depth bombings, it now had to knock out Egyptian gun emplacements and other military targets along the Canal, as it had done in the first months of the War of Attrition.

An excellent example of the spirit of those days is provided by the events of March 24–25. On the morning of the 24th, IAF Skyhawks and Phantoms attacked nearly 20 surface-to-air missile sites, along with a large number of AAA guns, radar stations, and other installations. These represented the bulk of the Soviet air defense effort of the preceding two months. The Soviets were now faced with the problem of reconstructing their SA-3 screen as rapidly as possible, with the additional requirement that it afford greater protection for the now almost constantly besieged Canal Zone. This they did, incredibly, in a single night. The first step was the positioning of several Russian-staffed AAA regiments as close as 30 kilometers from the waterline. Behind this protective screen the Soviets readied two complete air defense regiments; these were to move at first light into sites constructed by thousands of Egyptians, working at fever pitch throughout the night, under cover of darkness and protected by Soviet interceptors flying night missions from the Delta airfields of Mansoura, Bilbeis, and Beni Suef. At dawn on the 25th, the air defense regiments were in position and operative, which meant, of course, that Israeli intelligence had no difficulty spotting them in its morning reconnaissance check. Immediately, IAF aircraft were sent to demolish the air defense line. This resulted in a pitched air/ground battle with the Soviet troops, the first battle fought by any Soviet expeditionary force since World War II. While Israeli aircraft pounded the missile sites and gun emplacements, the Russians manning them fired frantically at the IAF attackers. Within hours, however, the IAF had gained the upper hand, reducing the new air defense positions to rubble for the second time in two days. The Russians, taken aback by their inability to defend their sites, flew in top experts from Moscow to devise a new operational plan.

Less than a month later, on April 18, IAF aircraft had their first definitive encounter with Soviet pilots. During an Israeli incursion into Egyptian airspace south of Cairo, the IAF pilots overheard the Soviets talking with their home base—in Russian. (At the time, the Soviet forces in Egypt were not yet equipped with data-link systems, which would have obviated the necessity for voice communication.) A quick check revealed that all MiGs in sight bore Egyptian Air Force markings; a second glance, however, made it evident that some of them were not ordinary MiG-21s. The IAF Command put two and two together, realized that Soviets were flying MiG-21Js to protect Egypt's airspace and, to avoid direct confrontation, called off all deep-penetration bombing at once. The new policy of confining IAF aerial activity to the Canal Zone itself was breached only once. Following Egyptian attacks on the port of Eilat and on an Israeli fishing boat in the Mediterranean in early May, the IAF decided to launch a retaliation raid. On the afternoon of May 16 IAF aircraft (Phantoms, according to subse-

quent Egyptian reports) sank an Egyptian destroyer and missile boats off Ras Banas near the Sudan border. Despite the distance and difficulty involved, both targets were hit without incident, and the IAF aircraft returned to base unscathed.

During the night of June 29, the Soviets began what then Israeli Defense Minister Moshe Dayan termed the "electronic summer." Newly organized Soviet SAM regiments were moved forward into the central sector, some 30 kilometers west of the Canal Zone, in an all-night operation reminiscent of the one they had staged in March. However, this time the results were slightly different. The following morning, a few minutes after the start of the customary Egyptian artillery barrage, the Israeli aircraft showed up on scene as usual, only to be confronted by scores of SA-3 missiles fired from clusters of six launchers apiece, instead of the former single-launcher technique. One Phantom was immediately downed, its pilot taken prisoner; a second soon followed. The shaken Israelis, unused to the cluster system, in which the launchers protected each other, were forced to withdraw without having damaged the missile batteries.

In the days to come the Soviets reinforced their air defense even further. More and more MiG-21Js were flown into the Delta area, enabling the Soviets to fly high cover on every Egyptian air strike. Hundreds of SA-7 *Strela* surface-to-air missiles, operated by infantry troops, on top of scores of radar-controlled quick-firing anti-aircraft guns, were added to the impressive array of Soviet-made weaponry gracing the Egyptian front line. The Israelis put through a top-priority request for ECM (electronic countermeasures) equipment to the Pentagon; United States officials ignored it, leaving Israel to cope with this new development on its own.

On July 3, the IAF began attacking the new SAM regiments, using a new form of flying tactics: They would zoom in extremely low, release the payload just inside effective range, then climb as steeply as possible to evade the SAMs. Several aircraft would attack each cluster base, starting from the launchers on the fringes of the cluster and working their way in, until they met for a combined attack on the command and control center. These tactics resulted in the immediate destruction of two SA-2 batteries; one Phantom, however, was lost to an SA-3 missile. Several days later a second Israeli request for electronic countermeasures was answered in the affirmative, a fitting reward for IAF valor, though perhaps more to test their effectiveness under combat conditions prevailing on the Canal.

Meanwhile, as June progressed into July, the Soviet pilots had begun to take a more active role in the defense of Egypt's airspace. No longer confining themselves to high-cover missions, they had begun chasing Israeli Phantoms home from bombing sorties in Egypt. The IAF High Command instructed its pilots at first to refrain from challenging the Soviets, hoping this new audacity would cease with the passage of time. On July 25, however, Israel realized the Russians were out for a fight. That afternoon two MiG-21Js piloted by Soviets fired on an IAF Skyhawk in the middle of a bombing run. Although they did not down the aircraft, they did manage to damage its tail assembly; only through consummate skill was the Israeli pilot able to coax his plane home and crash-land unhurt.

It did not take the IAF High Command long to decide that Israel would not sit still for a repetition of this incident. Five days later, on July 30, the IAF's chance for revenge came up. Two Phantoms and two Mirages were ordered to attack an Egyptian radar station at Ras Gharib, the same location from which the P-12 had been spirited away by Israeli commandos seven months before. By the time the reconnaissance aircraft had made two passes over the target, the Russians had scrambled three flights of MiG-21Js. The IAF pilots, realizing the odds were against them, had no choice but to jettison their fuel tanks. Within minutes, however, more IAF aircraft had arrived on scene. By the end of the battle four of the Soviet planes had been downed; a fifth exploded in midair. On the Israeli side, one Mirage was hit by a Russian missile but managed to reach home safely.

This incident is retold here by a veteran IAF combat pilot (and, as of this writing, squadron leader). Although relatively young, he has flown many combat missions in the Six-Day War, the War of Attrition, and the Yom Kippur War; but to him, as to the other pilots who took part in the events of July 30, 1970, that day remains unique in his memory:

We had been waiting for a long time for something like that to happen. When they attacked the Skyhawk, we knew the next step could be for us to take them on in combat—and frankly, many of us welcomed the chance. We'd been doing a lot of bombing, and nothing had happened to us in weeks and weeks—nobody fired on us, hardly anybody even chased us. But now the Russians had broken the agreement, and we hoped something would come of it.

None of us knew what degree of skill to expect from them. The Egyptians weren't the best fliers in the world—that's why they had orders to stay out of dogfights with us. I assumed the Russians couldn't be all that much better, especially as they'd had no combat experience since World War II. They might have a numerical advantage, of course; but that was nothing new for us.

On July 30, we were sent to attack a radar station at Ras Gharib, south of the Gulf of Suez. Our reconnaissance aircraft went in close to the target. On their first pass the Russians scrambled four MiG-21s; on their second pass three foursomes were in the air and two of them headed straight for our reconnaissance aircraft. We didn't lose any time—we had none to lose—but jettisoned our fuel tanks and pounced on them. By the time they realized what we were up to, the fight was on.

I was Number Two of a pair of Phantoms; we and two Mirages were up against about 10 MiGs. It was a little unsettling to see so many aircraft at once, so many fuel tanks being jettisoned all over the place. I didn't care about numerical superiority; I was just afraid someone might bump into my aircraft!

One of the Mirages fired an air-to-air missile seconds after the battle began. The missile hit a MiG and set it on fire. The pilot bailed out; the aircraft went into a spin and dropped like a stone from 30,000 feet. The Russian pilot's parachute didn't open right away.

It's not supposed to: Chutes are designed to open automatically at 10,000 feet, so their wearers don't freeze or suffocate at high altitudes. But this pilot used the manual apparatus and opened the chute himself! Maybe he didn't want to be taken alive . . . or maybe he just didn't know any better.

Now some more of our aircraft had joined the battle; the Russians no longer had numerical superiority. I started looking for a MiG to kill. Finally, I found one—its pilot was making a right turn, trying to close in on my Number One. I broke to the right. The MiG left my Number One and started chasing me! We stuck together for a while, dropping to about 15,000 feet; at that point he was only about 500 feet from me. I could see the pilot's helmet clearly.

By this time I'd realized the Russian pilot was inexperienced; he didn't know how to handle his aircraft in a combat situation. At 15,000 feet he proved this fact by trying to escape in a steep dive to 7,000 feet. All we had to do was follow him and lock our radar onto him—and fire a missile. There was a tremendous explosion, but the MiG came out of the cloud of smoke apparently unharmed. That made me mad and I fired a second missile, which turned out to be unnecessary. The Russian aircraft had, in fact, been severely damaged by the first missile; suddenly it burst into flames and fell apart. By the time the second missile reached it, it wasn't there any more.

On my way home something interesting happened. I noticed my Number One had two missiles missing. But I couldn't ask him about it over the radio, not with Russians so close to us and possibly listening to every word. I pointed at his missiles, hoping to catch his eye. He grinned and spoke into his radio: "I hit one with your dog." Because my dog's name was *Shafrir,** the same as that of our missiles, but the Russians couldn't possibly know that. No one could, except a friend like my Number One.

According to another Israeli fighter pilot, the Russians flew "by the book," making themselves easy game for the experienced Israeli pilots. He recounts:

> They came at us in pairs and we let them pass in order not to be sandwiched between the pairs, as they had anticipated we would. They passed one after another as couples in a procession. We waited and got in behind, now sandwiching them, and had before us 16 MiGs!
>
> The sky was filled with planes as the formations broke up, and the danger of collision was very acute. Also flying about were a lot of jettisoned fuel tanks, so you could hit anything if on our side. Then I saw my Number One fire a Shafrir missile, and then another. Soon his target was on fire, spinning down from 9,000 meters and the pilot bailed out fast.
>
> The melee continued, planes turning and twisting around, and firing guns and rockets at each other. More Israeli planes joined the battle. Braking hard, I succeeded in getting my sights on a MiG. He had guts and turned into the fight, but I quickly realized he was inexperienced. He made elementary mistakes. Diving down to 2,000 meters, I cut him off and soon locked on my radar—then we had time. It was clear that he could not get away. At a range of 1,000 meters we fired a missile. The MiG exploded into a flaming ball but, surprisingly, flew on. We fired another missile, but this was no longer necessary. The Russian plane suddenly disintegrated in the air. The pilot ejected and I observed him swinging down in his parachute. Breaking off combat, I returned to base.

Five Russian planes were shot down in a battle that lasted only a few minutes. There were no Israeli losses.

This was the last great battle of the War of Attrition. Eight days later, on August 7, 1970, the UN cease-fire between Israel and Egypt went into effect. However, incredibly, this cease-fire was breached the very day it was signed—by a deliberate collusion of the air defense forces of Egypt and the Soviet Union. Scant hours before it was to have gone into effect, the Egyptians, with a good deal of "help from their friends," moved a large number of dummy missile batteries up close to the Canal. This move, of course, was intended to enable the Egyptians to replace the fake batteries with real ones as soon as possible, which they did. Although both Israel and the United States were aware of what was going on, they preferred not to intervene, restricting their reactions to verbal protests. In the words of one American electronics expert:

> It became increasingly obvious that the Egyptians were rushing SAMs into the cease-fire zone to construct a solid SAM box, a firm barrier, that was slowly creeping towards the Canal. This was confirmed by a report on September 5, which stated that 45 missile sites had been constructed within the cease-fire zone since August 7, of which 30 had been armed since the cease-fire.

It was this move that later prompted former IDF Air Force Commander Ezer Weizman to state that the Yom Kippur War actually started in August 1970 and not, as most of the world believed, in October 1973.

---

*Its name means "Dragonfly," and it is a deadly air-to-air missile manufactured in Israel at one-quarter the cost of a U.S. Sidewinder.

Chapter 6
The Yom Kippur War, 1973

At the start of the Yom Kippur War IAF pilots had to face a veritable wall of fire, the greatest depth and mix of air defense systems ever deployed in battle. More than 10,000 systems, including conventional anti-aircraft guns that supplemented the latest Soviet SA-6 and the mobile SA-8 missiles, were positioned to provide a murderous cross fire and to cover both high- and low-altitude attacks. The Israeli Air Force was practically immobilized. The Egyptian Army used its temporary advantage to make a preemptive strike across the Suez Canal.

Within ten hours after the War of Attrition cease-fire became effective, the Egyptians advanced their missile bases right up to the Suez Canal, in defiance of the military stand-still agreement. The lack of a forceful Israeli or American reaction seemed to confirm the view that the cease-fire indicated an Israeli weakness, despite the crushing defeat handed to the armed forces of the four Arab nations. The War of Attrition was the first Arab–Israeli conflict that did not end with a complete victory for the Israelis. This had great influence on Arab military strategy, bringing to an end, it was thought, the long period of deterrence by Israeli's military superiority. The belief in Israel's weakness encouraged the attack on Yom Kippur, in 1973.

With the possible exception of the Vietnam conflict, the Yom Kippur War was the world's first real electronic war. In it modern weapon systems were put to the test, in quality as well as in density. But although most of the systems were effective, their actual combat evaluation was usually overestimated and conclusions were found to have been drawn hastily through unprofessional or exaggerated reports.

One of these reports dealt with the efficiency of Arab air defense systems and, especially, of their Soviet SAMs. In considering the worth of these systems, it is well to remember that the Israeli Air Force was initially put to an extremely difficult test: having to stem, as the only major defense force available at the time, overwhelming armored assaults on two fronts simultaneously. This mission, of vital importance, placed the IAF under extreme pressure, as did the inconvenient modus operandi forced upon

This Soviet-built SA-7, NATO code-named GRAIL, a shoulder-launched anti-aircraft missile, was first seen in the Middle East during the War of Attrition. The lightweight (20 pound) weapon, with a range of about 4 kilometers and a speed of Mach 1.5, is designed for defense against low-level attacks.

Egyptian SA-3s captured by Israeli forces on the west bank of the Suez Canal, October 1973. More modern than the SA-2, the SA-3, NATO code-named GOA, is effective from low to medium altitudes—100 to 4,500 meters—supplementing the higher-flying SA-2s. These missiles were integrated with radar-directed anti-aircraft cannons and machine guns, creating a tight anti-aircraft network.

it: flying front interdiction missions against the best-defended enemy sectors. Losses under these circumstances were inevitably heavy.

Following the Israeli preemptive surprise attack of the Six-Day War, which resulted in the destruction of several Arab air forces within a few hours on the morning of June 5, 1967, Egyptian air defense (with Soviet assistance) had grown to considerable proportions. During the drawn-out War of Attrition, between 1968 and 1970, the first SAM belt system on the Suez Canal came into being; in the early 1970s the whole of the Nile Delta and the Egyptian rear areas were covered by a dense air defense system, including over 60 SAM batteries deployed in well-chosen and protected sites. The shape of the system was perfected by Soviet advisors during the last stages of the War of Attrition, following combat experience gained in Vietnam and the Middle East. The latest addi-

tions to Egyptian air defense were the tactically operated SA-6 *Gainful*, of which several batteries operated with the Egyptian ground forces in the Suez Canal bridgehead, and scores of newly arrived ZSU-23/4 mobile, tracked radar-directed anti-aircraft cannons.

The SAM sites on the west bank of the Suez Canal operated in an integrated, mutually protective defense system. All missile sites were built with earth-protective walls and concrete shelters, the perimeter defended by anti-aircraft gun positions. The whole system worked within a well-planned radar surveillance network spread over wide areas and situated on well-chosen vantage points. Control centers and sector command posts, in underground dugouts, supervised the integrated air defense and interceptor operations.

A typical SAM site would have looked somewhat like this: Situated in a circular position are the SAM launchers, missiles deployed in pairs and protected by a round earthwork wall, fortified, if necessary, by concrete. The missiles—SA-2 *Guideline* or SA-3 *Goa* types—are usually placed directionally for better control from the command post dugout, located in the center. This structure, containing the *Fan Song* for SA-2 *Guideline,* or *Spoon Rest* (P-12) and *Flat Face* (P-15) for SA-3 *Goa* radar trailers and the control caravan, is the heart of the site. The center is well protected by earth and concrete walls, including vents for air conditioning; additionally, all-around light anti-aircraft protection is deployed. Around the site are scattered skillfully interspaced decoy ramps made of wood, making the identification of the real launcher positions sometimes extremely difficult. In an outer circle, multibarreled anti-aircraft guns cover all possible approaches. The whole site is served by an extensive communication network consisting of underground telephone cable and radio. Several SAM sites and their all-around AAA are integrated into a mutually protective sector system, controlled by a sector coordination site, which supervises the whole area with the aid of additional radars. These centers are again defended by densely deployed AAA. Some 60 of these sites were deployed along a strip 160 kilometers long and 20 kilometers deep, with one large concentration north of the swamps near Port Said, a second near Ismailia in the center, and a third in the southern center between the Bitter Lakes and the town of Suez. Deeply influenced by Russian defense concepts, the Arabs regarded this missile array as a counter to Israeli air supremacy. Now possessing hundreds of the latest Soviet SAM launchers, the Egyptians constructed an interlocking air defense system that was the thickest and most effective ever deployed—superior even to that protecting Hanoi during the American bombing offensive over North Vietnam.

The older SA-2 *Guideline* with its 30-kilometer range against high-flying aircraft was supplemented with the faster, more agile SA-3 *Goa* batteries with a 27-kilometer range, to combat low-flying aircraft, by scores of the ultramodern and mobile SA-6 *Gainful* missiles mounted on armored carriers. The SA-6 is capable of rapidly changing position and radar frequency, thus making its location and des-

Egyptian MiG-21 exploding from a hit by Israeli cannon fire. IAF fighter pilots preferred sharpshooting with their 30-mm cannons over using their expensive and less personally satisfying air-to-air missiles.

truction extremely difficult. An abundance of SA-7 *Grail* shoulder-fired light anti-aircraft missiles, also mounted in eight-barrel launchers on an armored chassis, together with the thousands of anti-aircraft machine guns and radar-controlled multibarreled cannons, completed the network. This complex formed an almost impenetrable air defense system.

But the Israeli Air Force had already encountered similar sites during the War of At-

Bomb attack on Nazaria air base in the north of Syria during the Yom Kippur War.

trition, mostly containing SA-2 *Guideline* batteries. At the time, tactics were devised to destroy these sites by direct attack, as the IAF lacked the sophisticated electronic equipment and armament available to American airmen in Vietnam. The Israeli tactics were quiet efficient and succeeded in destroying most of the Egyp- tian missile sites, thus clearing the area for anti- artillery strikes—at the time urgently needed to silence devastating Egyptian artillery barrages on the Bar-Lev Line. But following Soviet inter- vention in the Canal war, new SA-3 *Goa* missiles and unknown radar and electronic equipment had arrived, rendering the previous tactics in-

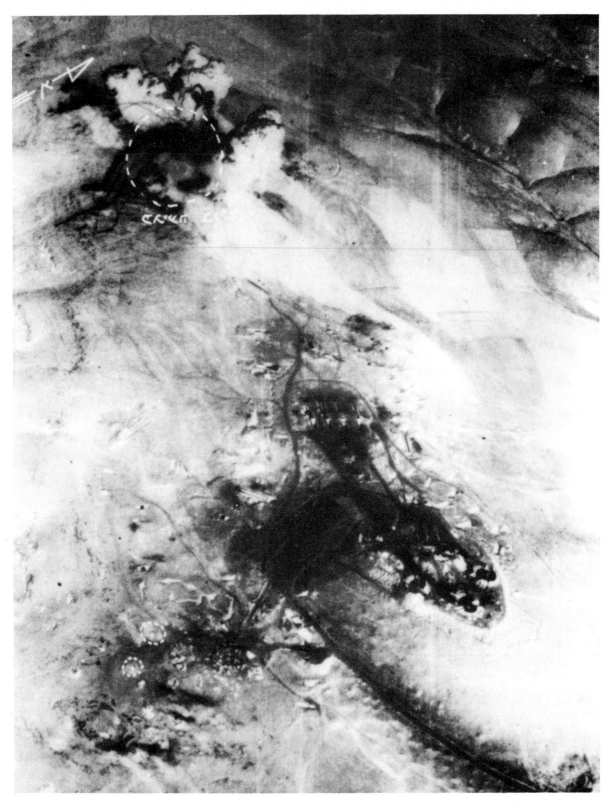

Syrian anti-aircraft missile site, some 40 kilometers southeast of Damascus, under heavy bomb attack. Note the many emplacements and trenches to guard it against attacks from the ground.

An A-4N Skyhawk II returning from a strike mission.

effective and causing heavy losses to the IAF. True, in the last stages of the war, the Israelis had captured a sophisticated Soviet radar (P-12) by a daring commando attack, and even acquired some effective anti-SAM armament. Nevertheless, the war itself ended with a draw and the missile sites remained in position.

The commander of the IAF at the time of the Yom Kippur War was Gen. Benjamin Peled, a highly experienced fighter pilot who had been shot down and rescued near Sharm el-Sheikh in the Sinai campaign of 1956. (During the Yom Kippur War, his son, flying a Phantom, was also shot down and rescued.) The Arab air offensive began with Egyptian attacks on major installations in the Sinai. Many of the attacks cost the Egyptian Air Force dearly. For example, on a fighter-bomber sweep by 12 MiGs against Sharm el-Sheikh, patrolling Israeli fighters shot down seven of the attacking Egyptian planes. At the same time scores of Syrian fighter-bombers swooped in low over Israeli positions on the Golan Heights, attacking

troops, vehicles, and military camps. The Arab air strategy was to prevent the IAF from concentrating its efforts. This was achieved by forcing it to spread its forces widely between distant battle fronts in order to support the scores of surrounded Israeli positions both in the Sinai and on the Golan Heights. The air force was also called on to destroy or beat back the columns of invading armor and to retain air superiority over the battlefield. A desperate battle ensued in which the IAF had to fly thousands of sorties through the thick of the Arab air defense system.

The Egyptians crossed the Suez Canal on October 6, 1973, under a most effectively planned and implemented air defense umbrella. As the IAF roared into the attack to destroy the bridges spanning the Canal, it encountered defense of unprecedented density and accuracy, and losses were extremely heavy. At the time there was little the IAF could do except to go in lower. Here, however, it encountered an even more deadly and devastating fire by thousands of light anti-aircraft weapons ranging from tank- and BTR-mounted 12.7-mm *Dushka* and the heavier 14.5-mm *AAMG,* to 23-mm shells from highly accurate ZSU-23-4 and ZSU-57-2. To make matters worse, several SA-6 *Gainful* batteries operated from changing positions on both banks.

The situation was very dangerous, and several Phantoms, Skyhawks, and Super Mystères, flinging themselves against the many targets massing along the Canal bridgeheads, were lost. During the next few days, as the battle raged in the Sinai, the IAF recuperated. New ECM equipment was received and, as tactics improved, losses decreased considerably. But as the plans for an all-out effort to regain initiative proceeded, the problem of air support to ground operations became acute. In order to cross the Canal to the West Bank and drive a wedge between the two Egyptian armies deployed in their bridgehead along the East Bank in the Sinai, a daring and massive armored operation was envisaged. One of the prerequisites was the early destruction of the SAM sites. Some 150 of these SA-2 and SA-3 missile batteries had been set up in Egypt, more than 60 right along the Canal. Quite effective when fired in salvos at targets at higher altitudes, they forced the Israeli planes to come in low, where they encountered a seemingly solid wall of anti-aircraft fire from thousands of guns, SA-7 shoulder-fired missiles, and volleys of SA-6s. All IAF plans to deal effectively with this anti-aircraft umbrella were coming to naught, as most of the sorties flown were of ground-support character. Realizing the grave situation of the country, the Israeli pilots repeatedly flew into the heavy fire. Losses in the first days were so heavy that Israeli ground forces, seeing the planes subjected to the shattering barrage of Arab missiles, refused to call for more air support.

A most ferocious battle developed on the Syrian front, where the missiles were all concentrated along the border. Each attacking Israeli plane was subjected to salvos of dozens of SAMs. More planes were lost over Syria—30 in one day—than in any combat zone thus far, but the pilots continued to attack the advancing Syrian armor columns. As the IDF's holding action eventually stabilized the front, the hard-pressed IAF could reorganize and systematically attack the missile sites. Damaged planes,

many of them crash-landing on their return, were repaired as quickly as possible and sent back into action.

On the Egyptian front, IAF pilots attacked the Canal bridges. But no sooner had they damaged a bridge than the Egyptian engineers repaired it. It was a seemingly endless battle, and losses were very heavy. During the fierce battles of the first few days, the IAF lost half of the planes that were brought down during the entire war—all from ground anti-aircraft guns and missiles. The Israeli Air Force commanders were presented with two choices: one, to destroy or at least neutralize as many sites as possible by air attack—a matter that could be achieved but would entail substantial losses of aircraft; second, to launch a combined air and ground SAM-destruction campaign. The second seemed both attractive and feasible under the circumstances and the plan of operations. Several tactics were considered. One of these entailed a heliborne commando strike against major radar and control sites followed by attacks on SAM sites. Another plan called for destruction by tanks that were to cross the Canal on barges immediately following the infantry assault.

The first option was scrapped because the units envisaged for the mission had to be used for other, more urgent jobs to clear and hold the

Gun camera photo of MiG-21 hit by IAF interceptor. Israeli pilots preferred to use their 30-mm cannons instead of air-to-air missiles—especially in large-scale melees with many planes dodging in and out.

An IAF Phantom closing in on an EAF MiG-17 over the Sinai. A rare photo taken by the Phantom's wingman.

bridgehead. Accordingly, the SAM destruction became a mission for armor. Following the assault 28 Patton tanks from "Bren" Adan's division crossed on barges into the bridgehead at Deversoir. Once over they refueled and, grouping several M-113 APCs (armored personnel carriers) into their ranks, made for the bridge over the Sweetwater Canal, which was already secured by Israeli paratroopers. Racing over the bridge, the tanks formed into small teams, each making for a predetermined SAM base. Operating with complete secrecy—the whole crossing operation was still undetected by the Egyptian command—the Israeli tanks approached the missile bases and opened deadly accurate direct fire on the sites. The outer earthworks and missile launchers were destroyed by combinations of HESH (high-explosive) and APDS (armor-piercing shells). As

they were hit the SAMs exploded in a yellow flash; some, launched by electric faults, spun crazily into the air. Within a few hours five active SAM sites were destroyed by tanks and several decoy sites were overrun. Once the skies were clear of the SAM danger, the IAF screamed into action, pouncing on the Egyptian tank reinforcements that, alerted by the debacle, had raced to the area.

By the following day, a complete Israeli armored division had crossed over the Canal on the first constructed bridge. This division, commanded by Maj. Gen. "Bren" Adan, directed its three brigades into the open, with primary orders to destroy all missile sites in the southern sector, the rear of the Third Egyptian Army area. During the following day scores of SAM sites were destroyed by tanks, supported by artillery and mortars; some of them were also

A MiG-21 on an IAF Mirage. Both aircraft are armed with air-to-air missiles.

taken complete by armored infantry. The Egyptians, realizing the danger, displaced several of their far sites to the rear, thus clearing the skies over the entire battlefield for the IAF, which came into the battle in force, operating against reinforcements and rendering close support for the roaming tanks. On several occasions, the Egyptian SAM-site crews, devoid of ground protection, tried to engage the tanks with direct SAM fire launched at lowest angle. The giant SAMs usually exploded in a deafening roar soon after launching, a shattering experience to the tankers watching these monsters coming at them; none of the IDF tanks, however, were actually hit by SAMs. More effective was the direct fire by anti-aircraft artillery; nevertheless, as the crews were not trained for ground action, this fire was too erratic and inaccurate to do much damage.

Altogether, the combined action had destroyed 75 percent of the SAM bases; one-fourth of the remaining ones were hastily taken

to the rear. Now the IAF was in control of the skies, and the Egyptian armor reinforcements were in trouble. In several instances, the Egyptian Fourth Amoured Division, lying in reserve not far away on the Suez–Cairo road, was repeatedly called to counterattack Adan's division. However, intercepted radio messages reported that the Egyptian division was under constant and severe air attack and unable to move.

Following the SAM destruction in the south, the IAF now flew SAM-suppression missions from both south and north on the remaining SAM belt in the central area. By the cease-fire most of the batteries had been neutralized. Both Israeli military arms had gained considerably by the combined operation. First, the tanks had cleared the corridor for the air force, knocking out the deadly SAM sites for them; when clear of danger, the IAF had swung into the area and prevented enemy reinforcements from endangering the armor and its newly gained

SA-6 GAINFUL transporter/launcher vehicle and Egyptian SA-6 STRAIGHT FLUSH fire control radar. Electronic and electronic countermeasure (ECM) weapons became an important element of the war between the IAF and the Arab defense systems, reaching its highest level during the Yom Kippur War.

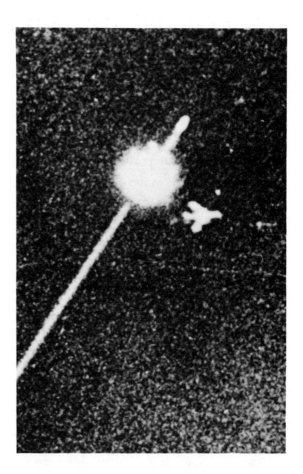

An unusual photo of a surface-to-air missile exploding near an IAF Super Mystère during the Yom Kippur War. Though not actually hit by the missile, the plane was disabled by fragments and crashed.

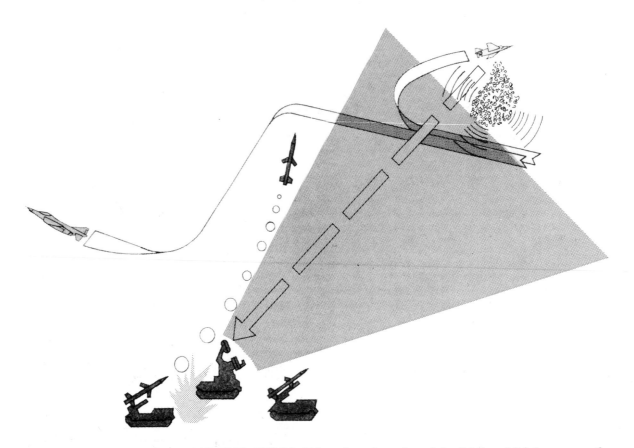

ELECTRONIC COUNTERMEASURES (ECM).* Able to jam the radar of the SA-2 and SA-3 systems, the lack of wide-bank ECM gear made effective jamming of the SA-6 and ZSU-23-4 mobile gun impossible. To cope with this very acute problem the IAF developed several relatively effective defensive techniques. The weakness of the SA-6 system was its limited search capacity and altitude discrimination, which the IAF exploited by high-altitude approaches followed by steep-angle attacks to release bombs on the target. Great quantities of "chaff"—thin, metal-coated strips—were released in the air to confuse enemy radar.

*Based on foreign sources only (*Air Warfare Book*, etc.).

freedom of action. The IDF came once more into its element and was able to contribute largely to the overall battle, encircling the Egyptian Third Army before the cease-fire came into effect.

Clearly, it was no longer a one-sided battle. The losses had mounted on the other side as well. On October 8 alone, 29 enemy aircraft were shot down. In contrast to the Six-Day-War, when most of the enemy planes were destroyed on the ground and the pilots left unhurt, the majority were now shot down in combat and the pilots killed. The Arabs did not relish air combat, and most air battles took place when enemy planes flying ground attacks were caught by Israeli interceptors. By the end of the war, of a total 222 Syrian planes downed, 162 were shot

down in air combat, while the Egyptians lost 300 aircraft, 180 in dogfights in the air. Israeli losses in air-to-air combat were six, out of a total of 99. The remainder were hit by surface-to-air missiles and anti-aircraft guns. In comparison, during the Six-Day-War only 50 Arab planes were shot down in aerial combat, compared to the loss of ten IAF aircraft.

As part of the Arab offensive, scores of giant Russian-built helicopters filled with commando troops tried to seize strategic positions behind the Israeli front lines. Many of these helicopters were destroyed by defending Israeli aircraft. In all, some 40 helicopters were downed. However, these audacious efforts by the Egyptians produced little effect on the course of the battle.

Another IAF feat was the shooting down of

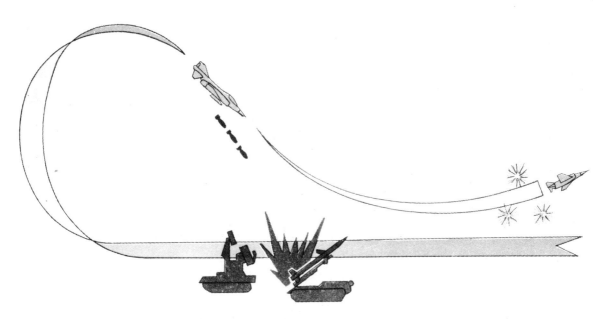

TACTICAL COUNTERMEASURES. ECM available to IAF pilots proved to be only partially effective against the new Russian-built SA-6 in the hands of Arabs, and there were many strikes directed against the mobile radar-launcher system itself. One of the riskier, but effective, techniques was the lo-hi-lo attack flight profile, which takes advantage of the SA-6's slow elevation and depression rates. Thus the IAF fighter-bomber would come in directly against the launcher on a very low-level flight trying to hide from the anti-aircraft radar in the "ground clutter," pop up just past the target, then dive steeply, releasing his stores. As he breaks away, again at a very low altitude, he drops flares to confuse the heat-seeking missile.

an airlaunched *Kelt* missile fired at Tel Aviv from long range by an Egyptian Tupolev heavy bomber. The missile was observed in flight by two patrolling Mirage pilots, who shot it down over the sea. A Syrian air attack on the northern settlements near Safed was foiled by interceptors who shot down three of the attacking Sukhoi-20 fighter-bombers. This was the first time that this kind of plane had been seen in combat.

The Israeli Air Force had turned to the offensive. It set about attacking targets of strategic importance, mainly in Syria, systematically destroying oil installations, electric power stations, and military camps throughout the country. In a retaliatory attack following Syrian bombardment of Israeli towns in the Jezreel Valley with *Frog* surface-to-surface missiles, heavy damage was caused in Damascus. No more *Frogs* were launched. In the Sinai the IAF flew many ground-support sorties, first cleaning out the Egyptian sites in the northern sector and then working southward. In all some 40 out of a total of 60 sites were destroyed, most of them by air attacks. As the armor advanced

into Egypt after crossing the Canal, the IAF was again operating freely over the battlefield. The enemy missile system, which had taken so great a toll of the IAF, was now broken and ineffective. Israeli control of the air was once more firmly established.

In the battles that raged throughout the Mideast's skies, the IAF flew four times as many sorties as it did in the Six-Day-War and shot down or destroyed more than 500 planes while losing over 100 of its own. The confirmed results of the Yom Kippur War showed that most IAF planes lost in combat were destroyed or damaged not by the highly sophisticated SAMs but by simple optically directed anti-aircraft fire. (The SAMs, mainly effective at high altitude, forced the attacking aircraft to operate at low level where they became prey to dense light flak, which, when concentrated, is devastating in its effect.) However, a clear and decisive victory was gained against the massive Soviet air defense system that defended the Arab battlefields. By the end of the war, the Israeli Air Force had again won supremacy in the air against the heavy odds.

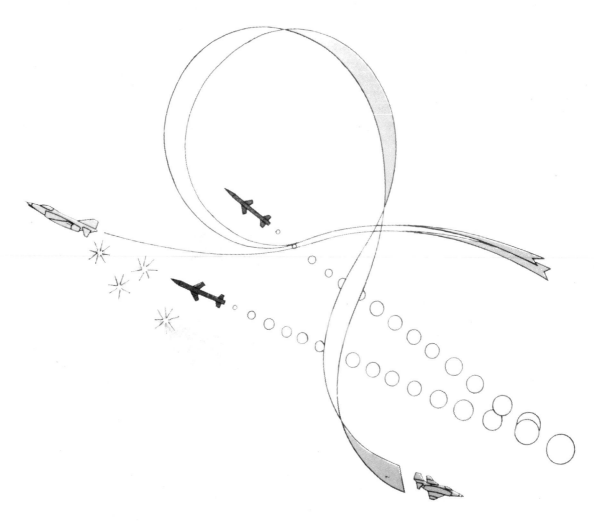

INFRARED COUNTERMEASURES. The IAF used several techniques to avoid the infrared (IR) tracking anti-aircraft missiles. Simplest was dispersing flares to attract the IR tracking missile by simulating the hot exhaust. However, the new and efficient IR filters were very difficult to spoof. More tricky to perform and requiring split-second reflexes and coordination was, upon sight detection or radio warning of missile approach, to fly a "cross" in the sky with two aircraft, with one plane intersecting the exhaust trail of the other, thereby creating a "hot spot" to attract the missile's heat-sending IR homing device. Other defenses were extremely violent maneuvers that the missile guidance system could not follow, or twisting the plane to present its "cool" side to the heat-seeking missile.

A very important part of the Yom Kippur War was the enormous airlift resupply missions that were flown by both the Soviet Union's Aeroflot to their Arab allies and by the United States to Israel.

This is how these operations were summarized by the official journal of the U.S. Military Airlift Command, in an article entitled "The Israeli Airlift (Oct.–Nov. 1973)" and written by Charles W. Dickens.

Early in the afternoon of 6 October 1973 on Yom Kippur, a high holy day in Israel, war erupted in the Mideast. It was a two-front invasion of Israel with Syria attacking from the northeast through the Golan Heights and with Egypt attacking across the Suez Canal and moving into the Sinai Peninsula. After initial successes by Syrian and Egyptian tanks and aircraft, the Israeli forces held and by 10 October counter-attacked, first in the Golan Heights area where they pushed to within 30 miles of Damascus, and a week later in the Sinai where

The Latakia oil terminals on the Syrian Mediterranean coast under heavy air attack. Retaliating with intensive air strikes after the Syrian surface-to-surface Frog missile attacks on Jewish towns in northern Israel, the IAF struck a heavy blow at the Syrian economic infrastructure during the Yom Kippur War.

they eventually pushed the Egyptians back across the Suez Canal.

The intensity of the fighting severely depleted the combat equipment and military supplies of both sides. The need for resupply was urgent. First to respond was Russia in behalf of Syria and Egypt. While American observers looked on with growing apprehension, the Russians flew supplies and weapons into Syria and Egypt aboard their AN-12 and AN-22 transports. As diplomatic talks to end the war continued, it became apparent that for those efforts to succeed a massive resupply of war material to Israel would be necessary to reestablish the balance of military strength. Plans for accomplishing the airlift of supplies to Israel were quickly drawn; items to be airlifted were identified, located, and

collected at onload ports, and MAC crews were alerted. On 14 October the first aircraft, a C-5, landed at Lod International Airport, Tel Aviv, Israel; the American airlift was underway.

The aircraft were routed from the CONUS onload bases to Lajes in the Azores for refueling and crew changes and then on to Tel Aviv. The route of flight through the Mediterranean was carefully chosen and flown to avoid African and Arab air space and to avoid overflying other foreign territorial space. With traffic flowing in both directions, Lajes became the choke point of the entire operation.

Much of the cargo airlifted to Israel could be carried only by the C-5. The large and sometimes extremely heavy items included the Army's M-60 and M-48 battle tanks, each weighing nearly

100,000 pounds; 175mm cannons at 56,000 pounds each; 155mm self-propelled howitzers at 48,000 pounds; CH-53 helicopters; and fuselages for A-4E attack aircraft.

By 2 November, 19 days after the airlift was initiated, the MAC aerial resupply had approximately equalled that of the Soviet airlift to the Arabs, even though the Soviet effort was underway well in advance of American activities, and by then totalled over 900 missions. Comparing the Soviet airlift with that of MAC, the Soviets flew 935 missions over a distance of 1,700 miles, lasted 40 days, and carried about 15,000 tons. MAC aircraft, on the other hand, flew only 566 missions over a distance of 6,450 miles and delivered over 22,000 tons in 32 days.

The impact of MAC's airlift was evidenced by the speed with which the supplies were moved from the aircraft to the front lines. Military ammunition and equipment reportedly reached the northern front within three hours after off-load. One source reported that 155mm shells delivered by MAC actually reached combat units on the Sinai front and were fired within 20 hours after offload.

Another, and perhaps an even more significant example of the impact of the airlift on the war, was the efectiveness of the Tow and Maverick missiles. According to the Defense Intelligence Agency, the great majority of Israel tank kills came from using the Tow and Maverick (Arab losses were estimated at 1,900 tanks during the course of the war). Since the Tow and Maverick were not present in the Israeli inventory in any significant numbers before the war began, it is apparent that the MAC airlift made the difference.

The assessment by Israeli Prime Minister

Golda Meir was probably the most meaningful: "For generations to come, all will be told of the miracle of the immense planes from the United States bringing in the material that meant life to our people."

Airlift had possibly saved a country.

The dramatic events of this war were summed up on a day-by-day basis in an official publication by the historical branch of the Israeli Air Force and the Israeli Ministry of Defense.

Following is *The Israeli Air Force in the Yom Kippur War:*

FOREWORD

This . . . deals with the activities of the Air Force during the Yom Kippur War, from Oct. 6th, through Oct. 24th, 1973. The war began with the premeditated assault by the Egyptians and Syrians on both fronts, along the Suez Canal and the Golan Heights, apparently giving them an initial advantage. However, anyone studying the events of the war a little closer, considering its results, will see things in a totally different light. Despite the extensive preparations by the Arab armies, led by Egypt and Syria, the unprecedented amounts of weapons employed in the battle, the coordinated opening of two fronts and above all the very short notice we had in the opening move, the Arab armies were unable to achieve any meaningful military gains. Zahal, the Israel Defense Forces, led by its striking force—The Israeli Air Force—upset the enemy plot:

a. Despite repeated attempts, the Egyptians did not succeed in reaching the Baluza–Romany route north east of the Canal because of the massive air attacks on the Egyptian bridges, plus the attacks of our tank units and armored troop carriers, as well as air attacks against the Egyptian infantry.
b. The retreat of Zahal from the artillery route along the Canal was avoided due to the intensive action of our Air Force.
c. The advance of the Egyptians army toward Rass-Sudar and Sharem El Sheik was also halted thanks to continuous attacks of enemy positions at Rass-Massala and Eyun-Mussa, by our aircraft.
d. The destruction of the Egyptian commando units in the Sinai was done mostly by the Air Force.
e. The Syrian plan of occupying the sources of the Jordan River, and the Sea of Gallilee was upset when their armor was repelled by intensive Air Force assistance to our forces.
f. Jordan avoided going to war due its fear of the Israeli Air Force.
g. Above all, the Air Force totally upset attempted enemy air-raids on strategic targets in Israel; such as large cities, ports, air fields, power and water plants.

The intensive activities of the Air Force during the first two days of the war, while engaging in a difficult and decisive battle to stop the advancing enemy, enabled Zahal to call up its reserves, have them reach the fronts, beat back the enemy, drive him back beyond the "purple" line, and then transfer the war into his own territory and occupy a sizeable area of his land.

The Israeli Air Force strikes on the enemy were heavy and decisive:

a. Many airfields were raided and deactivated for long periods, thereby eliminating enemy interference in the air.
b. Strategic targets in Syria, such as electric plants, fuel and water installations, were bombed.
c. The Air Force initiated and gained control of many air battles in which hun-

dreds of enemy aircraft were downed, giving the Air Force absolute superiority on both battle zones.

This . . . is unclassified. For obvious reasons we are unable to publish information about special operations, methods of attack, details on quantity or quality, and the method of operation and management of Air Force activity, due to the classified nature of this information. However, a close study of the contents will reveal the tremendous achievements of the Air Force during this war. The actions of the Air Force in the war are put down chronologically and according to the various stages of the battle.

February 1975

Joseph Abboudi—Major
Historical Officer of the
I.D.F.—Air Force

ISRAELI AIR FORCE ACTIVITIES DURING THE "YOM KIPPUR WAR"

1. The Yom Kippur War broke out on the 6th of October, 1973, at approximately 14.00 hours, with the invasion by Egyptian and Syrian forces into the Sinai and the Golan Heights and their attack on Israeli targets in the Sinai and the Golan Heights and their attempt to deploy air-to-ground missiles against Tel-Aviv.

2. The Israeli Air Force was immediately deployed to defend the country's air space, and to stop the invading enemy forces. Our Air Force first attacked the Egyptian forces crossing the Canal and assisted in stopping the Egyptian and Syrian advance. The Air Force then proceeded to attack strategic enemy targets and airfields in Syria and Egypt.

3. As our forces pushed the Syrian army back across the Purple Line, the Air Force assisted by attacking armor units, infantry, vehicle concentrations, and camps, as well as the numerous missile batteries covering the enemy forces.

4. When Zahal proceeded to repel and destroy the attacking Egyptian forces, and cross the Canal and surround the Third Army, the Air Force joined in, providing intensive support and assistance to its advancing forces and maintaining the skies "clean" of enemy aircraft.

5. Many air battles took place in this war. These were mostly battles initiated by the Israeli Air Force, although some were developed by intercepting enemy aircraft who tried to attack our forces, or enemy aircraft flying cover for other attacking aircraft.

6. In addition, many missions were flown by helicopters and transport aircraft, moving troops and supplies and evacuating casualties whose condition required quick transfer to medical centers. Light aircraft flew reconnaissance missions, and were extensively used by VIPs and commanders for travel and reconnaissance.

7. Following is a concise review of the activities of the Israeli Air Force during the Yom Kippur War, chronologically and by battle sectors.

OCT. 6, 1973 — THE FIRST DAY

A. The Egyptian Sector

1. The Egyptian attack (coordinated with the Syrians) began at approximately 14.00 hours. The Egyptians deployed artillery and aircraft to attack military targets including airfields, in the Sinai. Vast numbers of infantry and armored units kept crossing the Canal while transferring large amounts of military equipment to the east side.
2. The regular forces of Zahal began a braking battle against the intruders.
3. THE AIR FORCE
   The primary mission of the Air Force during the first day of the war was to stop the advance of the enemy. The Air Force attacked the Egyptian forces on both sides of the Canal, which included armored and infantry forces at the following locations:
   a. at Ismailia
   b. at Port Said
   c. south of the large Bitter Lake
   d. near Kabrit
   e. near the "Budapest" stronghold, in the north of Sinai
   f. bridges along the Canal
   g. Egyptian vessels near Zafrana
4. The following results were achieved in these attacks:
   a. Egyptian armored units, vehicles and infantry were hit near Port-Said.
   b. Good hits were seen near the "Budapest" stronghold.
   c. Missile batteries south of Kantara were hit.
   d. Bridges built by the Egyptians were hit.
   e. A Kelt missile, deployed from a Tupolev aircraft toward Tel-Aviv, was successfully intercepted and downed by an Air Force plane.
   f. 37 Egyptian planes were downed in air battles between our aircraft and the enemy aircraft. (Some were shot down by our ground-to-air missiles and some by anti-aircraft fire).

B. The Syrian Sector

1. The Syrian attack in the Golan Heights began parallel with the Egyptian attack, using the same method of massive bombardment, air attacks and penetration by massive infantry and armored forces into our territory. Most of the pressure was on the Hushnieh sector and a secondary effort was made toward Kuneitra.
   The Hermon outpost was captured by enemy commando forces.
   The Syrians deployed "Frog" ground to ground missiles during the night, hitting civilian settlements in Migdal-Ha'emek.
2. The Air Force was engaged in battles to repel the enemy.
3. Navy missile boats attacked enemy vessels during the night in the Latakia sector.
4. THE AIR FORCE
   The Air Force participated in repelling the attacking enemy forces, bombing and strafing armor and infantry units on the Kuneitra–Damascus route. Enemy forces south of Rapid were also attacked. Good hits were observed.
5. Five Syrian aircraft were downed in air battles.

C. Summary

Most of Air Force activities during the first day of the war consisted of repelling the attacking enemy forces on both fronts. The Air Force in conjunction with our ground forces stopped the advance of the enemy forces into our territory.
The Air Force also completed numerous patrol missions within Israel, and along the borders to engage and destroy intruding enemy aircraft.
42 enemy aircraft, including attack aircraft interceptors and helicopters, were downed on that day.

D. Our Air Losses

A number of our Air Force planes were hit by anti-aircraft missiles and by conventional anti-aircraft fire, falling in the Syrian and Egyptian sectors.

OCT. 7, 1973 — THE SECOND DAY

A. The Egyptian Sector

1. Our forces continued repelling the enemy forces.
2. The Air Force concentrated its activities on assisting our ground forces and attacking the bridges on the Canal. In addition, our aircraft, attacked the following targets:
   a. Egyptian infantry and armored units on both sides of the Canal, at the great Bitter Lake, the Gidi Pass and near the "Budapest" stronghold.
   b. Vessels near the island of Shaduan and near Ras-Zafrana.
   c. Bridges along the Canal.
   d. Egyptian airfields at Beni-Suef, Bir-Arido, Tanta, Mansurah, Shubrah-hit, Gankelis and Kutamieh.
   e. Missile batteries.
3. Good results were observed of infantry and armored units being hit in these attacks, while many bridges were hit as well. Good hits were observed on runways and missile batteries at the airfields.
4. 12 Egyptian aircraft were downed in air battles and by anti-aircraft fire.

B. The Syrian Sector

1. On the second day of the war, Syrian forces reached the area by Ramat-Magshimim. The Syrian force which attacked in the Kuneitra sector was stopped.
2. As a result of the Syrian advance, a number of our strongholds were evacuated. The civilian population of the settlements in the Golan Heights was also evacuated. The Jordan River bridges were covered by our forces.
3. The Air Force continued attacking and repelling the enemy forces. It attacked and hit enemy concentrations at Hushnieh and near Ramat Magshimim where the Syrian force was stopped. The Air Force also attacked enemy forces near Ahmedieh, Tel-Pharas and the oil road along the border.
4. In addition to assisting our forces, the Air Force massively attacked anti-aircraft batteries SA-2 and SA-3 aircraft missile sites. Good hits were observed and numerous anti-aircraft batteries were put out of action.
5. 19 Syrian aircraft were downed in fierce air battles in the area.

C. Summary

1. During the second day of the war, the Air Force continued its assault on enemy forces in order to stop their advances. Both Egyptian and Syrian forces were attacked.
2. The Air Force also attacked targets deep in enemy territory, including Egyptian airfields and Syrian conventional anti-aircraft and missile batteries.
3. The Air Force flew numerous patrol and interception missions.
   31 aircraft were downed by our aircraft, by Hawk missiles and by conventional anti-aircraft fire.

D. Our Losses

The Egyptians and the Syrians set up a very dense wall of anti-aircraft guns and missiles on both fronts, trying to protect their attacking forces.
Some of our aircraft were downed in both sectors by these guns and missiles during their attacks.

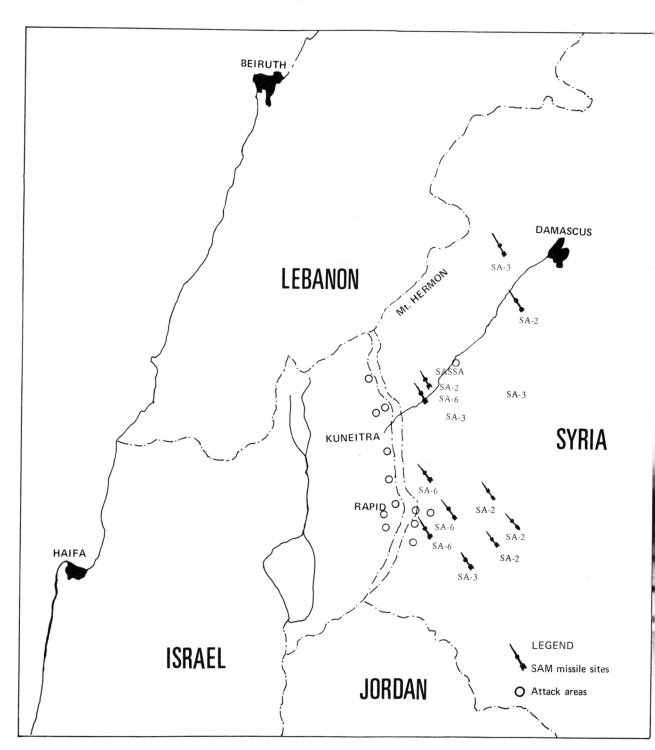

LEBANON

BEIRUTH

Mt. HERMON

DAMASCUS

SA-3

SA-2

SASSA
SA-2
SA-6
SA-3

SA-3

KUNEITRA

SYRIA

SA-6

RAPID
SA-6

SA-2

SA-6

SA-2

SA-2

SA-3

HAIFA

ISRAEL

JORDAN

LEGEND

SAM missile sites

O   Attack areas

OCT. 8, 1973 — THE THIRD DAY

A. The Egyptian Sector

1. Our forces began their assault on the Egyptian forces.
2. The Air Force attacked enemy concentrations, bridges and assisted our ground forces. The targets attacked were:
   a. Bridges built along the Canal.
   b. Military targets in the area of Ismailia.
   c. Conventional and missile anti-aircraft batteries and fuel dumps at Port Said.
   d. Military targets in the southern sector of the Canal.
   e. A radar station.
3. Good hits were observed at most targets and anti-aircraft gun batteries at Port Said were hit and destroyed. Egyptian infantry and armored units on the east side of the Canal were hit.
4. Many air battles took place between our interceptors and Egyptian planes. Egyptian planes, trying to attack our forces, were also downed by our anti-aircraft fire. Altogether, 35 Egyptian aircraft were downed.

B. The Syrian Sector

1. The advance of the Syrian forces was decisively stopped and counter-attacking action began to move them back across the "Purple Line" (the old border).
2. The Air Force participated by assisting our forces and attacked military targets deep in Syrian territory, which included:
   a. Dmeir, Halhul, Nasserieh, and Seikel airfields.
   b. Radar stations.
   c. Missile batteries.
3. The following results were achieved in these attacks;
   a. Good hits were observed at tank concentrations on the Oil line.
   b. Hits on buildings, anti-aircraft guns and runways at the airfields were observed.
   c. Syrian armored units were hit in the area of Hushnieh.
4. 36 Syrian aircraft were downed in air battles and by anti-aircraft fire.

C. Summary

1. On the third day of the war, the Air Force concentrated primarily on the attack of targets on the east side of the Suez Canal as well as targets deep in Syria. The Air Force also massively attacked enemy infantry and armored units in both sectors.
2. 71 enemy aircraft were downed in air battles and by anti-aircraft fire on that day.

D. Our Losses

Some Air Force planes were hit by Syrian and Egyptian conventional and missile anti-aircraft fire, and were downed in both sectors.

OCT. 9, 1973—THE FOURTH DAY

A. The Egyptian Sector

1. Beginning Oct. 9th our forces began battles with the Egyptians who tried to advance, with the primary purpose to tire them out. Break-through attempts by Egyptian armor through the Gidi pass toward Ras-Sudar were stopped.
2. The Air Force massively attacked infantry and armored units on both sides of the Canal. Bridges, anti-aircraft guns and airfields were also hit.
   The following targets were attacked by the Air Force:
   a. Armored and infantry units near the lakes, near Ismailia, and near Kantara.
   b. Bridges along the Canal.
   c. Anti-aircraft guns at Port Said and along the Canal.
   d. Manzura and Kutmieh airfields.
3. Following are the results of these Air Force attacks:
   a. The runways, the radar, aircraft and other targets at the Manzura airfield were hit.
      Runways at Kutmieh airfield were also hit.
   b. There were good hits of the bridges on the Canal.
   c. Egyptian forces near the "Budapest" stronghold were hit.
4. Six Egyptian planes were downed in air battles.

B. The Syrian Sector

1. All of the Golan Heights (except the Hermon stronghold) were returned to our control during the day.
2. The Air Force attacked many targets in Syria, including military targets near the border and strategic targets deep in Syrian territory. These targets included:
   a. Syrian armor at Tel-Ashur, Tel Achmar, Ein Manshic, Sarunah, Jedidat, Hushnieh, Achmadieh and near the Hermon Stronghold.
   b. The Syrian General Headquarters and Air Force Headquarters building in Damascus, and the refineries.
   c. An Iraqi convoy moving from the east toward Damascus.
   d. Missile batteries and radar stations.
3. Following are the results of these attacks:
   a. Good hits of the Syrian General Headquarters building and the Air Force Headquarters were observed, also observed were hits at the Homs refineries, and at nearby power station.
   b. Missile and conventional anti-aircraft batteries were hit.
   c. A military camp near Hushnieh was hit.
   d. Good hits of Syrian armored units near the border were observed.
4. Ten Syrian aircraft were downed in air battles.

C. Summary

1. The Air Force continued its attacks on Egyptian and Syrian armored and infantry units and continued assisting our forces. Also attacked were deep and strategic targets in Egyptian and Syrian territory, including airfields, missile sights, and other economically valuable targets.
2. Sixteen enemy aircraft were downed in air battles and by anti-aircraft fire.

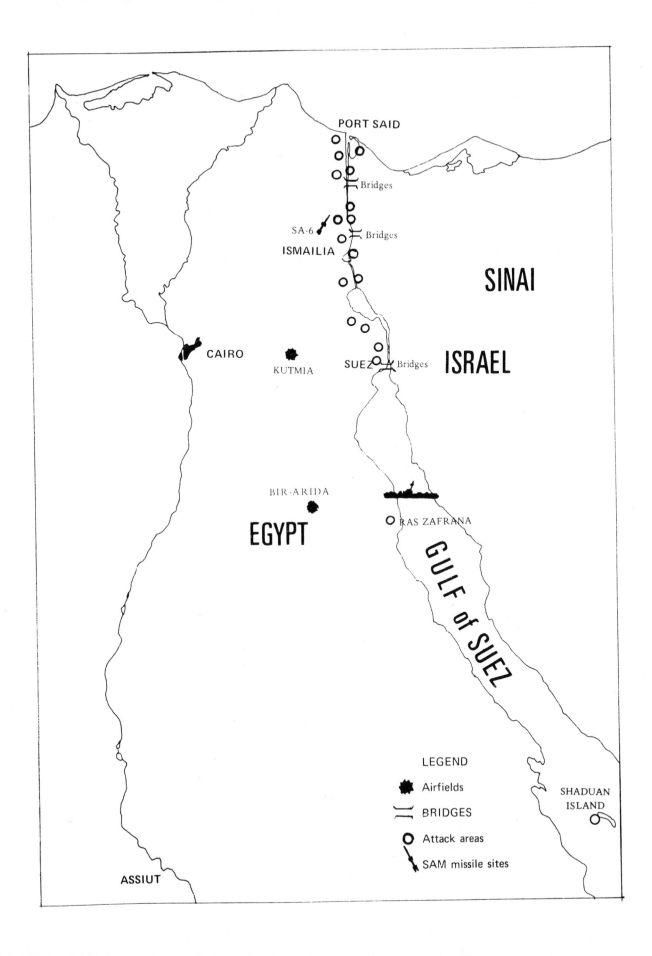

PORT SAID

Bridges

SA-6

Bridges

ISMAILIA

SINAI

SUEZ   Bridges

ISRAEL

CAIRO

KUTMIA

BIR-ARIDA

EGYPT

RAS ZAFRANA

GULF of SUEZ

ASSIUT

SHADUAN
ISLAND

LEGEND

Airfields

BRIDGES

Attack areas

SAM missile sites

OCT. 10, 1973—THE FIFTH DAY

A. The Egyptian Sector

1. Our ground forces continued their defense while breaking up enemy forces trying to advance toward the east.
2. The Air Force attacked armored units, tanks and other strategic targets in this sector along the front. The targets attacked were:
   a. Airfields at Kuisna and Abu-Hamed.
   b. Bridges on the Canal.
   c. Armored units near Ismaila.
   d. Anti-aircraft missile batteries.
   e. Radar stations.
   f. Ground assitance for our forces battling the enemy.
3. The following results were achieved in these attacks:
   a. Good hits were observed at the Kuisna and Abu-Hamed airfields.
   b. Egyptian armored units on the east side of the Canal were accurately hit.
4. At dusk, the Air Force massively attacked Egyptian armored units trying to advance toward the Gidi and Abu-Rodes. The Egyptian attacks were repelled.
5. Five Egyptian aircraft were downed in air battles and by anti-aircraft fire.

B. The Syrian Sector

1. Our forces on the Golan Heights continued putting the pressure on the retreating Syrians and cleaned up all the remaining pockets in the Golan Heights (except for the Hermon Stronghold).
2. As the Syrians were preparing for defense east of the ceasefire line, the Air Force continued attacking strategic targets deep in Syria. These targets included:
   a. The refineries at Homs.
   b. Airfields at Damascus, Haleb, Halhul and Blei.
   c. Mont-el-Bida Port.
   d. In addition, the Air Force continued close assistance to our forces near Mount Paras, east of Kuneitra.
3. a. The following results were achieved in these attacks as good hits were seen at the Haleb, Blei and Halhul airfields.
   b. There were good hits against the Syrian armored units.
4. Syrian aircraft tried attacking our forces. In the ensuing air battles between our aircraft and the Syrian aircraft, the Syrian lost 18 aircraft, some of which were downed by ground anti-aircraft fire.

C. Summary

1. The Air Force concentrated primarily on attacks of strategic targets in Egypt and Syria. Attacked were airfields, missile sites, radar stations and other economically vulnerable targets. The Air Force also performed many attacks to assist our ground forces.
2. Twenty-three Egyptian and Syrian planes were downed on the fifth day of the war.

OCT. 11, 1973 — THE SIXTH DAY

A. The Egyptian Sector

1. Our forces continued their defensive battle. The Egyptians concentrated their efforts in the central sector of the Canal and tried to advance toward the Gidi, the Mitla and in the direction of Abu-Rodes. Their efforts failed after fierce battles, and they retreated to their positions suffering heavy casualties.
2. Most of the Air Force activities on that day focused on the attack of armored and infantry units in the northern sector. The Air Force also assisted our forces in repelling the enemy forces.
3. The airfield at Zalahieh was raided, and hits were seen in the center of the main runway.
4. Missile sites west of the Canal were massively attacked and accurate hits were observed.
5. Good hits of the Egyptian armored units in the northern sector were observed.
6. The Egyptian aircraft tried to attack our forces on this day.
   Twelve (12) Egyptian planes were downed in the ensuing air battles.

B. The Syrian Sector

1. While our aircraft continued softening enemy targets and attacking airfields, our ground forces began a general attack toward enemy territory in the northern sector on the Kuneitra–Damascus route.
2. Our forces advanced about 15 kilometers into Syria and reached the outskirts of Mizreat-Beit-Ghan and Tel-Shams.
3. Early in the morning, the Air Force began concentrated attacks on Syrian airfields and missile sites east of the border. It also assisted our forces in their advance and attacked Syrian armor and armored vehicles.
4. The Air Force attacked airfields at Blei, Seikal, Halhul, Dmeir, Maza, Nasarieh, Damascus and T-4. Good hits were observed at all targets, and most airfields were closed for long durations, due to accurate hits on their runways.
5. Good hits were also seen at the missile sites, and most sites were destroyed.
6. The Syrian Air Force activities were disturbed due to the many attacks on its airfields, resulting in its deactivation most of the day.
7. A fuel dump north of Damascus was attacked in the afternoon, and was badly damaged. Two (2) Syrian planes were downed in air battles.

C. Summary

1. On the sixth day of the war, the Air Force participated in the attack of armor and infantry along the fronts, but also massively attacked Syrian airfields, badly disturbing the Syrian Air Force's activities.
2. Our forces on that day penetrated deep into Syrian territory, where forces went into defensive and retreating action.
3. The Egyptian forces who tried to advance on that day were beaten and began retreating after suffering heavy casualties.
4. Our Air Force downed 14 enemy planes.

OCT. 12, 1973—THE SEVENTH DAY

A. The Egyptian Sector

1. The Egyptians continued digging in on the east side of the Canal, but their efforts to "bite-off" parts of our force's defense formations failed again, this time in the area of the Gidi.
2. Beginning on that day, the Air Force began shifting its fulcrum of activities to the Egyptian sector. It massively attacked missile sites at Port Said, assisting our forces along the front, and attacked Egyptian armor and infantry at Ismailia, near the lakes and in the southern area of the Canal.
3. The Egyptians lost 3 planes on that day.

B. The Syrian Sector

1. Our forces took Beit-Jan and the village of Nassag.
2. The Syrian Air Force tried unsuccessfully to attack our forces on the Golan Heights.
3. The spearhead force of the Iraqi division arrived on that day and placed itself in front of our forces.
4. The Air Force attacked the following targets in Syria:
    a. Airfields at Al-Meza, Blei, Latakieh, Babila, Seikal, Damascus, Nazarieh and Dmeir.
    b. Bridges.
    c. Missile batteries.
    d. Tank and armor concentrations.
    e. The Air Force also assisted our forces at Mizreat Beit-Ghan.
5. Good results were observed at the attacked targets.
6. The Syrians suffered heavy aircraft losses to anti-aircraft fire and in air battles. A total of 16 planes were shot down.

C. Summary

1. As mentioned, the Air Force shifted the fulcrum of its activities to the Egyptian sector, and massively attacked Egyptian missile sites and armor. But the Air Force was also active in the Syrian sector, attacking airfields, missile sites and armor.
2. Nineteen (19) enemy aircraft were downed that day.

OCT. 13, 1973—THE EIGHTH DAY

A. The Egyptian Sector

1. The following targets were attacked by the Air Force on that day:
   a. Missile sites on the west side of the Canal near Port Said.
   b. Infantry forces west of the Mitla Pass.
   c. Egyptian armor and vehicles in the center and southern sectors of the Canal.
2. The following results were achieved in these attacks.
   a. Missile sites west of the Canal and at Port Said were destroyed.
   b. Egyptian vehicles and armor at the center and southern sector of the Canal were hit.
   c. Large numbers of Egyptian armor were hit on various movement routes and roads.
3. The Egyptians lost 9 aircraft; mostly in air battles and some by anti-aircraft fire.

B. The Syrian Sector

1. Our forces destroyed about 40 Iraqi tanks in an ambush near Mashara. The Syrians tried to develop an attack near A-Teiha, but were repelled.
   Meza airfield, near Damascus, was shelled by our artillery units.
2. The Air Force attacked Syrian airfields including Meza, Blei, Halhul, Damascus, Dmeir and Seikal, as well as missile sites and Syrian armor.
   Our forces received great assistance from the Air Force.
   Syrian airfields were hit, some at their runways, others at vital installations.
   Good hits of missile sites and of Syrian armor were observed.
4. Twelve (12) Syrian aircraft were downed in air battles.

C. Summary

1. On the 8th day of the war, the Air Force attacked strategic targets deep in enemy territory including airfields and missile batteries. It attacked armor and other vehicles along the border and interfered with the flow of enemy forces to the front.
2. Twenty-one (21) enemy aircraft were downed on both fronts.

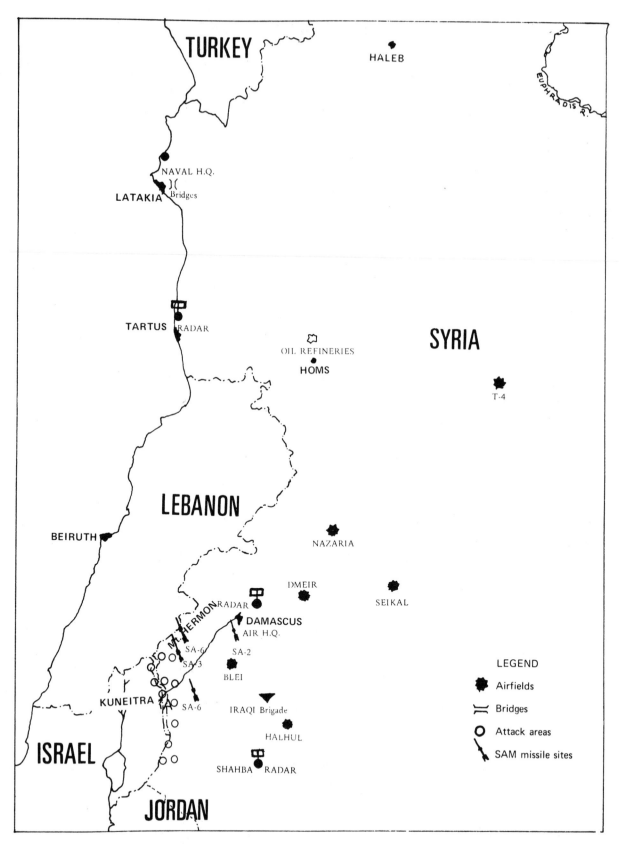

AIR FORCE ATTACKS IN THE SYRIAN SECTOR, OCT. 8th–OCT. 12th, 1973

OCT. 14, 1973 — THE NINTH DAY

A. The Egyptian Sector

1. At 05.30 hours the Egyptians began a massive armor attack on all sectors. Those attacks were repelled by our Southern Command divisions, while destroying over 200 enemy tanks.
2. At dawn the Air Force began attacking military targets, including:
   a. Egyptian armor and infantry south of the Canal, near Rass-Massala, Eyun-Mussa and in the central sector.
   b. Missile batteries west of the Canal.
   c. Salahieh, Mansura and Tanta airfields.
   d. Bridges.
3. Good hits were observed at most targets.
4. The Egyptians lost 10 planes; some in air battles and some by ground fire.

B. The Syrian Sector

1. The gap in this sector became an enclave. Our forces advanced to the outskirts of Sassa after taking Tel-Arum and the village of Kefar Shams. Syrian attacks near Mizreat-Beit-Ghan and Nassag were repelled.
2. The Air Force attacked the Meza airfield and assisted our forces on the front. Good hits were observed and the runways at the airport were damaged.
3. The Syrians lost 4 aircraft. Three in air battles and one by ground fire.

C. Summary

a. The Air Force operated massively, especially in the Egyptian sector, attacking airfields, missile sites and bridges. Air Force missions in the Syrian sector were relatively few.
b. A total of 14 enemy aircraft were downed on that day.

OCT. 15, 1973—THE TENTH DAY

A. The Egyptian Sector

1. The breaking of the Egyptian attack began and the Southern Command began taking the attack initiation into its own hands. A bridgehead was started at Dwer-Sueir.
2. The Air Force massively attacked the Egyptian ground forces east of the Canal, as well as airfields and ground-to-air missile sites including:
   a. Armor concentrations at Kantar, Port Fuad, near Firdan, near the Bitter Lake, Suez, north of Dwer-Sueir and near Ismailia.
   b. Airfields, including Kutmieh, Shubra Hit and Tanta.
   c. Missile batteries east and west of the Canal.
   d. The railroad tracks between Cairo and Suez.
3. Good hits were observed at the airports; runways, aircraft pits, warehouses, etc., were damaged.
4. The Egyptians lost 4 aircraft in air battles.

B. The Syrian Sector

1. The Iraqi armor was again beaten in armor battles. Our forces extended their control to Tel-Antar. The Syrians employed long range artillery to attack settlements in the Hula Valley.
2. The Air Force activities in this sector were limited to assisting our ground forces and attacking fuel dumps at Tartus and Latakia. Good hits were observed.
3. Three (3) enemy aircraft were downed in air battles in the Syrian skies.

C. Summary

1. The emphasis of Air Force activities shifted to the Egyptian sector as of the tenth day of the war, even though the Syrian forces kept trying to break through Zahal's formation.
2. Military targets in Egypt were massively attacked and our forces near the Canal received much assistance from the Air Force. The Air Force also attacked economically vulnerable targets in Syria and continued assisting our forces in that sector.
3. Seven (7) Egyptian planes were downed in air battles.

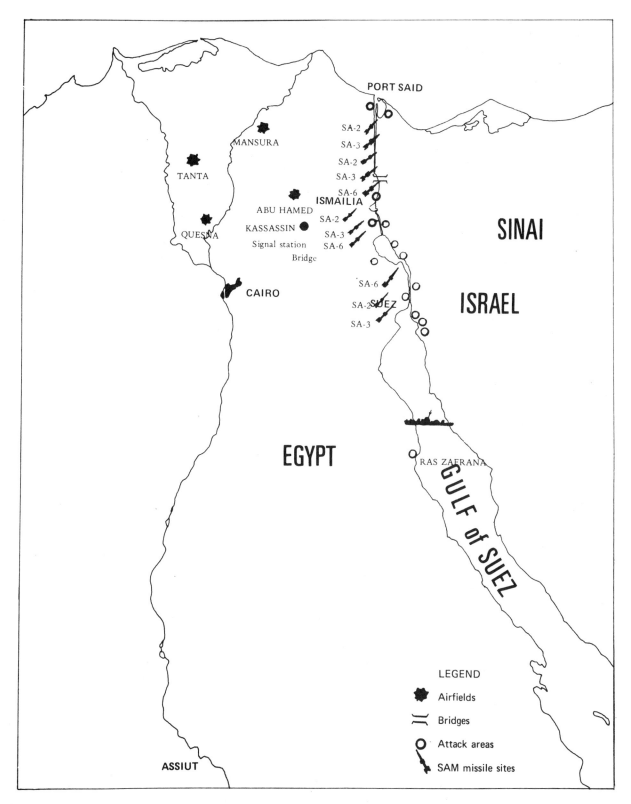

AIR FORCE ATTACKS IN THE EGYPTIAN SECTOR, OCT. 10th–OCT. 15th, 1973

OCT. 16, 1973—THE ELEVENTH DAY

A. The Egyptian Sector

1. In the early hours of morning a bridgehead was taken, and the first tanks of Zahal began crossing the Canal westward near Dwer-Sueir. At the same time, our forces stopped the enemy's attempts to "plug" the breakthrough by pressure from the north and south.
2. The Air Force continued attacking Egyptian armor and infantry, and assisted our forces along the Canal and in other areas on the west bank of the Canal.
3. At Port Said, the Air Force attacked artillery positions and missiles sites.
4. Egyptian radar stations were also attacked from the air.
5. Good hits were observed at most attacked targets:
   a. Numerous missile sites were damaged and put out of action.
   b. Radar sites were damaged and put out of action.
   c. Large Egyptian infantry forces and many vehicles were hit near the lakes, near Ismailia and on the west bank of the Canal near breakthrough area.
6. Following the breakthrough, the Egyptian Air Force began a continuous attack on our forces. Despite their losses, their aircraft performed tens of attack missions, and some of their planes were downed by our anti-aircraft fire. Heavy air battles followed and a total of 21 Egyptian aircraft were downed that day, by ground fire and in air battles.

B. The Syrian Sector

1. Our forces in the Syrian sector found themselves facing three armies which tried to attack at dawn (the Syrian army, the Iraqi and the Jordanian army). The Syrian and Iraqi attacks were repelled. The first encounter with Jordanian forces began to take place in the form of armor battles near Tel-Hara. The massive Syrian shelling continued and Zahal employed 175mm cannons to shell Syrian camps.
2. The Air Force attacked Syrian targets, including:
   a. The Hermon stronghold, where good hits were observed.
   b. Two bridges in northern Syria. One bridge was destroyed, the other damaged.
   c. An economically valuable target near Harasta was attacked and accurate hits were observed.
   d. The Air Force assisted our forces at Sassa, and hits on enemy armor and vehicles were observed.
3. Eight (8) Syrian planes were downed in air battles which developed during the day.

C. Summary

1. On the eleventh day of the war, the Air Force provided massive assistance to our forces who broke through to the west bank of the Canal, and attacked armored vehicles along the Canal and on the Golan Heights. Strategic and economically valuable targets deep in the enemy territory were also attacked.
2. The enemy lost 29 aircraft, mostly in air battle, and some to conventional ground anti-aircraft fire, and to our Hawk missiles.

OCT. 17, 1973—THE TWELFTH DAY

A. The Egyptian Sector

1. Our forces widened the approached sector to the Canal, while battling heavily with enemy armor. Other forces continued widening the break on the west side of the Canal. A stable bridge was put over the Canal in the afternoon and armored forces began crossing the Canal to the west.
2. The Air Force aircraft attacked Egyptian targets since dawn, including:
   a. The Egyptian Navy Headquarters and anti-aircraft guns at Port Said. The Navy Headquarters was damaged.
   b. Missile batteries west of the Canal. Good hits were observed and a number of missile sites were put out of action.
   c. Kutmieh airfield.
   d. Vehicle armor concentrations, as well as anti-aircraft batteries along the Canal, both east and west of it.
3. Egyptian aircraft, trying to intervene in the attacks or attack our forces, suffered losses. Five (5) enemy aircraft were downed in the developing battles.

B. The Syrian Sector

1. Syrian armor tried to develop a counter attack at Mizreat-Beit-Ghan, but was repelled and beaten.
   The Syrians continued their heavy shelling on the Golan Heights.
2. The Air Force attacked military targets at Nabek, bridges at Latakieh and the Iraqi armored units. Good hits were observed. Ammunition dumps at Nabek were damaged and one bridge was destroyed near Latakia.
3. The Syrians lost 7 aircraft during these attempts to intervene in the attacks.

C. Summary

1. The Air Force concentrated its efforts in the Egyptian sector while massively assisting our forces east and west of the Canal. Strategic and economically valuable targets deep in enemy territory were also attacked, with the intent of weakening enemy efforts.
2. Twelve (12) Egyptian and Syrian planes were downed in air battles and by ground fire.

OCT. 18, 1973—THE THIRTEENTH DAY

A. The Egyptian Sector

1. Our forces continued their advance on the west side of the Canal in a south-westerly direction, and penetrated 10 km., while destroying enemy armor and infantry, and damaging missile sites in the area. Another force moved north, paralleling the Canal.
2. Our aircraft attacked the missile formations in the northern sector of the Canal. Some of these missile sites were damaged and put out of action in this assault.
3. Our aircraft also attacked the airfield at Salahieh. Good hits on the runways were seen and the field was paralyzed.
4. Egyptian radar stations were attacked.
5. Military and economically valuable targets at Port Said were attacked. Good hits were observed at the port, at the fuel dumps and at the gun emplacements.
6. The Egyptian Air Force scrambled and sent many aircraft toward our forces, especially in the breakthrough area west of the Canal. Effective anti-aircraft fire was shot at them and interceptors were sent to meet them as well. In the ensuing air battles the Egyptians lost twenty seven (27) planes, including 6 helicopters.

B. The Syrian Sector

1. The Air Force was not used in the Syrian sector on this day, and there were no air battles with Syrian aircraft.

C. Summary

1. The Air Force limited its operations on this day to the Egyptian sector only. Massive assaults on missile batteries, anti-aircraft emplacements, airfields and other targets took place.
2. The enemy lost 27 aircraft.

OCT. 19, 1973—THE FOURTEENTH DAY

A. The Egyptian Sector

1. The west bank was reinforced by additional armored forces who participated in the advance to the west and southwest. There were also armored battles on the east side north of the bridgehead. On the south side of the canal were many armored battles and the Egyptians were pressed northward.
2. The Air Force massively attacked Egyptian ground forces west of the Canal near the breakthrough area, as well as east of the Canal and along its full length, particularly around Kantara, Ismailia, Ras-Massala and Port Said in the north.
3. Missile batteries and bridges near Kantara were attacked.
4. The Egyptians tried to attack our crossing forces from the air. In these attempts they lost twenty five (25) aircraft in air battles and to ground fire.

B. The Syrian Sector

1. Our forces captured Um-Butna in the central sector. Counter-attacks by the Syrians, Jordanians, and Iraqis near the village of Kfar-Shams, and Kfar Nasseg were repelled.
2. The Air Force assisted our forces in the northern Syrian sector.
3. Two enemy aircraft were downed in air battles.

C. Summary

1. On the 14th day too, the primary efforts of the Air Force were concentrated on the Egyptian sector. The Air Force attacked enemy forces on both sides of the Canal, as well as assisting our forces. It also attacked targets deep in enemy territory, including missiles, bridges, armor and vehicles.
2. In the Syrian sector, the Air Force attacked enemy armor.
3. Twenty seven (27) aircraft were downed in the air battles and by ground fire in both sectors.

OCT. 20, 1973 — THE FIFTEENTH DAY

A. The Egyptian Sector

1. Our forces continued their rapid advance, west and south of the breakthrough area, and even built a third bridge over the Canal. All that in spite of desperate efforts of the enemy to try to stop them by heavy artillery shelling.
   The Egyptians began preparing a defense line west of the penetration area, to prevent our forces from breaking through to the heart of Egypt. Our forces continued to move southward toward the city of Suez, destroying large amounts of armor and missile bases on their way. On the east bank, the attack and pressures continued to the south and north of the Canal.
2. The Air Force continued massive support of our forces on both sides of the Canal. Enemy strongholds, mobile artillery, batteries, armored vehicles and enemy tanks were attacked.
3. Bridges over the Canal, bunkers, and military camps were attacked.
4. Good hits were observed when an airfield was attacked. The Air Force also attacked missile sites far west of the Canal.
5. The Egyptians tried desperately to launch many air attacks on our forces. Effective ground fire and interceptors downed 11 of the attacking Egyptian aircraft.

B. The Syrian Sector

1. The Syrians continued shelling the Golan Heights.
2. The activities in this sector slowed down a bit, but the Air Force continued assisting our forces.
3. One Syrian aircraft was downed in an air battle.

C. Summary

1. The main efforts of Zahal were concentrated on the Egyptian sector.
2. The aerial activities also centered on massive and continuous assistance to the army in this sector and the Air Force attacked many Egyptian targets.
3. The Arab air forces lost a total of 12 aircraft on this day.

OCT. 21, 1973—THE SIXTEENTH DAY

A. The Egyptian Sector

1. Our forces continued moving south on the west bank toward Suez, while destroying enemy armor and missile bases. On the east bank, pressure on enemy forces continued toward the south and north.
2. Air Force activities concentrated on massive assistance to our ground forces. The following targets were attacked:
   a. Mobile artillery batteries near and south of Kantara.
   b. Armor and infantry concentrations near Kantara and El-Balah.
   c. The camps of Faid and Kasprit west of Canal.
   d. Armor and vehicles on routes west of the Canal.
   e. Missile batteries near Port Said, Ismailia and Suez.
3. The Egyptians sent many aircraft to the area to attack our forces. These aircraft were met by effective ground fire and by our planes, resulting in the loss of 25 Egyptian aircraft.
4. An air base opposite Faid was activated on that day and for the first time, transport aircraft landed there with supplies for our forces on the west bank.

B. The Syrian Sector

1. The enemy formation was reinforced by a Jordanian armored division and an Iraqi mechanized division. A Syrian attack in the north section of this sector was repelled in the morning hours. The battle for the Hermon strongholds began in the afternoon. The Syrians also tried to land forces on the Hermon with helicopters.
2. The Air Force attacked Syrian military targets near the Hermon stronghold and near the border.
3. The Syrians tried to attack our forces from the air, but their planes were met by our Air Force interceptors who downed 9 of them in air battles.
   Eleven (11) Syrian aircraft were shot down that day.

C. Summary

1. On the sixteenth day of the war, the Air Force planes continued their massive attacks in the Egyptian sector, but also attacked in the Syrian sector and destroyed many enemy targets in both sectors. Our aircraft attacked armor, infantry, mobile artillery, conventional anti-aircraft and missile batteries and continually assisted our ground forces.
2. The enemy tried to activate his aircraft and attack our forces in both sectors. They lost 36 aircraft to ground fire and in air battles.
3. The Air Force activated the air base at "Faid" west of the canal, on that day, naming it "Nachshon."

OCT. 22, 1973—THE SEVENTEENTH DAY

A. The Egyptian Sector

1. Our forces advanced in all areas of the front on the west side of the Canal, trying to beat the ceasefire deadline at 18.50 hours.
   One force reached the southern Suez-Cairo route, another force reached Ismailia and controlled the route Ismailia-Cairo and a third force arrived at a point north of the town of Suez. Our forces' control expanded to include the area of Shluffa.
2. The Air Force attacked Egyptian positions east of the Canal and various forces west of the Canal since the early morning hours. These air attacks were massive attacks to assist our forces to break the enemy. The attacked targets included:
   a. Anti-aircraft and mobile artillery in the area of Port Said.
   b. Blocking the route along the east side of the Canal.
   c. A base south east of the Bitter Lake.
   d. The Gidi Pass.
   e. Bridges along the Canal.
   f. Military camps west of the Canal, along the shores of the Bitter Lake, infantry and armored bases.
   g. Blocking routes of the Canal, especially at the Cairo-Suez route.
   h. Missile batteries west of the Canal.
4. The Egyptians tried to attack our forces west of the Canal, but were met by effective anti-aircraft fire, and by our interceptors. A total of 11 Egyptian planes were downed.

B. The Syrian Sector

1. Our forces captured the Syrian and Israeli Hermon strongholds. (The Israeli stronghold was captured by the Syrians at the beginning of the war).
2. The Air Force assisted our forces in capturing these strongholds.
3. The Syrians tried to attack our forces, even using attack aircraft, however these aircraft were met by interceptors and 5 Syrian planes were downed in the resulting air battles.

C. Summary

1. The Air Force attacked many targets, mostly west of the Canal to assist our forces, who were advancing rapidly in order to reach dominant areas and surround the Third Army before the ceasefire deadline. In the Syrian sector, the Air Force also assisted our forces in capturing the Hermon strongholds.
2. The enemy tried to attack our forces from the air in both sectors, but was engaged in air battles by our interceptors resulting in the loss of 16 Egyptian and Syrian aircraft.

OCT. 23, 1973—THE EIGHTEENTH DAY

A. The Egyptian Sector

1. The ceasefire which took effect on the 22nd of October, was violated by the Egyptians who tried to gain better positions and especially to break the siege on the Third Army. As a result, our forces continued their advance attacking the Egyptian both west and east of the Canal.
2. The Air Force continued attacking Egyptian targets, including:
   a. Egyptian ranges west of the Bitter Lake and north and south of the town of Suez.
   b. Third Army Headquarters.
   c. Military camps west of the Canal.
   d. Bridges on the south end of the Canal.
   e. Egyptian vehicles moving on the Cairo-Suez route.
3. The Egyptians tried to attack our advancing forces west of the Canal, and also tried to intercept our attacking aircraft. A number of air battles took place, and 11 Egyptian planes were downed.

B. The Syrian Sector

1. There was no ground action in this sector.
2. In the early morning hours, the Air Force attacked Syrian tanks and armor moving toward the Hermon stronghold. Missile batteries were also attacked.
3. Fuel dumps northeast of Damascus were attacked during which the Syrians tried to intercept our aircraft. In two large air battles, the Syrians lost 9 aircraft.

C. Summary

1. Because of the Egyptian break of the ceasefire, our forces continued their advance. The Air Force attacked many military targets west of the Canal and assisted our forces. The Air Force also attacked Syrian targets.
2. Twenty (20) enemy aircraft were downed in air battles and by ground fire in both sectors.

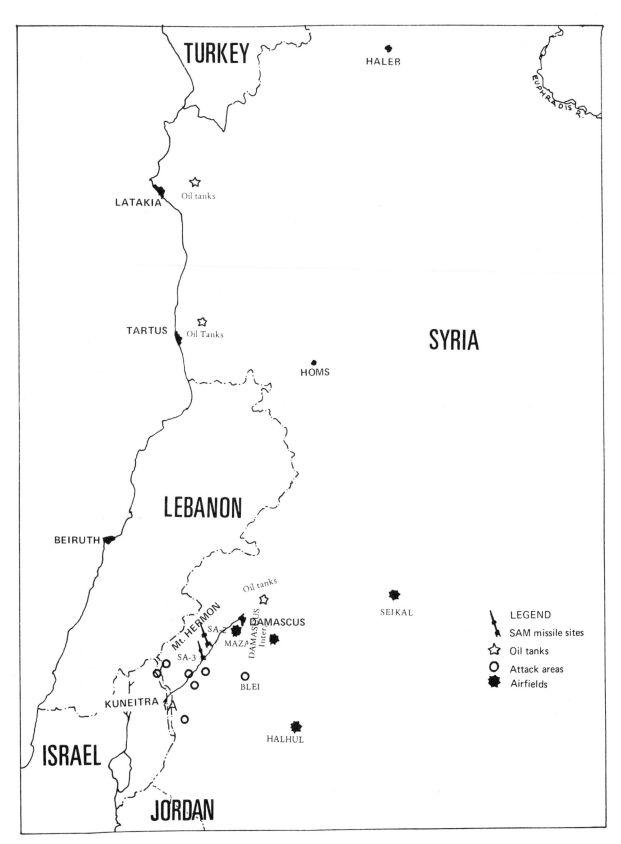

AIR FORCE ATTACKS IN THE SYRIAN SECTOR, OCT. 13th–OCT. 23rd, 1973

OCT. 24, 1973 — THE NINETEENTH DAY

A. The Egyptian Sector

1. Until the ceasefire deadline, set for Oct. 24, at 17.00 hours, our forces continued their fast moving advance and reached the northeast beach of the Gulf of Suez, Ras-El Abadieh, completing the total envelopment of the Egyptian Third Army and the town of Suez.
2. On this last day of the war, the Air Force completed the following missions:
   a. Massive attacks on enemy forces west and east of the Canal.
   b. Attacks of bridges at Suez and at Port Said.
   c. Attacks of fuel dumps south of the Canal.
   d. Attacks of armor, vehicle concentrations, infantry forces, mobile artillery and anti-aircraft batteries along the Canal.
   e. Attacks of military camps on the west bank of the Canal.
   f. Concentrated assaults on the Suez-Cairo routes.
   g. Attacks on camps and strongpoints in the town of Suez, Port-Ibrahim and near Ras-el-Adabieh.
3. The Egyptians tried to interfere with our attacking aircraft by sending large numbers of interceptors to meet them. In the ensuing air battles which took place, the Egyptians lost 14 fighters.

B. The Syrian Sector

There was no activity in the Syrian sector on that day.

C. Summary

1. The Air Force participated by massive attacks on Egyptian targets on the last day of the war as assistance and cover for our advancing forces. Many enemy concentrations were attacked on both sides of the Canal.
2. The Air Force fought serious air battles on this last day, during which 14 Egyptian interceptors were downed.
3. The ceasefire went into effect on that day, and all firing stopped at 17.00 hours by the orders of the Israeli Chief of Staff.

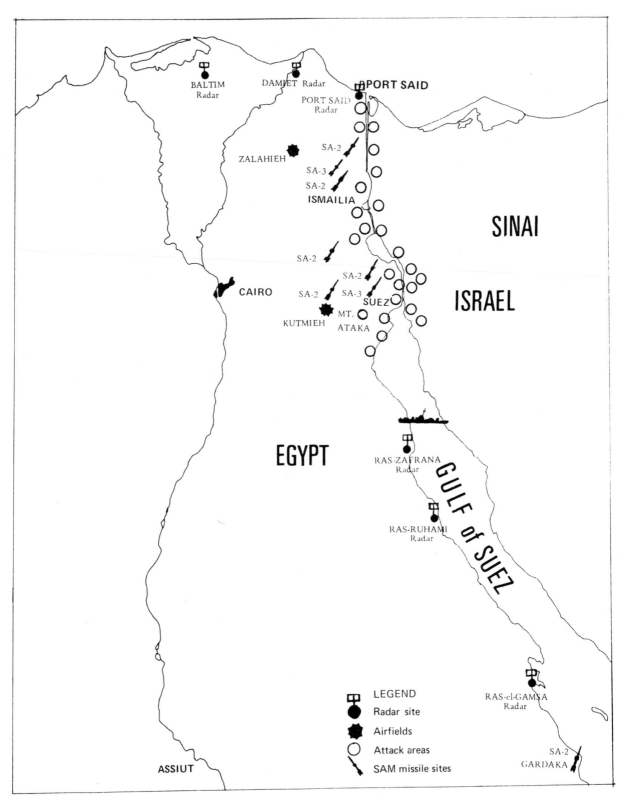

BALTIM
Radar

DAMIET Radar

PORT SAID

PORT SAID
Radar

SA-2

ZALAHIEH

SA-3

SA-2

ISMAILIA

SINAI

SA-2

SA-2

SA-2   SA-3

ISRAEL

SA-2

SUEZ

KUTMIEH   MT.
ATAKA

CAIRO

EGYPT

RAS-ZAFRANA
Radar

GULF of SUEZ

RAS-RUHAMI
Radar

LEGEND

⬟ Radar site

✴ Airfields

◯ Attack areas

➚ SAM missile sites

RAS-el-GAMSA
Radar

SA-2
GARDAKA

ASSIUT

AIR FORCE ATTACKS IN THE EGYPTIAN SECTOR, OCT. 16th–OCT. 24th, 1973

SUMMARY OF AIR FORCE ACTIVITIES IN THE YOM KIPPUR WAR

1. The Yom Kippur War began suddenly and without sufficient notice, as far as the state of preparedness of the forces of Zahal was concerned. The war broke out on Yom Kippur, the Day of Atonement, October 6th, when the Egyptian and Syrian armies, with the aid of other Arab forces, invaded the Sinai along the Suez Canal and the Golan Heights along the Syrian border and attacked our forces.

2. Zahal, the Israel Defense Army, is an army which is founded and based on its reserve forces. Because of this, it can operate at full strength only after sufficient warning period, so as to enable it to call up the reserves, arm them, and place them along the borders.

3. Since the war began with no warning at all, Zahal met the massive enemy attacks and invasion with only its regular forces, who could not, because of their limited numbers, prevent the enemy from attaining first advantages, during the first stages of the war.

4. The enemy performed his attacks while being almost completely covered by an aerial umbrella of missile batteries and this, as a result of their conclusive understanding, that the Egyptian and Syrian air forces have a slim chance of fighting against the Israeli Air Force.

5. Therefore, in the beginning stages of the war, the Air Force attacked the enemy infantry and armor forces, stopping their advance; at the same time engaging in a hard and ruthless battle with the enemy's ground-to-air missiles, fired at them by the hundreds.

6. During the first stages of the Yom Kippur War the Air Force massively attacked enemy armor and missiles, participating in very effectively stopping the enemy's advance.

7. At the same time, the Air Force fulfilled its primary responsibility of guarding the country's skies and engaged in many battles with enemy aircraft, trying to attack targets in the country and along the borders.

8. After the reserves were called up and fought armored battles with the enemy and went into the repelling stage, the Air Force joined in and provided large assistance to our advancing forces, all that while destroying the very closely positioned Egyptian and Syrian missile battery formations.

9. The Air Force also performed many raids deep in enemy territory, destroying strategic and military targets, including airfields, fuel dumps, radar stations, missile batteries, bridges, vessels and transportation routes. Many enemy airports were attacked and paralyzed in these raids, and most economically valuable strategic targets were damaged. During these raids, the enemy sent tens of aircraft in an attempt to intercept ours. In the air battles which developed the enemy lost many aircraft.

10. A large number of Egyptian and Syrian planes were downed by effective fire of conventional aircraft guns and Hawk missiles during their attempted air attacks on our forces.

11. When Zahal moved into the phase of repelling the enemy, pushing him back across the border and taking territory across the Purple Line. The Air Force, as mentioned, participated in providing effective and massive assistance to our forces. In that, the Air Force helped in breaking the enemy's resistance, who changed from an attacking army into a defending and retreating army.

12. All units of the Air Force operated in this war with all their might and with maximum efficiency. The enemy lost a total of 451 aircraft in this war. Most of them in air battles, and some by ground fire and Hawk missiles (283 Egyptian aircraft and 168 Syrian aircraft).

13. The Air Forces' helicpoter and transport aircraft were used very effectively in this war, participating in many operations involving the rescue and evacuation of hundreds of casualties of Zahal, who were moved to the rear and to medical centers, thus saving hundreds of lives.

14. The war on the Syrian front ended, with our forces positioned about 40 km. from the capital city of Damascus. The Air Force gained total aerial superiority on this front, and toward the end of the war the Syrian Air Force could not operate in a manner that could endanger our forces.

15. On the Egyptian front the war ended with the Egyptian Third Army completely encircled; the Egyptian army completely weakened and our forces controlling the west side of the Canal from Ismailia to the Port of Adabieh on the Gulf of Suez and Zahal stationed about 100 km. from Cairo. The Egyptian Air Force was badly beaten and lost hundreds of its aircraft. Toward the end of the war, the Egyptian Air Force tried desperately to stop our forces advancing on Egyptian soil, but was badly beaten by the Israeli Air Force which completely controlled the air space in this theatre of operations.

16. The Air Force participated in the Yom Kippur War in an efficient and decisive manner during the first stages; to stop the enemy forces breaking through and then together with Zahal's armor and infantry repel the enemy far beyond its lines.

Chapter 7

Entebbe—The Impossible Rescue, July 4, 1976

For the sake of security many brave deeds of Israel's airborne forces must remain forever untold. But one incredible action, top secret throughout its feverish planning, may now be published in great detail. The victory scored by the IDF paratroopers and commandos at Entebbe has gone down in history as the most incredible raid ever accomplished by any army in the world.

The story of Entebbe began on June 29, 1976. Air France Flight 139, en route from Tel Aviv to Paris via Athens, was hijacked by terrorists operating under the aegis of the Palestine Liberation Organization (PLO). After landing at Benghazi, Libya, to refuel, the pilot of the Air France Airbus was directed to head for Uganda.

On landing late that evening at Uganda's Entebbe International Airport, the passengers were taken to the airport's old terminal under heavy guard. During the seemingly endless week the passengers spent as "guests" of the smiling dictator Idi Amin, the non-Jewish hostages were released and flown to safety. The Jews, however—along with the courageous crew of the Airbus, who elected to stay with them— were not to be released unless the government of Israel decided to accede to the terrorists' demands. These—especially the liberation of 54 convicted terrorists—were unthinkable. So was what at first seemed the only viable alternative: letting the hostages be murdered. Out of the seemingly insoluble dilemma arose a third alternative: to free the hostages by military action.

This third choice would have been impossible for any other government. Entebbe, some 4,000 kilometers from Israel, was guarded by the Ugandan Army—not to mention the terrorists themselves. But Chief of Staff Lt. Gen. Mordechai "Motta" Gur, himself a veteran paratrooper, had confidence in his men. Gur delegated the planning of the land forces' role in the action to a young and energetic officer, Brig. Gen. Dan Shomron. Shomron, a veteran of many bloody battles and now O/C Paratroop and Infantry Forces, was assisted by the O/C Israeli Air Force, Maj. Gen. Benjamin Peled, whose job it was to plan the mission of the IAF. The final plan, approved by Israel's cabinet at the last possible moment, involved a hand-picked team of paratroopers and commandos, to be flown out to Entebbe in four C-130 Hercules transport aircraft. Once the aircraft had landed on the old runway, the troops were to rush out, storm the old terminal, dispose of the guards and terrorists, and escort the hostages to the Hercules waiting to fly them home.

The leader of the team, Lt. Col. Jonathan "Yonni" Netanyahu, was a truly remarkable character. This odd mixture of intellect and guts was brought up in New York by Zionist parents. On reaching the age of 18, Yonni went to Israel to join one of the elite units of the IDF. Rising quickly in rank, he distinguished himself in the Six-Day War of 1967 and again in the fighting on the Golan Heights during the October War of 1973. In a daring operation Yonni rescued his best friend, an armor battalion commander

King of the transports is the C-130 Hercules, which proved itself in combat during the Entebbe raid in 1976.

wounded and left to die by the Syrians, but was himself wounded grievously in the process and was discharged from the IDF with a 30 percent disability. Technically, he was still 30 percent disabled when he returned—after years of excruciating operations—and convinced the chief of staff to let him have command of his old unit, a crack commando force. Now, squeezed into the front seat of a black Mercedes lashed down inside the lead Hercules, Yonni faced the toughest mission of his life.

As the first Hercules, piloted by the transport squadron leader, rumbled along the runway, Yonni's men settled down in their bucket seats, preparing for the long journey ahead. Their commander had trained them to the utmost: Time and time again, they had sprinted down a training course matching the distance from the aircraft to the Entebbe terminal, until they could finish the sprint in less than 120 seconds. Now, hanging by its turboprops, the lead air-

craft took off, followed closely by the other three transport planes, and headed south.

As they headed down the Gulf of Eilat, the four Hercules took necessary evasive action, in an effort to dodge the watchful radars of Egypt and Saudi Arabia. Once over the Red Sea, they set course on the route that would take them deep into Africa. The lead pilot, listening in on the radio, tensed as he heard the latest weather report: clouds and thunderstorms over the African airspace. This could ruin the timetable, scotch the entire mission, he thought. Then, glancing back into the cabin, he saw the calmly dedicated faces of the paratroopers and was himself reassured.

Thick clouds covered the sky, driving rain beat down on the windshields; the monotonous sweep of the windshield wipers alternated with the fitful pitching of the airframes in the turbulence. Unearthly flashes of lightning illuminated the black sky; rolls of thunder vied with the noise of the engines. The pilots, fighting the controls, kept the aircraft in strict formation. As they approached their target, Yonni slid out of the Mercedes and joined the lead pilot in the cockpit for a moment. A reassuring hand on the shoulder, a confident wink, and the young commander returned to his station, readying his men for action.

Over Lake Victoria the formation split up, each pilot taking his station for landing according to plan. Amazingly, Entebbe Airport was fully lit, runways ablaze with easily visible landing lights. The lead aircraft crept warily into the final leg of the approach, glided silently onto the runway and stopped precisely on the spot IAF intelligence had planned. Incredibly, the landing was 30 seconds late, an achievement rarely matched even by veteran airline pilots who have flown the Africa run for years.

Yonni and his men rolled down the lowered ramp of the first aircraft in the black Mercedes, followed by two unmarked Land Rovers.* Scant seconds behind them, paratroopers poured from the other aircraft. The black Mercedes rolled past the Ugandan sentry, who, standing at attention and unable to perceive the whiteness of the faces, mistook the car for that of his president and, saluting, stepped back to let Yonni through. Now the assault parties had a clear path to the terminal. Surprising the terrorists before they could shoot, they gunned them down one by one. Then, shouting for the terrified hostages to lie low, the airborne forces stormed into the terminal, submachine guns blazing. Support groups silenced the Ugandan guards, who had begun to concentrate fire on Yonni's men. A bazooka smashed the control tower searchlight. Under cover of the resulting darkness, the paratroopers began to assemble the hostages for the journey home.

Suddenly, horrifyingly, a single shot rang out in the darkness and Yonni Netanyahu toppled forward. Swiftly his second-in-command took over; within minutes, the hostages were inside the aircraft, ready to take off. As the heavily laden transports rolled down the runway, the entire airport was suddenly illuminated in a vast display of fireworks. A special demolition team had blown up the seven MiG-21s and four MiG-17s constituting Uganda's fighter strength. Now the Israeli aircraft were safe from pursuit.

Hours later, early on the morning of July 4, 1976,† four IAF Hercules aircraft flew over the towns and cities of southern Israel to land at Ben Gurion Airport. The rejoicing, unparalleled in Israel's history, grew even wilder as a tide of excited Israelis literally swept the intrepid soldiers off their feet. Crowds danced *horas* on the tarmac; flowers and champagne were showered on the victors. It seemed as if the whole nation were one large carnival. But this was not quite the case. Inconspicuously, in incongruous silence, a stern, sad band of tired men filed out a side exit. On their shoulders, in an unwitting parallel to the red-bereted troops carried shoulder-high by the jubilant crowd, they bore the lifeless body of their commander, Yonni Netanyahu, the only man lost in the raid.

PRESS CONFERENCE‡

The Defence Minister, Mr. Shimon Peres Sokolow House, July 4, 1976

Ladies and Gentlemen, I do not need to introduce Gen. Gur, the Chief-of-Staff or Brig. Dan Shomron, who commanded last night's operation in Entebbe. I believe that, when the force left

---

*Israeli intelligence reports identified Idi Amin's official car as a black Mercedes-Benz. He was always accompanied by his PLO bodyguards, who rode in Land Rovers. Amin had made several visits to the hijackers at Entebbe in this fashion. This was an aspect of the "cloak and dagger" part of the operation. Another report, unconfirmed, had an American female spy "occupying" Amin in his bed that night.

---

†It is interesting to note that, although the day was not selected for that reason, this mission for freedom was accomplished on the 200th anniversary of the independence of the United States of America.

---

‡This is an official statement made by the Israeli minister of defense at a press conference on the day of the rescue at Entebbe.

Israel yesterday afternoon—they were leaving an anxious country, and when they returned this morning, it was to a proud nation. This night and the change that it brought was achieved by an IDF force that unveiled one of the army's most brilliant pictures—of intelligence and wisdom in planning, boldness in approach, surprise in conception and courage in execution. From Israel's point of view, this was a supreme test of command ability, planning and performance by the IDF. The nation, its Government and Knesset have expressed their appreciation to the Chief-of-Staff, the General Staff and the officers and men who carried out this act of exceptional courage.

What faced us was that, in the terror war, for the first time a State and its President, Field Marshal Idi Amin, with his army cooperated with the terrorists in order to extract blackmail by threat and murder. In the history of terror there is no mention or memory of such a complete cooperation. The fact that there were only four terrorists in the aircraft, and something like double that number at the airfield, is an indication that terrorists were brought by the Government of Uganda to help in the implementation of this serious act.

Their operation was carried out by an organization headed by Wadia Hadad. We know this organization as one that does not hesitate to shoot at innocent aircraft, and kill all the passengers that they carry.

This is not the first nor the second occasion in which we have been placed in a critical situation but, this time, the situation was made worse because in addition to the demands made of Israel, the hijackers posed demands to other States. There was a demand addressed to the Government of Kenya, which says that it does not have the requested terrorists. There was a demand of the Government of Germany, because among the hijackers were two Germans from the Terror Internationale. This factor was also to be seen in the separation carried out at the airport, not between children and adults, not between men and women, but between Israelis—and those suspected to be Israelis—and all the others.

The entire world is today celebrating the Bicentennial of the greatest democracy of all—the United States of America. The concept inherent in American democracy—of freedom of man and his equality before the law, of recognition of his existence and liberty as a supreme value—was to a very large extent put to the test in these last few days.

I must note, and I do so willingly, a few words about the behavior of the French crew of the aircraft. All the passengers, without exception, made a point of praising the captain and his crew for their comportment during every minute of the hard days which they had to endure.

The IDF this time had to cope with, on the one hand, the greatest distance ever over which it had been called on to stage an operation—more than four thousand kilometers from the home base—and, on the other hand, the very short time at its disposal, which was in fact a matter of one or two short days and nights. Within this very short time, the General Staff had to find answers to problems with which they were not familiar, training the forces, finding the means and carrying out the operation itself—an operation which the Chief-of-Staff defined as a calculated risk that the country could take. We see in this operation a decisive battle in the war against terror. But we do not delude ourselves; the terrorists can still try their hand elsewhere and at other times. But, as in all wars, the one who is resolute, daring and determined not to surrender must eventually win.

And, finally, this was an operation by the IDF—a purely Israeli operation, decided on by Israel, at her responsibility, with her knowledge solely, and at her risk, with all the success therefore solely to her credit.

PRESS CONFERENCE§

The Chief of Staff, Lt.-Gen. Mordechai Gur Sokolow House, July 8, 1976

This conference is taking place today because, since the Entebbe operation, we have succeeded in holding debriefings and—during the last days—have already applied some of the lessons learnt from the operation. This means that we can be even more ready for such incidents if they were to occur this week or in the near future, and—with completion of the debriefing and of application of the lessons—we can paint a clearer and more responsible picture of what happened during the operation.

---

§An official statement by the Israeli chief of staff summing up details of the Entebbe operation.

I have no intention of referring to the political aspects involved in this operation, nor to the politico-military aspects. I believe that this function of politico-military decision making is too secret, and that the interaction between the two planes which eventually results in a decision in favour of such a mission should not be a public matter—certainly not through the agency of myself. I will, therefore, be concentrating on the military aspect, and on many of the elements involved, without of course divulging professional secrets of which there were many. I am sure that you will forgive me if I say that this is the reason that I asked that no questions be posed. In other words, what I will not say I have no intention of saying, and what I will say is on this paper, which I will cover point by point. Accordingly, what I consider worthwhile and important for the public to learn—you will know.

It can now be said that the operation was successful both militarily and politically, and these are in fact the two main objectives in a mission of this kind—beyond, of course, the concrete objective of rescuing the hostages. We certainly view the mission as a successful operation—yet I can say that the risks we took were very many and in fact covered almost every aspect of planning, execution and of the situation that could have developed afterwards. I am glad to say now that the risks were calculated—and that to no small extent the success was greater than we could have estimated—and that we took into account in recommending implementation of the operational plan.

However, it must be remembered that we took no risk beyond what was calculable, particularly in view of the national danger involved in capitulation to terrorist demands. It is also important to remember that the planning was entirely an IDF matter, that the performance was entirely by the IDF including in certain reasonably marginal aspects about which I will be speaking, and that no other party or body took part.

The units that took part in the operation were a cross-section of the entire IDF. There is frequent mention of the apparent need for a special counterterror unit. Of course we did not invent this operation to disprove that argument, yet if we speak about conclusions and lessons, it could be said that when the entire army is prepared and alert, there is no need to entrust jobs such as these to one or other small unit. Taking part in this mission were paratroops from a variety of units, infantrymen, members of Golani, different elements of the Air Force, squadrons of differ-

ent kinds and varied means, and operational and maintenance echelons such as Communications and the Medical Corps, the entire maintenance complex, Military Intelligence—of course—with the whole intelligence community which in this case pooled their work effort to help each other, achieving exceptional results.

There is no doubt that a mission like Entebbe, and the speed at which it was mounted and with the precision of its execution, was the result of a well-oiled military system—and the basic capability of the army is the result of hard work, put in over a long period by a great many men, work carried out quietly and modestly and seriously. The most important thing is that it is performed with a responsibility that does not show itself other than when necessary. If anyone was in need of proof that Israel's restraint in various political and military situations is based on military might, then Entebbe is that proof. A nation does not need to strike matches as proof that they will light, when we have shown that there is a great flame which burns properly whenever it is needed. I believe that the message is clear. The extent to which the plan was good and complete can be learnt from the simple fact of the closeness of performance to the plan. Most of the details reviewed in preliminary exercises proved themselves in practice, and it may be said that 90% of the planned operational detail was carried out in the field—including everything connected with the timetable.

A point which in my estimation is most important of all is that this operation could demonstrate the full moral posture of the fighting Jewry of a fighting State of Israel. This entire mission was based on "purity of arms" and battle morality. I will make do with only one example: it can be said that our main weapon system in the operation was a group of 33 doctors, with civilian and military medical equipment, with milk churns for abdominal cases, with water—in other words with "weapons" not fundamentally of the combat variety, but rather for treating human beings even in the middle of the operation itself. This while the men were faced with questions of combat morality. And the orders were explicit: not to harm men who are clearly not offering resistance or bearing weapons. Indeed, all those in the new terminal building (of Entebbe) who were not active in the battle—were also not attacked or harmed.These are my main introductory remarks, and I now want to move on to a description of the timetable of how it all developed.

On the night of Sunday—the day the aircraft

was hijacked—the Defence Minister and I spent the entire night keeping careful watch on the flight plan of the plan, to be able to give appropriate orders at any moment according to where it would land. Once it landed in Uganda, operational planning began to keep abreast of developments at every stage.

On Monday there were almost no dramatic developments, because it was impossible to know clearly what was happening to the plane, or the nature of the terrorists' demands. Activity really began at a greater intensity on Tuesday. At noon, I was called to a meeting in Jerusalem. On the assumption that the subject was the hijacked plane, I stopped on the way to give orders to have a unit ready for the same evening. At the Tuesday afternoon session in Jerusalem I was asked, and replied, about whether a military option was possible. This was of course dependent on more thorough and basic directions, and we began ongoing planning of the operation. That evening a number of planning teams were set up in the General Staff, to work on the various possibilities—with most of the planning contained within the General Staff mainly for reasons of secrecy; we did not wish at this early stage to involve other elements.

On Wednesday morning a number of plans were submitted to me, all of them in keeping with the objectives of the operation, and all capable of hitting the terrorists, but there were weak points and I could not clearly and singlemindedly support and recommend them as operations for execution. The main point was that I could not satisfactorily guarantee the non-vulnerability of the hostages. After all, the operation was being planned to release the hostages, and we are experienced in this type of mission and have seen more than once that they are difficult and complex. There is a certain degree of risk that can be taken, with a good chance that the hostages will not be hurt. But, on Wednesday, I could not yet promise myself that the plan amply covered this aspect.

A second point was that intelligence data was not sufficiently complete, and for an operation of this kind—with all its possibilities—it is very important that intelligence should be as precise as possible. I will give an example, which I bring because it was bearing on all the rest of the plans: there were at the Airport between one to two Ugandan battalions, or 500–1000 men, and we needed to know where they were located. Their assembly points. How they were guarding, and with what weapons, instruments and so on.

I am prepared to note that, in all this planning,

the danger to our soldiers was certainly a risk that we could take. In other words, the problem was not the safety of the force, but of the hostages—and the intelligence picture enabled us to take a responsible decision for an operation of this kind.

On Thursday the picture was clearer, and we could put together a more informed operational plan, which was presented in the Defence Minister's office that afternoon. The whole afternoon was devoted to marathon debates, under pressure from the Minister to reach the optimum of feasible operational schemes. By the evening, we indeed had a certain plan, but I must say that I could not yet offer it as operative, and there were still aspects that I called "charlatan and irresponsible." I explained that I was not about to recommend the plan until there were additional data.

Throughout all these hours, the Head of Operations Branch directed the planning work while, at this stage, the Senior Paratroop and Infantry Officer was brought into the picture, and he proposed one of the plans on which the final version was based. The differences between the various versions was not great, but in an operation of this sort every detail is of great importance and might have drastic significance when it comes to performance. And so, the Head of Operations conducted this work, when in practice he was matched against two major factors—one of which was the Commanding General Air Force, with Air Force Headquarters and all the pilots. The head of the Air Force, from the first moment, confirmed clearly and unmistakably that an operation over this range could be carried out, and the problem was only to find the right way to use this air detachment.

The second factor matching the Head of Operations was the ground force, under the Senior Paratroop Officer, who came in only at this stage as commander of the operation. One way or another they discussed all the possibilities on the ground, while a number of central points demanded an answer: the correct and fastest control over the entire area, quick and correct break-in to the terminal building, in order to guarantee that a minimum of hostages would be hurt. Of course, the factor which constantly accompanied the planning was the intelligence community, in all its arms, which had to complete the picture as it could.

Although, as I have already noted, I still saw holes in this plan and did not yet intend to offer it as a plan for execution, we ordered the units to prepare because there was a minimum of preparation needed, and we wanted to see how it was done. On Thursday, in the afternoon, the force began to organise and the planning moved into the very detailed stage.

On Friday morning a picture took shape which allowed me to conclude that I could recommend the plan. During the day we checked a number of tactical aspects, and some weapons system questions, then—towards evening—I asked to see two aspects that I considered central. We made a model (practice) flight, because I wanted to see how the air component would function almost without any external air help. I flew with the squadron commander and the pathfinder navigator, and posed them certain problems to see how they would be solved. After two hours of flight, I decided that the air aspect was strongly enough covered.

The second subject was that of the ground forces, and the speed of their arrival at the point of action—in other words, at the hostages. In this exercise, I saw that all the units were fully conversant with the plan, knew the terrain, and had developed enough operational techniques to permit a maximum security in everything connected with quick arrival and control over the building.

When these aspects were clear, it was possible from my personal viewpoint to put together a far more basic recommendation. And here for a moment permit me to deal not with the chain of events but with the influences on decision making within the army.

It is nothing new that a commander is influenced by his men and influences them. Confidence is radiated from an officer to his subordinates, and very often, at the most decisive moments, there is a spirit that radiates up from the ranks to him. I must say that, on Friday, more than I was impressed by the professional achievements of the men, I was impressed by their confidence—a responsible confidence that they were going to carry this operation out as we wanted to be done, while they recognised the full responsibility of the decision.

The first subject that for me was very important was the air aspect. The personal confidence of the Commanding General Air Force, which influenced his men or perhaps derived from them has already been mentioned. But in my conversation with the four captains and their navigators before their flight, with all the complexity of bringing their planes to the Airport, they spoke quietly and confidently and impressed me with their navigational capabilities and confidence in their powers of improvisation. This in fact could give me the feeling that, in the air

aspect, it would be alright, and that if there would be hitches these boys would overcome. This was true of the pilot, the navigators and the overall Air Force system. In fact we felt the same thing after taking part in the ground exercise, after which I brought them in for a short summing-up and improvement of a few professional matters—and I asked the officers, Dan Shomron, Yanosh, the commanders of paratroops, infantry and Golani, in all seriousness whether they felt that this was an operation they could carry out in their professional fields of expertise. Were they all least able to create the option of achieving a maximum? And the answer from all of them was unmistakeably positive.

I would say that a similar conversation took place with the Defense Minister two days earlier—with officers of a higher rank, who also expressed their confidence. But I wanted to get the feeling from the men who would have to run on the spot, who would have to find the terrorists, deal with them and hit them before they hit the people—and we have had no little experience in this field.

And so, the feeling of confidence that we got from all the men was such that, with minor corrections the following morning, I could recommend this as an operation for execution. On Saturday morning a series of discussions began, and from the beginning I was able to present the plan with the opening remark that this time it was operational. The discussions went on a number of hours, in parallel with advanced operational preparation, and I can tell you that a part of the movements were made before we had the final decisions—of course with the ability at any moment to stop the operation. But we slowly learnt that the direction was indeed that of going ahead.

And yet, at the hour when we received final approval, I must say that a great many of the men involved did not quite believe it, despite all the preparations and their self-confidence. The conception was so daring and dangerous that they were not certain until the last minute that it would be approved.

I want to analyse a number of major considerations and then I will go on to the actual performance on the battlefield. An initial consideration was of course to reach the hostages as fast as possible. I must remind you here that we are speaking of some 10 terrorists and 60, 80, or 100 Ugandan soldiers who were near the building. And so, we had to overcome a not insignificant force. Of course the basic consideration that guided all the planning was how to get there quickly. How to arrive at the place where the hostages were to be released as a total surprise? I also want to mention that, according to the information, the aircraft and the building were prepared for demolition, or at least contained explosive charges.

The second consideration was correct navigation and arrival at the spot as far as the air operation was concerned. I have already said earlier that I will not go into detail on this aspect, because we developed a complete system of forces and means which are better not discussed, but all were to guarantee that the first force would arrive at the objective in conditions of surprise. The entire flight, flight plan and navigation had but one objective—to bring in the planes to a situation of absolute surprise.

The third consideration was how precise the intelligence picture needed to be. Operations such as these in fact stand or fall on precise intelligence, and I must say that the cooperation of all aspects of intelligence, of the whole intelligence community, in fact bore exceptional fruit, but it must be remembered that any intelligence system, especially at such a distance from home, had its problems and difficulties, and one of the major considerations was to what extent we could take a risk on one or other picture? And of course we were looking at the intelligence picture at our disposal when the decision was made.

The fourth consideration is that of field security. When I mentioned before that nobody participated in this operation other than the IDF, this was not only because of political considerations. I specifically forbade any foreign element, no matter how essential it may be, from participating in anything that meant knowledge about an operation that might take place. And we prepared to take our internal operational risks on the clear and specific condition that no external body would be party to it with us, and that no such party should have any idea that a mission was being planned.

Now I want to go on to the mission itself. Firstly, the flight lasted 7 hours, and there were no few interferences by weather, since we flew in differing conditions according to the terrain. There were storms and it was necessary to deviate from the flight plan. Yet, despite a certain difficulty with the weather close to target, which compelled a change, and despite the distance flown, the boys arrived at their objective within a minute of plan. I think that there are few precedents for that.

When they arrived, the complex plans we had prepared in advance to allow them to land the

planes worked properly according to plan, and the touchdown of the first aircraft was exactly as planned. Dan Shomron, the operation commander, who was in the first plane, could look out the doors and check the correct navigation on the ground, and was able to tell himself what he had told the Defence Minister three days earlier that: from his point of view, if the first plane succeeds in making an innocent landing, the operation will succeed.

The plane did indeed reach the appointed place, and the pilots say that they have never seen a force disembark so quickly. Within tens of seconds, the force was outside and immediately moving towards the target. That was Yoni's force which had to reach the building, surprise and hit the terrorists. They were on their course immediately because the pilots told them exactly where they were, and what direction to go. And because the boys from the plane were already conversant with the area, they did not lose a second in moving out. While travelling they encountered two Ugandan soldiers on guard not far from the building, who signalled them to stop. Yoni and the boys with him hit them and kept moving. They succeeded in getting within proximity of the terminal building at a fantastic speed and with almost total surprise.

When they arrived on the spot, the force deployed immediately, their intention being to break in simultaneously through all the entrances, and reach the hostages as fast as possible, hitting most of the terrorists with the first burst. The first terrorist in fact came out of the building. I must mention at this point that the area was floodlit, and the building was illuminated inside. The first terrorist came out, and the deputy commander of our force fired immediately, hitting him, and the teams burst in simultaneously through all entrances. According to estimates, four terrorists were killed within 45 seconds. Two were immediately to the left of the door—apparently the German couple, another was beyond the hostages, about 10 yards away, and a burst from one of the boys got him in the middle of the body. A fourth terrorist was on the other side of the room, and was hit by another burst. He fell, tried afterwards to rise, and was hit again. With that the hostages were in fact free—as a result of a sharp, fast and completely smooth strike. The four terrorists who were guarding them and who could have hit them, were in fact eliminated much faster than we had thought could be done.

Additional forces burst through two entrances in order to get on to other floors and adjoining rooms, and one of the forces did encounter two more terrorists hiding in the toilets, and hit both of them. A third force working in the more northern wing of the terminal building sought terrorists who could have hostages. These were hit immediately, two others within seconds, and the last a few seconds later. The terrorists managed to fire very few bullets in this exchange of fire before they were hit. At the same time another force was guarding the perimeter of the terminal, near the MiGs, and fired on the Ugandan soldiers in the neighborhood and in the building. Some of them were trapped and killed inside, some of them ran out, and others were outside. According to the instructions, the boys hit the MiGs and saw them catch fire and explode one after the other at a distance of 100–150 meters.

While this was going on, the vehicle with the doctors arrived, and the boys began immediately to evacuate the wounded. At this point there was a firing incident from the control tower, and it was apparently a Ugandan soldier. He was struck from behind. The boys opened fire on the tower to silence the fire, and began to bring out the hostages. The hostages behaved perfectly, because from the first seconds the boys shouted to them to lie down and not raise their heads. Most of them did, but there were some who did not obey the order and were wounded. The moment an order was received to move out of the building, they behaved quietly and responsibly, most of them moving on foot in the direction of the planes, those who were wounded being carried by the boys or put on vehicles to take them to the plane, which was to receive them and take off first.

The whole operation lasted two minutes, less than in the Friday night exercise, up to the moment that the plane with the wounded took off. In other words, the operation was perhaps 5 minutes less, with 2–3 minutes taken up in the plane taxiing to the main runway. That in fact ended the main part of the operation. When the hostages were on the plane, the doctors began to deal with the wounded. There were 10 doctors with the hostages and this permitted maximal treatment as early as possible. As I told you before there were 33 doctors in all, but they were distributed in various places, with ready operating theatres, in order to drop in at various places at our instruction, and deal with people wherever they could be brought. The medical treatment was covered from every direction, with some of the best medical teams that we have in Israel and the most modern operating theatres. According to these preparations you can understand that

we at least feared results far worse than what actually happened, and I am happy that we did not need all of them, though every loss in this battle is a loss, but we saw the risk when we suggested the operation, and I cannot but mention that we were overjoyed not to have to use more than a small part of the medical setup that we prepared.

After the MiGs were set on fire and began to explode, and the hostages were on the plane, the men moved to the planes and prepared for evacuation. While this main operation in the old terminal was taking place, other forces took control of the new terminal and the whole complex by the control tower, gained good control over various areas of the airport, and allowed the aircraft to move from place to place according to the operational requirement. I can tell you that we spent 20 tense minutes, but that the tension was reduced somewhat as a result of accurate detailing of the men on the field.

The operation on the ground was commanded by Dan Shomron and a team of officers, and from interim stations by the Head of Operations branch and the Commanding General Air Force, both of whom could give immediate operative solutions to any problem which might crop up. They were in a situation where they could hear the conversations between all the forces in the field and the secondary units. Since I have worked with Kuti (Adam) for a few years previously and in a good many operations, I could know that as long as he is silent it is going well, and I will not tell you what a curse he got from me when I finally got his report that the hostages were on their way out. But the first thing he said was—you sent me, and you knew who you were sending, and you know me well. But it is a fact that the communications worked exceptionally well, though there were a few hitches on the ground because of aircraft noise. However, the network was quiet and responsible, all questions were brief and answers were brief. There were quite a few occasions in which officers changed the plan according to needs on the spot, and I must say that the best of values found expression in all the little details, and in all the bigger decisions, as they were heard over the communications system through all stages of the operation. And the decisions taken down below by Dan Shomron, by the aerial commander attached to him, by the pilots who had to make a number of far-from-simple decisions—and their complaint in exercise was that they were not given enough responsibility—but they did at a number of very delicate points have to take decisions on what to do and how to continue—I must say that all this system when you hear it recorded is a cause of enjoyment professionally, from the point of view of control, of coolness and of the ability to give to-the-point answers to unexpected developments.

And so one of the forces took control of the terminal building, and in the course of mopping up, one of our boys, Hershko, was hit at close range by bullets fired by two Ugandans who were racing towards him. He then hit them—he is still gravely wounded. Taking control of the building was completed fairly quickly as was the area around it, and silence in fact prevailed. Then the soldiers and airmen began to move around to check a number of essential points concerning the operation of the aircraft, then waited for the forces to return. Because the evacuation of the hostages was faster than planned, and permission was given for the aircraft with the wounded to take off immediately, the officers on the spot decided—and this in parallel, both Dan Shomron and his orders group, the commander of the four aircraft and the ground commander who was by his side—that it would be more correct to leave immediately, and this takeoff of course obliged us to make a decision that was anything but simple. We decided to force ourselves on the Kenyans, because here was a possibility for refuelling, which did exist and which could be done. We made a consideration of timetable as against forcing ourselves on the Kenyans, and this was most difficult for, as I mentioned earlier,

I had given a clear and strict instruction against any contacts with outsiders which could indicate a mission of any sort, because no one could rely on it not being leaked. In other words, the moment we gave permission to the aircraft to take off from Entebbe, we decided to force ourselves on the Kenyans, and indeed on the basis of all the days of preparation, we did just that and prepared the landing of the aircraft, the medical teams to deal with the wounded with all the equipment that was ready for the operation, and the system of refuelling in such a fashion that it would be as little burdensome as possible for the Kenyans. Then they were to come home as fast as possible, and that indeed is what happened. The planes arrived. The doctors decided who needed more immediate attention in hospital. The planes were refuelled fairly quickly, and began to return home keeping to the timetable but for a delay of half an hour because, after all, when you force yourself on a refuelling system, it does not always serve you at 100% of its speed, so it took a few more minutes.

Thus far the operation and its details, and according to my estimation this is what we can give without arousing questions which are best not brought up in the political or field-security aspects of the operation—and I found it correct, as I told you in the beginning, to give you all this, because this is undoubtedly an exceptional operation, and everything that we can tell I thought it best to tell.

Thank you.

Chapter 8

Baghdad—The Osirak Reactor, 1981

The time was 1600, June 7, 1981. In the afternoon light, eight General Dynamics F-16 fighters, heavily laden with fuel and external weapons stores, took off from Etzion air base in the Sinai to the south of Israel. This in itself was not an unusual sight—the IAF is constantly flying training and combat missions, more than any air force in the world. This mission however, was different.

Why? Because, at the same time, a formation of six McDonnell Douglas F-15 Eagles also took off fully loaded; other F-15s had been readied to provide aerial refueling. Because both formations linked up and disappeared over the hills *to the east*. Because these takeoffs, seemingly innocuous, were actually the first move in one of the most daring and difficult air-attack missions in history.

Streaking at zero feet (about 30 meters) over the desert, the two formations headed for their target—the Osirak nuclear reactor at Tuwaitha, Iraq, on the west bank of the Tigris, 17 kilometers southeast of Baghdad and over 1,000 kilometers east of Israel. The pilots, tense at the controls in their air-conditioned cockpits, had been training for this assignment for many months, flying countless simulated combat missions and poring over numerous intelligence reports and data between sorties. The flight plan itself, with all its contingencies and alternatives, had been drilled into the flight leaders and their pilots in briefing after briefing, yet both the target and its mission profile had always been kept under strictest secrecy by its many participants, all painfully aware of the consequences of even the slightest breach of security.

Now, as they thundered over the wasteland of the Middle East, the pilots were confident. Knowing they were capable of fulfilling the mission as briefed, and realizing its vital importance, they pressed on toward Baghdad. They had no doubt of their ability to destroy the reactor, and they were all too aware that, should they fail, there would be no second chance.

After flying for over an hour, the pilots approached their target. Climbing to 600 meters, the F-16s lined up for weapon delivery. Suddenly they spotted the reactor—familiar from the detailed practice sessions—just below them. The leader picked his target and released his bombs; the other pilots followed suit, each aiming for the exact part of the target area assigned to him at briefings before the mission. The huge dome, 20 meters in height and 32 meters in diameter, began to crumble instantly. Additional bombs soon followed, battering the entire objective, including its laboratories, computer stations, and sensitive installations. The subsequent chain reaction totally destroyed the nuclear core, located deep underground at the center of an 11-meter pool of water, covering core and pool with tons of debris. Within four minutes the entire complex had been reduced to rubble.

By then the IAF attackers—their mission a complete success—were already on their way back. Covered closely by the F-15 Eagles, the F-16s streaked toward home on their long, dangerous flight over unfriendly territory protected by many hundreds of supersonic interceptors and SAMs. The pilots' eyes darted again and

IAF Eagle landing at an IAF air base. Note the pilot's excellent view of the runway compared with that of the Mirage or Phantom.

again to the radar screens, but all was clear, and remained clear during the long flight westward. As they came in over the Israel coastline a pair of F-15s shattered the evening silence with a sonic boom, startling the few bathers on the beach below. The latter, ignorant of the deadly mission from which the planes had just returned—a mission that saved them and their children from possible annihilation—went on peacefully splashing in the waves. The pilots, observing them smiled grimly. That, after all, they thought with satisfaction, is what it is all about.

Amazingly, the entire time spent over the target had been barely two minutes, and the mission had been accomplished with a single pass by each of the light, bomb-carrying F-16s. It had happened so fast that the Iraqis had not had time to respond.

The 14 Israeli aircraft had flown 1,000 kilometers eastward for one-and-a-half hours, over three hostile countries. On their way to the target they had succeeded in avoiding the three Boeing AWACs aircraft flown by U.S. crews in Saudi Arabia, the Saudi and Jordanian air forces, and Iraq's 300 ultramodern Mirage F-Cs, MiG-23s, and MiG-25s, plus an entire brigade of Soviet- and French-manufactured SAM missiles and radar-guided anti-aircraft artillery at the nuclear site; and they had traveled home for another hour and a half over this hostile territory. Despite all this they had returned safely to base—after successfully destroying the Iraqi nuclear reactor with surgical precision.

Some of the success of Operation Babylon, as it was officially called, was due to the months of preparation and training of the aircrews and the accuracy of their intelligence reports. Most

Returning from the mission, the F-15 pilot is assisted by the ground crew.

important, perhaps, was the skill of the pilots. To confuse the enemy the attacking planes had varied their flying formations. Some aircraft had flown individually at low altitudes; others had flown at extremely high altitudes. The remaining fighters had flown in tight formations that resembled the pattern of a commercial airliner on the radar screen.

Using an old fighter-pilot tactic from World War I, the Israeli fighters had come over target at approximately 1830 hours Iraqi time, with the setting sun behind them, lighting up the target sufficiently for them to see, but blinding the defenders.

Another factor in the pilots' success had been the complete laxity of the Iraqis. Having been at war with Iran for some time, they had ignored or paid little attention to Iranian air attacks, which up to that time had not been very effective. The Iraqis looked upon the air raids from their Moslem neighbors as something, to quote Macbeth, "full of sound and fury, signifying nothing." This may have been a case of

"crying wolf." However, this time the "wolf" was not the one they were expecting, but one with real fangs.

The decision to "take out" the Osirak nuclear reactor was arrived at after a great deal of deliberation and a lot of give and take by the leaders of a responsible democratic government. Clearly, the reactor was in the hands of Saddam Hussein, a chief of state who had sworn to destroy Israel. (Following an earlier, superficial attack on the reactor by Iran, Saddam Hussein openly remarked that it was ridiculous for the Iranians to go after the reactor because it was being built solely for use against Israel.) Intelligence reports showed that Iraq's need for peaceful nuclear energy was negligible and that the reactor's logical use was more than likely to be the production of nuclear bombs. With the fear of another holocaust directed against them, the defensive cry "Never again!" came to the fore, and the IAF was given the task of neutralizing the threat.

Needless to say, the pilots were all hand-

The latest addition to the IAF inventory is the F-16, which played an active role in the attack on the Iraqi nuclear plant.

picked for the mission, although IAF officials would certainly maintain that any of their fighter pilots could have handled the assignment with equal effectiveness. Their commander was a young colonel, a veteran of three air wars against Arab adversaries. While it was stated earlier that a formation of F-16s taking off is not an unusual sight in Israel, the fact that each of the aircraft carried two 900-kilogram bombs might have raised an eyebrow or two if known. Clearly, the relatively small American-built F-16 Falcon was designed as a fighter, not as a bomber. It can outfly and outfight any other fighter in the sky today, with the possible exception of the F-15 Eagle, which flew top cover for it on the mission to Baghdad. But, then again, nothing is unusual in Israel. Their ingenious engineers have done many unusual and unorthodox things with tools of peace, as well as weapon systems, to adapt them to their needs.

It is interesting to note that at first military analysts had assumed that Israeli F-4 Phantoms using "smart" bombs had participated in the raid; but they were wrong on both counts. The IAF had used conventional "iron" bombs manufactured by the Israel Armament Industry, not the new exotic bombs that can be guided by the pilot directly to the target. Israeli pilots are superior marksmen, as they surely proved in the Six-Day War when they practically wiped out the air forces of three of their adversaries and eliminated a fourth using only pinpoint precision bombing. They had perfected their tactics during months of practice on a mock-up of the reactor in the desert. The first bombs had delayed-action fuses that had enabled them to penetrate the concrete-lead dome before exploding. The pilots of the F-16s that followed had placed their conventional bombs unerringly into the gaping holes made by their predecessors. These bombs had bored down into the guts of the reactor and torn it apart.

A French technician who had observed the raid attested to the surgical accuracy of the bombing, "The precision of the attack was stupefying! The central building is completely collapsed. The atomic reactor is hit and the radiation shield has disappeared." His eyewitness report was corroborated by U.S. satellite photos.

The concern of the Israeli government for human life must also be taken into account. The attack was carried out on a Sunday so that 100 to 150 foreign experts and advisors, who normally worked at the reactor, would not be there when the bombs fell. Unfortunately, one French scientist was killed.

The opening paragraph of the official Israeli government announcement, issued immediately following the raid, tersely summed up the situation: "The Israeli Air Force yesterday attacked and destroyed completely the Osirak nuclear reactor, which is near Baghdad. All our planes returned home safely."

Chapter 9
Lebanon—Operation Peace for Galilee, 1982

Following repeated PLO terrorist attacks across the Israel–Lebanon border and the attempted assassination and severe wounding of Shlomo Argov, Israel's ambassador to the Court of St. James in London, the State of Israel was finally provoked into action. Four IDF task forces—massive armored columns—roared north in a multipronged attack. Their mission, coordinated with Bashir Gemayel, was to drive the terrorists away from Israel's northern border. Clearing them 40 kilometers for the border would mean that the Palestine Liberation Organization's Soviet-made Katyusha rockets and artillery would be out of range of the peaceful settlements in Israel's northern Galilee and marauding bands of PLO terrorists would be prevented from continuing their murderous attacks on defenseless children and other unarmed civilians.

In 1970 the PLO made an attempt on the life of King Hussein of Jordan and sought to take over his country. Although supported by Syrian troops and tanks, the PLO was soundly defeated in battle by the king and the Jordanian Army. Many thousands of its followers were killed and the rest were driven out of Jordan during August and "Black September" of that year. The PLO then moved their base of operations to Lebanon and accomplished there what they had failed to do in Jordan. Lebanon, a much weaker country than the Hashemite Kingdom, fell easy prey to the PLO. Part Christian and part Moslem, Lebanon was split by bloody internal strife, and it was relatively simple for

the PLO terrorists to move in and impose their will on the nation; and that they did, and murdered large segments of the Christian civilian population. They did what they wanted and went where they chose to with complete impunity. They became a nation within a nation and thrust themselves, by force of arms, on the people and government of Lebanon. They set up schools funded by the Soviet Union for foreign terrorists, which were attended by German, Italian, Japanese, and other nationals. They built up massive stores of arms supplied by the Soviet Union, Saudi Arabia, Libya, and others. These they used to maintain their hold on Lebanon and to attack Israel, launching their deadly rockets and shells across the border.

The Israeli military machine moved across the border only after clear provocation. While the immediate reason for committing its aircraft, tanks, and troops to battle was the serious wounding of the Israeli ambassador to Great Britain by Arab terrorists, the IDF (Zahal) had been acting with more than due restraint for some time. The attempted assasination was, in effect, "the straw that broke the camel's back."

Nearly one year before, on July 24, 1981, there had been a cessation of hostilities between Israel and the PLO that was supposed to have put an end to those senseless, unprovoked attacks. However, since that time, more than 25 Israeli men, women, and children had been killed and 250 wounded in 150 attacks by PLO terrorists in Israel and against Jews in Europe.

A pair of F-15 Eagles returns from mission. The 20-mm twin anti-aircraft gun is deployed here as part of the basic wartime security.

Returning from mission, this Phantom is momentarily shrouded by the smoke of the tires' touchdown.

The Grumman E2C Hawkeye, one of the IAF keys for modern deployment of combined airborne force.

These bloody attacks had escalated in May 1982. There had been 26 attacks in the month preceding Operation Peace for Galilee alone. And commencing on June 4, during a 48-hour period the PLO had directed massive fire barrages (including Soviet Katyusha rockets, 130-mm and 152-mm artillery rounds, and tank shells) at 23 Israeli towns and villages, killing, wounding, and causing heavy damages. They fired 600 Katyusha rockets alone, forcing the civilian population along Israel's entire northern border to live in bomb shelters, in constant fear for their lives.

It is interesting to note that Lebanon is the only Arab neighbor with whom Israel had had any semblance of a long-standing friendly relationship. But, as has been stated, the Lebanese political situation was an unusual one—one that invited disaster. The weak government had been forced to tolerate a number of dissident armed forces in addition to the PLO. These forces roamed freely through the country, often molesting (wounding and killing) and making demands of the Lebanese people. These forces included other Palestinian paramilitary groups, the Syrian Army, the Druse, and the Christian Phalangist militia, who had once been allies of the Israelis.

Each of these forces had its own substantial geographical sphere of influence, or territory, within Lebanon itself. The area on the border with Israel, for a depth of about 30 kilometers, was controlled by the Lebanese Christians under the command of Maj. Saad Haddad. Immediately to the north of this sector, stretching to the Litani River, was the UN zone, which also sheltered some 700 PLO guerrillas. It was this group of terrorists that had constantly violated the Israeli border and attacked and murdered Israeli civilians by infiltration and with artillery and Katyusha rocket barrages. A large area above the UN zone, extending on the west along the Mediterranean coast to the environs of Beirut, Lebanon's capital, was the stronghold of more than 8,000 well-armed PLO terrorists. Surrounding the capital in a wide area, except for a Lebanese Christian enclave to the north of Beirut, were some 30,000 regular Syrian troops with tanks, missiles and other heavy military equipment. The Syrian-controlled area extended to the east and north to the Syrian border. Within this territory (the largest part of Lebanon, including the Bekaa Valley) the Syrians allowed an additional 6,000 PLO terrorists, some of Colonel Qaddafi's Libyan Army troops, and notorious international terrorists: the German Bader-Meinhoff gang, the Italian Red Brigade, the Japanese Red Army, and others.

Of obvious immediate concern to the Israelis was the zone closest to their border that harbored the PLO terrorists, the one from which Katyusha rocket barrages were launched. The Russian Katyusha is a particularly dangerous and destructive conventional weapon system that fires a salvo (a large quantity of rockets launched simultaneously from a rapid-firing multiple-barrel launcher); it inflicted heavy casualties on the Israeli civilian population. (During World War II, British and American troops called similar Soviet weapons "Stalin's Organs" because of their resemblance to the musical pipe organ.) Today they are called multiple-launch rocket systems (MLRS).

With the merciless shelling continuing and the attack on a member of its diplomatic corps, the government of Israel was left with no alternative. A new war of attrition could not be endured. According to the official statement, they made the decision on June 5, 1982, to:

1. Order the IDF to place the civilian population of the Galilee beyond the range of the terrorists' fire from Lebanon, where they, their bases, and their headquarters were concentrated.
2. Name the operation "Peace for Galilee."
3. Order that the Syrian Army not be attacked unless it attacks our forces.
4. Aspire to the signing of a peace treaty with independent Lebanon, its territorial integrity preserved.

Under a partial mobilization, the Israeli armed forces rolled into action. As the four columns of IDF armored vehicles, self-propelled artillery, and mechanized infantry pushed north in pursuit of the PLO terrorists, the IAF operated over all the advance routes, flying combat missions against PLO armored vehicles, artillery emplacements, anti-aircraft, and command posts. Later the IAF flew close-support sorties, especially against PLO blocking positions. Amphibious landings were also supported from the air. Over the ground combat Israeli air-superiority fighters flew intercept patrols against intruding Syrian combat aircraft. Reconnaissance aircraft flew photographic sorties over most Lebanese and other areas to detect enemy movements and gain intelligence.

Once the Syrian Air Force decided to intervene, the IAF intercepted them and shot down several Syrian MiGs. On the ground, activities along the central region axis, as well as the Bekaa Valley, involved the IAF in the fighting, with growing numbers of close air-support missions flown by the fighter-bombers and attack helicopters in support of the advancing armor formations. Repeated attempts by the Syrian Air Force to attack Israeli ground forces were foiled by IAF fighters, which shot the attackers out of the air before they could cause serious damage. The IAF not only destroyed 17 out of 19 Syrian SAM batteries in a single attack but flew battlefield interdiction missions, destroying a large part of the vanguard of the Syrian Third Armored Division advancing on tank transporters along the main Damascus–Beirut road. Later, after knocking out newly deployed SA-6 mobile batteries, the IAF pounced on Syrian ground reinforcements advancing from the north into the Bekaa Valley, destroying tanks and artillery. In air-to-air combat, IAF air-superiority fighters destroyed at least 85 Syrian aircraft, including MiG-23BM Flogger F, MiG-21 PF/MF, and Sukhoi-20 fighter-bombers. A few more were downed by ground fire.

Matching the superb performance of the IAF air and ground crews in combat was the unequaled performance of their equipment, including: the two new U.S.-built fighters, the multirole F-16, and the F-15 air-superiority fighter, which had seen action on the long-range raid on the Osirak nuclear reactor in Iraq and which had been victorious in many battles

F-16—a top MiG killer—displaying five roundels. Four MiGs were killed in one sortie over Lebanon.

IAF F-16 with two kills in battle.

against the Syrian MiGs prior to Operation Peace for Galilee; the amazing Grumman E-2C Hawkeye, airborne early-warning and battle-control aircraft that can track 600 air targets over 620,000 square kilometers of land and water; the battle-tested, older but still effective F-4 Phantom and A-4 Skyhawk, veterans of the Yom Kippur War, which came through with flying colors in action above Lebanon (despite the fact that the new F-16 can do what the Phantom does on half the fuel); the home-grown Kfir C-2, manufactured by Israel Aircraft Industries, which was employed successfully en masse for the first time in Lebanon; the IAI Scout RPV pilotless drone, which provided continuous mobile surveillance over enemy missile sites; and the Hughes Defender and Bell Huey Cobra helicopters, which were magnificent in anti-tank and other support missions. (These combat helicopters were in action for the first time on the Israeli side, as were Mi-24 HINDs and

Aerospatiale Gazelles on the side of the Syrians. Helicopter losses were two for the Israelis versus six on the Syrian side.)

Israeli MEDEVAC helicopters lifted more than 1,000 casualties from the battle zone directly to Israeli hospitals, saving many lives. IAF transports flew resupply missions with fixed-wing and rotary aircraft, supporting ground formations having supply difficulties over the mountainous routes. Later, a forward logistical air base was prepared to which IAF C-130 Hercules and "ancient" C-47 Dakotas flew cargo missions.

The Lebanon war was unique not only in the length of time it took but in the fact that the IDF had to fight on only one front. Despite that fact, the variety of combat and logistical missions flown by the IAF gave it ample opportunity to demonstrate its exceptional combat effectiveness, leadership, and technological infrastructure. These place it second to none

F-15 Eagle with four kills has the inscription "Skyblazer" in Hebrew on its nose cone.

among the leading air forces of the world.

One of the most impressive acts of the war was the complete destruction of the Syrian SAM batteries in the Bekaa Valley. Several of these air defense systems had been deployed there since the spring of 1982, when the IAF had downed two Syrian Air Force Mi-8 helicopters that had been part of the Syrian pressure of the Lebanese Phalangist defenses on Mount Lebanon. However, during Operation Peace for Galilee the Syrians deployed 19 SAM batteries in a dense air defense complex to cover the movements of two of their armored units into the combat zone. The majority were SA-6 *Gainful*s, with some SA-2s and SA-3s deployed as well. The batteries tied into the existing and reinforced early-warning system situated on vantage points overlooking the battle area. Judging by its density, the deployed air defense complex in the Bekaa Valley that IAF pilots faced on Wednesday, June 9, was a formidable

objective. Experiences during the Yom Kippur War had demonstrated the deadliness of the Soviet SAM, especially the mobile SA-6, and the IAF planners took this particular mission extremely seriously, integrating hard training, technical ingenuity, and original thinking into a brillant plan that made the most of the advanced equipment in hand.

The Israeli planners did not leave anything to chance. As already demonstrated in the highly successful mission against the Osirak nuclear reactor in June 1981, effective operational planning and careful, realistic training ensured a flawless implementation of the most difficult combat missions. Here again, such preparations were envisaged to prevent anything from going wrong.

According to their practice, to meet their particular needs the Israelis made modifications to acquired matériel. Based on the combat experiences of the October War, improvements

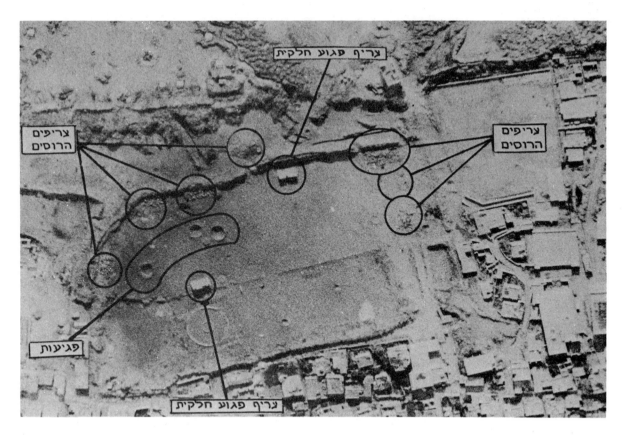

צריף פגוע חלקית

צריפים הרוסים

עריפים הרוסים

פגיעות

צריף פגוע חלקית

The PLO combat training center, on the outskirts of Beirut, hit by IAF aircraft on June 4, 1982.

were made to the Texas Instruments Shrike air-to-surface anti-radar missile. The AGM-45A proved to be a major weapon system in the destruction of the SAMs. Although many attacks were made during the latter stages of the Yom Kippur War against the Syrian SAM batteries, results were limited and achieved at high cost. These experiences were studied carefully, especially those that were successful near the Suez Canal. It turned out that where combined air and ground action was implemented success was maximal; an important factor was the introduction of the Shrike and—finally—an integrated attack combining low-level approach with effective electronic countermeasures (ECM) and decoy systems.

The Israeli Air Force implemented these lessons into an exhaustive and realistic training program involving low-level flight under combat configuration as well as advanced modifications to existing matériel. These measures, combined with extensive preparations before the mission, paid off in full. In fact, the results

achieved were far above expectations. Some of this overwhelming success must be accorded to the fact that most of the Syrian SAM batteries recently deployed had not been fortified in emplacements. As the attack commenced they started a defensive smoke screen, which aided the attackers in pinpointing the targets.

However, the attack on the SAM complex was far from easy. The Syrians had deployed a dense air defense system with a complete array of advanced and sophisticated matériel. In fact, the Bekaa Valley SAM system was similar in density to the air defense encountered in the Yom Kippur War. And the Syrians could call on their entire air force from bases in Syria scant minutes away. The IAF used all kinds of attack aircraft in the mission. The durable F-4E Phantoms and A-4 Skyhawks played leading roles with Kfirs, F-16s, and F-15s also taking part in the battle. As the Israeli fighter-bombers screamed into the Bekaa Valley, Syrian interceptors swooped into the fray from nearby air bases in Syria, just over the mountains to

Above and right: *Smoke rises over the Bekaa Valley from the ruins of the Syrian surface-to-air missile (SAM) sites destroyed in a devastating attack by the IAF.*

the northeast. Soon a tremendous air battle developed, with more and more aircraft being drawn into the fight.

A young Israeli captain led his formation in an attack on a SAM battery; as he approached, he identified Syrian MiGs over the target. The immediate dilemma was whether to go into the attack as planned or deal with the MiGs first. A quick decision convinced the leader that he should complete his mission, and the formation dropped its warload on the SAM as briefed. As they emerged from the objective, they set onto two Syrian MiGs and shot them out of the sky. From above, the covering F-15 Eagles intervened with devastating effect, knocking down scores of MiGs as they swarmed over the Bekaa like moths drawn to a candle. During the engagement, which took two hours and lasted until around midday, hundreds of aircraft

reportedly took part. The IAF fighters shot down 29 Syrian MiGs while destroying 17 out of 19 SAM batteries and radar installations without loss of their own aircraft. Even the tough IAF planners were surprised by the unprecedented success of operations in the Bekaa Valley. Casualties had been expected, especially from the deadly ZSU-23-4 air defense guns, which had wreaked havoc on many IAF aircraft in the Yom Kippur War.

According to foreign reports, the successful attack was made by the integration of aerial surveillance, precision strikes by attack aircraft and new, advanced surface-to-surface weapons that employed radar-homing sensors from ground deployments within range. The use of remote-piloted vehicles (RPV) designed for special mission applications enabled the planners to receive near real-time intelligence and elec-

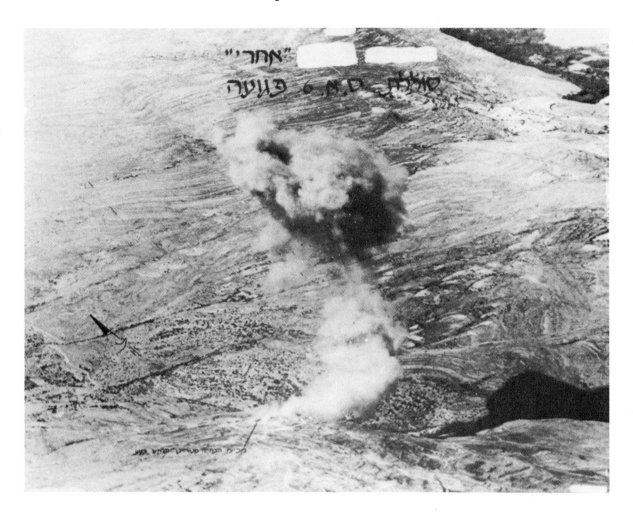

tronic battlefield capability over the target area. These systems tied into the overall air warfare control systems of the Grumman E-2C Hawkeye and ground EAW infrastructure, allowing full control over the combat airspace, including the key Syrian airfields from which potential threat aircraft could be located prior to its taking off. The RPV, used in their advanced mission capacity for the first time in combat, provided zoom magnification and high-resolution imagery, allowing full display at various command levels on screen or overlay maps of the combat area. According to these foreign sources, Israel fielded a new Zeev-type (Wolf) ground-launched missile designed to be fired against air defense radars, using a sensor to home on radiation emissions. Based on the continuous real-time information, the coordinated air attacks achieved unprecedented success.

Following the experience gained in the October War, the IAF planners thoroughly researched the method that offered the best chance of taking out advanced SAM systems and their infrastructure with acceptable losses. In the Yom Kippur War, the IAF—insufficiently equipped and trained—had been badly mauled by these enemy systems. During the late stages along the Suez Canal, there had been some partial successes against the SA-6, but in Syria the air defense system had kept the IAF severely limited in its action and had caused heavy losses to close-support aircraft operating in the combat zone.

The main conclusions drawn from these activities were that the best chance against the SAMs would be offered by integrated air and ground action using tanks, artillery, and paratrooper assault teams to clear the way for air

F-16 Flying Falcon and a display of weapons it can carry.

action. This aim was dramatically achieved by the combined operation over the Suez Canal as spearheads of an armored division destroyed most of the Egyptian SAMs in the area, opening the way for extensive air action over wide ranges in Egypt. However, it was also realized that the use of advanced technologies employed with imagination and skill could overcome many of the problems attacking aircraft had to face from the extensive and powerful Soviet-type air defense.

Western concepts for such action, drawing from experience gained over Vietnam and the Middle East, advocated different methods of combat. The American concept favors a medium-level approach, taking out the Soviet air defense by sophisticated means, including a pathfinder technique with special "Wild Weasel" ECM and SAM suppression aircraft, followed by saturation attacks from attack aircraft. The West German and British approach to the problem prefers low-level penetration with contour-hugging supersonic aircraft outflying the SAM and radar cover—an "under the fence" approach, as the new Tornado program is called.

The actual tactics employed by the Israelis to neutralize the Syrian SAMs still carry a high security classification and have not yet been disclosed even to the U.S. Air Force. However, reliable sources attribute the IAF's spectacular victories to a combination of factors: superior air and ground force coordination; effective electronic countermeasures; the U.S.-built Grumman E-2C Hawkeye miniature AWACs and battle-control aircraft; U.S. Shrike anti-guided-

Frontal view of Kfir C-2.

missile missiles; F-15 and F-16 air-superiority fighters; F-4 Phantoms employing "Wild Weasel" counter-missile techniques; Israeli-made small RPVs, or remote-piloted drones; the Israeli's own Kfir C-2 fighter; tremendous accuracy with the employment of conventional "iron" and cluster bombs; ground observers; and exceptional flying and combat skills.

The Hawkeye E-2C proved to be a key factor in the success of the strike. Its capacity for simultaneously handling multiple targets, in addition to its ability to pinpoint various electromagnetic emitters (PDS), could account for the tremendous success of the IAF in air-to-air and air-to-ground operations. As to the SAM batteries, the IAF had been evaluating possible attack tactics since April 1981. Exercises and training missions had been rehearsed. Special equipment had been modified, developed, and acquired, such as upgrading ELQ 119 ECM pods, improving Shrike anti-radiation air-to-surface missiles, and developing other ECM devices (installed in a modified B-707) and sensors installed in drones.

The IAF successfully integrated low-altitude attacks with sophisticated ECM and decoy techniques. Thorough, realistic training programs and imaginative planning did the rest.

Israeli-designed and manufactured RPVs equipped with special electronic warfare (EW) and ECM packages were able to illuminate precision targets so that they could be attacked accurately from stand-off range with laser-tracked weapons. Forward air controllers used the Scout RPVs, built by Israel Aircraft Industries to observe targets and guide attack pilots to preassigned objectives. Several RPVs used television images, relayed to distant ground stations and displayed on large screens, to provide real-time intelligence of the battle zone displayed.

But the Israeli pilots deserve most of the credit. Not even specially designed equipment, matériel, and devices could have ensured such smooth, well-coordinated missions in so dense an armed area. In fact, more than 150 aircraft from both sides were flown into a 260-square-kilometer area at various heights. Merely avoiding collisions was a distinct accomplishment.

As learned from several pilot interviews, the Israelis used a kind of improved radiation homing weapon (Shrike) for radar and guidance center destruction (*Straight Flush, Fan Song*). Missile battery destruction was accomplished by use of regular "iron" bombs. However, it is widely stated that the attack's success was made possible by the joint operation of ground-

Supersonic wing fuel tank and Shafrir anti-aircraft missile.

to-air forces (reminiscent of the Egyptian missile destruction in the Yom Kippur War).

The attack lasted two hours. It is assumed that the opening move was made against the Syrian Ground Control Intercept (GCI). As the IDF had decided to restrict the attack to Lebanese territory, the problem of neutralizing Syrian radar had to be solved in several different ways. Radars located on Mt. Hermon, in Anti-Lebanon, and elsewhere had to be jammed. Others, especially on the Khalde hills, were to be taken by ground forces. As the southern and/or western approaches to the Bekaa Valley through the Beirut–Damascus road were cleared, the IAF took out the missile control radars and Zahla GCI one by one, probably by means of Shrike missiles (under the cover of specially designed "diversionary bodies") and by utilizing constant, sophisticated jamming devices to protect the attacking force.

Even though all altitudes were open for the IAF, masses of interceptors were being sent into the area from Syria. As the SA-6 could also be operated optically, the IDF had to saturate the area with artillery barrages. Then scores of IAF fighters could destroy the batteries either by cluster bombs or regular "iron" bombs. In addition to their fighter-bomber mission the aircraft were also equipped for air-to-air battle.

Some of the dogfights took place after the ground attack was accomplished and 29 MiGs had been shot down. Pilots' orders were strict: First destroy the missile site, then take on the Syrian MiGs.

Probably the best analysis of this unprecedented victory of the IAF over the sophisticated Soviet air defense systems and the Syrian Air Force's Russian-built MiGs was presented by Maj. Charles E. Mayo in the U.S. Army's *Air Defense Artillery* magazine.

On June 9, 1982, the Israeli Air Force destroyed the Syrian surface-to-air missile (SAM) complex in Lebanon's Bekaa Valley without losing a single aircraft to Syrian air defense weapons. The success of Israeli warplanes against the same family of air defense weapon systems which had controlled the skies over portions of the Yom Kippur battlefield a decade earlier captured the attention of the air defense community.

Had the Israelis discovered an Achilles heel that might relegate air defense to a less dominant role on future battlefields than popularly supposed, or had the Syrians mismanaged their air defense assets?

An analysis of the Syrian air defense catastrophe reveals that the well-thought-out and brilliantly executed Israeli anti-SAM offensive took advantage of Syrian mistakes rather than

Test pilot about to enter his cockpit.

The Kfir, designed and built by Israel Aircraft Industries, is shown with its weapons systems.

any inherent weakness or unsuspected vulnerability of air defense artillery. The Israeli attack succeeded because the Syrian air defenders disregarded basic air defense countersuppression measures.

Prelude

The Syrian air defense force guarding the Bekaa Valley consisted of two SA-2 batteries, two SA-3 batteries and 15 SA-6 batteries. For more than a year before the attack and also during the attack, the Israelis sent remotely piloted vehicles (RPV) such as the Scout over the Bekaa Valley. These RPVs, equipped with electro-optical sensors, located Syrian missile batteries and relayed the data to ground stations for real-time analysis. The Israelis learned that the Syrian SAM batteries had, for the most part, remained static for many months, a tactical blunder that allowed the Israelis to precisely target known sites located in a confined geographic area. The intelligence gained through the use of Scout

RPVs gave the Israelis a decided edge on the eve of battle.

The Scout can carry a payload of 50 pounds. One of its principal elements is a gyrostabilized platform on which is mounted a television camera with a 15:1 zoom lens that can be aimed and zoomed by a remote operator via a radio data link. The camera transmits high resolution motion pictures at 50 frames per second. The Scout is tracked through its data-link transmitter and a parabolic antenna that determines range and bearing. From the information, the Scout's location is calculated and automatically plotted on a ground station mapboard. The ground station computer displays the coordinates of any object caught in the camera's crosshairs. The RPV's coordinates and altitude are continuously displayed, along with the time and date on the operator's TV console, and are taped.

At a typical cruise altitude of 3,000 feet, the camera provides surveillance of about 20 square miles (50 square kilometers), while at maximum zoom the area viwed measures approximately 130 × 160 feet (40 × 50 meters). The lens can

Israeli F-4 Phantoms launched anti-radiation missiles against SAM radar systems.

be zoomed from one extreme to the other in less than four seconds.

The use of remotely piloted vehicles enabled Israeli commanders to have a near real-time picture of the battlefield situation. Senior officers were able to watch the attacks on the SAM sites on their television monitors.

After thorough planning and preparation, the Israeli Air Force launched a coordinated four-phase operation against the Syrian air defense complex. The four phases were electronic warfare, deception, SAM attack and counterair.

Electronic Warfare

To execute the electronic warfare phase, the Israeli air force used modified Boeing 707s and other aircraft as electronic warfare platforms near the battle area. These aircraft carried a variety of electronic sensors and palletized jammers which could be reconfigured as the tactical situation dictated. The sensors, along with supporting equipment, automatically identified missile site radars and performed real-time analysis. The jammers disrupted Syrian communications nets and blanked out missile site radars.

Deception

Next, the Israelis initiated the deception phase. According to the Israelis, waves of decoy drones, which simulated strike aircraft, were sent over the Syrian batteries. The Syrians reacted by turning on their radars and tracking the decoy drones. They even engaged the drones, expending valuable, ready-to fire missiles. In some instances, once the radars were turned on, the Syrians continued to radiate long after there was a need for tracking information.

Additionally, the Israelis used rockets or other means to drop chaff which further confused the Syrian missile site radar operators.

SAM Attack

Once satisfied that the Syrian SAM batteries had been deceived, the Israelis began the SAM attack phase. First, F-4 Phantom fighter bombers armed with anti-radiation missiles (ARM) (including the AGM-78 Standard ARM and possibly the AGM-45 Shrike) attacked each SAM battery. These missiles were launched against

Other aircraft, including Kfir C-2s, attacked the missile sites with cluster munitions and regular bombs.

site radars by homing in on the radars' radio frequency beams.

The Standard ARM is a large missile that turns toward the target radar even when the aircraft is not pointed directly at it. By communicating with a radar homing system in the aircraft, the missile determines the target location before launch and can turn, after firing, to acquire and home on the target.

The Shrike is smaller than the Standard ARM and was designed to destroy a SAM battery's radar antenna. The missile is fired when the aircraft is pointed at the emitter. The Shrike finds the radar emitter, then locks on and homes on the signal until impact.

Once the Syrian missile battery radars were destroyed, other attack aircraft, which included Kfir C-2s, attacked some of the missile sites with cluster munitions and regular bombs. When the attack was over, the Israeli Air Force had destroyed 17 of 19 Syrian SAM batteries deployed in the Bekaa Valley and had damaged the other two while losing no aircraft. The Syrian air defense system in Lebanon had suffered a catastrophic defeat.

Counterair

To provide air cover for its attacking F-4s, the Israelis employed an E-2C Hawkeye as an airborne command post and F-15s and F-16s as counterair aircraft. The Syrian air force reacted to the attack on their SAM sites by launching MiG-21s and MiG-23s toward the Bekaa Valley.

The E-2C Hawkeye used an onboard radar system to track the Syrian MiGs as they took off. Consequently, as soon as the MiGs rose off runways, the Israelis knew how many were coming and from what azimuth. By continuously monitoring the MiGs in flight, the E-2C directed the Israeli F-15s and F-16s on intercept paths that enabled them to shoot down the MiGs with AIM 9-L Sidewinder heat-seeking and Sparrow radar-guided missiles. The Sidewinder is capable of an all-aspect attack; its infrared seeker homes on not only the target aircraft's exhaust, but also on the aircraft's surfaces that become heated from air friction.

The E-2C can scan three million cubic miles of airspace and its radar can detect fighters at ranges up to 250 nautical miles. It can control up to 130 separate engagements and can monitor more than 200 aircraft simultaneously.

Augmenting the radar is a passive detection system, a multiband, 360-degree, azimuth coverage receiving system that detects radar signals to a distance of 500 miles, thereby doubling Hawkeye's detection range. The detected radar emitter's characteristics such as pulse width, pulse repetition frequency and amplitude are analyzed by a digital signal processor that identifies the type signals, alerting the crew to new threats. A computer links all the detection systems, processes the radar signals in real time and automatically provides target intercept data, giving the Israeli F-15s and F-16s a jump on the Syrian MiGs as they approached.

Also contributing to the Israeli success in the air were the Boeing 707s. Their electronic equipment jammed the communications links between Syrian ground controls and pilots, causing the Syrian pilots to fly according to inflexible Soviet tactics without ground radar control or vectors to targets. The Syrians, therefore, were vulnerable to Israeli fighters from various azimuths.

Countersuppression Measures

The Syrians could have avoided the catastrophic loss of its entire SAM complex in Lebanon through proper use of air defense countersuppression measures such as movement, radar emission control, camouflage and deception. The most significant measure which Syria should have used to prevent a successful Israeli SAM suppression and attack operation was to move its SAM batteries as often as possible. More specifically, the Syrian batteries should have been moved after each overflight by Israeli remotely piloted vehicles or manned aircraft. Since hostilities existed with Israel, Syria should have moved its SAM batteries at least every 24 hours even if there were no known reconnaissance overflights. Also, these moves should have been conducted at night. The Syrians, however, kept many of their mobile SAM batteries in the same positions for more than a year, a clear violation of the air defense principle of mobility.

In conjunction with movement, the employment of radar emission control (with selected batteries remaining silent) would have enhanced the SAM units' survivability and mission accomplishment. Only the minimum number of radars in the air defense network should have been allowed on the air for acquisition coverage. Also, the Syrians should have minimized tracking time by waiting until Israeli targets were within engagement range before tracking.

After applying movement and radiation control measures, the Syrian air defenders should have heavily camouflaged their SAM equipment, doing everything possible to reduce the visual contrast between their equipment and the surrounding areas.

Finally, the Syrians should have implemented a deception operation by using dummy or decoy SAM positions to deceive the Israelis as to the actual number and locations of its SAM batteries. These could have included nonoperational items of SAM equipment or facsimiles of radars, launchers and missiles. Along with the dummy sites, the Syrians could have added more realism by integrating infrared radiators, radios and other electronic emitters into the sites to simulate the electromagnetic signature of real SAM sites. During the 1973 Middle East war, the Egyptians made extensive use of dummy sites. These elaborately detailed fakes, many of which included active radar transmitters, were used for two reasons: to lure the attacking Israeli air force away from real sites to attractive, but useless, targets; and to destroy the decoyed aircraft in ADA flak traps surrounding the dummy positions. These flak traps consisted of air defense guns and camouflaged SA-6 units. According to one report, there were more dummy sites west of the Suez than there were actual sites. In the 1982 Israeli-Syrian conflict, the Syrians made no attempt to use dummy sites.

Conclusion

Early reports of the Bekaa Valley campaign were characterized by half-truths and inaccuracies; many of them, apparently, purposely planted by Israeli briefing officers. *Newsweek,* for example, reported the first wave of reconnaissance drones was followed by "killer drones" armed with warheads that demolished the SAM sites. The Israeli program of disinformation, in fact, appears to have been so effective that some details of the battle may remain obscured for years. It seems clear, however, that the Israelis built on already existing technology and employed conventional rather than exotic techniques.

The Israeli Air Force's success in destroying Syria's air defense network in Lebanon must be credited to a number of factors. These include the intelligence gathering by RPVs, thorough planning and preparation and the skillful execution of a four-phase operation featuring electronic warfare, deception, SAM attack and counterair operations. More importantly, however, Israeli success was due primarily to Syria's tactical errors.

The failure of the Syrian air defense system in the Bekaa Valley underscores the absolute necessity for U.S. air defense units to actively practice as many countersuppression measures as possible on the modern battlefield. Failure to do so could result in catastrophic defeat for U.S. air defenders, just as it did for Syrian air defenders.

Cautioning against overconfidence, Maj. Gen. David Ivry, IAF commander during Operation Peace for Galilee, warned that the air force would start assessing future developments of air defense to prevent repetition of surprises as a result of this startling success. To underline his warnings the IAF was soon put to a new test as the Syrians deployed newly arrived Soviet-supplied SA-8 *Gecko* SAM batteries to replace the depleted air defense in the Bekaa.

On Saturday, July 24, IAF jets attacked and destroyed three of these systems, the first ever to go into action, without loss to the attackers, though an IAF RF 4E was shot down by a Syrian-based SA-6. A few days later the IAF destroyed a Libyan SA-9 *Gaskin* along the Damascus–Beirut main road.

In all of the air combat over Lebanon, the IAF destroyed 102 Syrian aircraft, including MiG-21s, MiG-23s, and SU-20s, and 50 SAMs, losing only two of their own aircraft to ground fire.

In addition to the aerial combat and anti-missile efforts, the IAF also did yeoman duty in support of IDF ground troops. They attacked PLO ground positions and helped to root the terrorists out of their hiding-places among the civilian population, and they dropped leaflets to guide Lebanese civilians to safety. The entire Operation Peace for Galilee was supported by Israeli Air Force fighter-bombers locating tar-

gets and bombing them accurately and with incredible speed. They knocked out fixed, dug-in targets as well as moving ones such as tanks and self-propelled artillery. Excellent interarm combat procedures were in evidence at all levels.The closely knit combat teams demonstrated high training standards and operational discipline, which inevitably reduced casualties and resulted in a speedy and clean-cut execution of the operation. In the end the Israelis succeeded in driving out 14,000 PLO and other terrorists to eight Arab countries in North Africa and the Middle East.

THE WAR IN LEBANON

The Sequence of Main Events

June 3, 1982, close to midnight—The Israeli ambassador to the United Kingdom, Mr. Shlomo Argov, is shot by Arab assailants as he leaves the Dorchester Hotel in Park Lane, London.

June 4—1515 hours—IAF aircraft attack PLO targets in Beirut. Among the objectives are the ammunition dumps at the sports stadium near Sabra and Shatila as well as 22 other targets nearby. The PLO retaliates immediately with Katyusha and artillery fire on Israeli settlements in the Galilee panhandle.

June 5—Heavy artillery bombardments continue across the whole Israeli northern border. Twenty-three settlements are attacked with continuous fire; several dead and injured are accounted for. Israeli artillery and naval units open a counterbarrage on the PLO artillery positions while the IAF intervenes to knock out point targets in South Lebanon.

June 6—While the artillery bombardment continues, four IDF armored columns cross into southern Lebanon and, with close air and artillery support, advance rapidly on four separate axes, outflanking resistance by PLO defenders. By nightfall the western IDF formations reach a line north of Tyre on the coastal road. On the eastern sector the IDF advances, carefully avoiding Syrian forces, while in the central sector, moving over heavy ground obstacles, the Israeli forces enter the mountain ridges, facing the Syrians there. An IAF Skyhawk is lost, its pilot captured by the PLO.

June 7—After midnight Israeli infantry captures the PLO stronghold, the Beaufort castle, in a *coup de main*; in other sectors the armor is advancing while the accompanying infantry starts to mop up the built-up areas where the PLO has constructed its main defense. To the north of Sidon, the Israeli Navy launches several amphibious landings, placing tanks, APCs (Armored Personnel Carriers), and fresh infantry units on vantage positions along the coastline. In the central sector, Israeli tanks clash with Syrian armor near Jezzin, while Israeli vanguards push the Syrian forward units back from the village of Kankaba at the entrance to the Bekaa Valley.

June 8—IDF armored spearheads link up with the units landed along the coast by amphibious vessels and push north towards Damour, while infantry supported by tanks continues mopping-up operations in the coastal towns and refugee camps—the main PLO redoubts. Heavy fighting between Israeli and Syrian armor continues in the Jezzin as PLO tank-killer teams and Syrian commando units exploit the excellent cover to retard the Israeli advance. IAF fighter-bombers fly close support missions and in three separate air battles six Syrian MiGs are downed, one pilot captured.

June 9—In a dramatic attack, 17 out of 19 Syrian SAM batteries, with their infrastructure, are destroyed in the Bekaa Valley. The attack is carried out by a combined air and ground action. During continuous air battles, 29 Syrian MiGs are shot down by IAF fighters. In the coastal sector, heavy fighting goes on in the towns where PLO defenders fight for their lives against advancing IDF paratrooper teams. Israeli spearheads reach a point 18 kilometers south of Beirut. In the central sector, Israeli armor captures vantage positions overlooking the Bekaa valley and the Damascus–Beirut main road. Heavy opposition from Syrian forces supported by ATGW (anti-tank guided weapons), anti-tank helicopters, and artillery.

June 10—In the coastal sector the IDF enters Kafr Sill on the outskirts of the capital, defended by PLO and the Syrian Eighty-fifth Armored Brigade. Heavy fighting as the Israelis enter the township. IDF engineers force a bypass over the mountain ridge, outflanking the Syrians from the east. In the central region an Israeli armored force is ambushed by Syrian commandos supported by T-62 tanks. The encircled Israelis are evacuacted under a combined armor and artillery barrage, at close quarters against heavy odds. IAF Cobra and Defender helicopters come into action against Syrian reinforcements in the northern Bekaa Valley, operating with IAF fighters, knocking out tanks and SP artillery. Several Syrian Gazelle helicopters are shot down and some captured almost intact. Twenty-five Syrian MiGs are shot down in continuous air battles, as two more SA-6 batteries are destroyed. In all, close to 90 Syrian fighter-planes are destroyed in air-to-air combat. No IAF aircraft are lost in all these air battles.

June 11—At noon a cease-fire is arranged between the Syrian and Israeli forces in Lebanon. Shortly before, an Israeli force ambushes a Syrian unit with T-72 tanks in the Bekaa Valley. Following a sharp clash, nine of the Syrian T-72s are destroyed and go up in flames. In the coastal sector the IDF reaches the outskirts of Beirut overlooking the airport. Fighting continues in the coastal towns as the PLO fighters are routed out in bloody battles.

June 12—The cease-fire with the Syrians holds, but heavy fighting continues in the coastal sector south of Beirut as the Israelis close in.

June 13—A cease-fire is arranged between the PLO and IDF but does not hold long as rapid firing exchanges escalate. IDF units enter East Beirut, taking the Baabde presidential palace and the nearby outskirts.

June 14—Following a six-day siege, IDF troops storm Ein Hillwe camp and capture it after a savage close-in battle with the PLO.

June 15—Sporadic fire exchanges escalate into artillery barrages by evening over West Beirut.

June 16—The new cease-fire holds temporarily as diplomatic efforts start to prevent an Israeli attack on Beirut.

June 17–21—Sporadic fire exchanges in Beirut and the east.

June 21—The cease-fire breaks down. IDF attacks the Syrian forces and PLO positions along the Beirut–Damascus road in the Alei-Bahamdoun sector, with heavy artillery and air support.

June 23—The battles along the main road continue as the Syrians throw in reinforcements. Syrian commando units are destroyed at El Mansourije.

June 24–26—Heavy fighting on the Damascus-Beirut road. The IDF pushes all Syrian forces from the high ground into the Bekaa Valley, links up with the Christian militia to the north, and closes the ring around Beirut from the east, encircling PLO and Syrian forces in the city. A cease-fire is arranged, which lasts, with sporadic fire exchanges, until the first week of July.

Early July—During the first half of July sporadic fire exchanges take place on the outskirts of Beirut, escalating into sharp artillery duels from time to time. Heavy sniper activity causes casualties to IDF troops in forward positions. Most of the fighting takes place around the airport where IDF positions are in the open, controlled by PLO in high buildings nearby. As losses mount, the IDF calls in air support to hit PLO positions unattainable by direct ground fire.

July 21—Repeated incidents and cease-fire violations in the eastern sector; five IDF soldiers killed by Syrian action.

July 22—IDF armor and artillery opens fire along the whole eastern sector, hitting Syrian and PLO targets on a broad front. Later, IAF fighter-bombers initiate an intense two-hour fire-fight; 72 Syrian tanks are destroyed.

July 23—IAF strikes at several PLO camps in Beirut as IDF artillery and tanks fire directly at targets on the outskirts.

July 24—IAF fighters destroy three Syrian SA-8 Gecko SAMs that had taken up positions in the Bekaa during the night. An IAF recce Phantom is hit by a Syrian SA-6 and crashes in flames.

July 25–27—Continuous air activity over Beirut. IAF attacks PLO targets at Sabra, Shatila, and Fakahany quarters where main PLO headquarters are based. A cease-fire is called on July 27.

July 30—Cease-fire broken as artillery duels start. IAF aircraft together with Israeli naval units attack PLO targets. Libyan forces take up positions with the Syrians.

August 1—Artillery duels in Beirut. IDF armor and engineers advance along the main runways of Beirut airport and capture the terminal.

August 2—IDF forces enter El Salloum camp at nightfall and capture it from the PLO.

August 3—IDF infantry assaults El Uzay camp north of the airport and starts mopping up. Heavy fighting during the night as PLO withdraws under pressure.

August 4—Israeli forces advance with fire support into the Museum complex, where the PLO has built a stronghold on the "green line" between East and West Beirut. In the afternoon heavy fighting as artillery and air attacks come in on the PLO concentrations.

August 5—Protracted exchanges of shoulder-fired ground-to-air missiles (RPG) and artillery fire near Beirut Port. IDF advances further north at El Uzay camp and encircles Burj-el-Barajne quarter housing the PLO HQ.

August 6—Further IAF attacks on PLO quarters, direct hits on HQ buildings at Fakahany soon after Yassir Arafat leaves.

August 8—IDF armor races to Junia port, north of Beirut, to take positions preventing landings of French forces from naval vessels off the coast. PLO artillery shells East Beirut and Junia with Katyusha and Grad rockets.

August 10—IAF aircraft destroy Syrian SA-9 Gaskin that entered Lebanon to stem depletion of air defense.

August 11—IDF armor advances towards the Hippodrome and its nearby woods. Heavy fighting with PLO. IAF intervenes, flying close support. In the afternoon there is a marked decrease in PLO fire due to shortage of ammunition. Large Israeli troop reinforcements are moved to Lebanon to exert pressure on PLO and Syrians.

August 12—The breaking point of PLO resistance in Beirut. IDF bombards the PLO quarters for 11 hours with artillery, air, and naval fire. In the evening, as the fire ceases, the PLO finally declares its willingness to withdraw on Israeli conditions. A cease-fire is arranged as final talks begin.

August 21—PLO starts its withdrawal from Beirut as multinational force takes position. In the port the Second Battalion French Foreign Legion takes charge, later relieved by a USMC Unit from the Sixth Fleet. An Italian contingent made up of paratroopers and Bersaglieri takes up position along the "green line" in the city.

August 23—Bashir Gemayel is elected Lebanon's new president.

August 30—The Syrian Eighty-fifth Armored Brigade withdraws from Beirut along the main road with its heavy equipment. At this stage half of the PLO have already withdrawn from the city and left for Arab countries. On the eastern sector the Syrians move in further reinforcements, building up to a two-divisional size force. Part of the Israeli reserve forces are moved to

Israeli territory. The Lebanese army enters West Beirut for the first time after eight years. The siege is over.

September 1—14,000 PLO and other terrorists expelled to eight Arab countries over a two-week period.

September 13—IAF pounds Syrian and PLO positions in the Bekaa.

September 14—Lebanon's newly elected president Bashir Gemayel is killed in an explosion by demolition charges placed at his HQ in Beirut by Murabitoun. (Later, his brother Amin is elected in his place.) Heavy Syrian and PLO troop concentrations in the Bekaa. IDF reinforcements take up positions as tension grows.

September 15—IDF enters West Beirut and begins taking vantage points in the city and former PLO concentrations. The IAF flies top cover.

Appendix I

The Missions of the IAF*

1. To protect the State of Israel and Israeli airspace, as well as IDF troops beyond the state's borders.
2. To maintain air superiority over enemy air forces and armies in the IDF's theater of operations.
3. To support ground and sea forces.
4. To fulfill IDF transportation, reconnaisance, communications, and intelligence needs.

The IAF is constantly upgrading its equipment and adapting it to the special fighting conditions of the Middle Eastern theater. The air force places continuous stress on the acquisition of new matériel and weapon systems and the development of new modes of combat. Likewise, the IAF pays special attention to the training of high-quality technical cadres at its own school as well as in specially coordinated pre-military programs offered at civilian institutions.

The IAF maintains its high operational level through repeated exercise alerts and operational employment, as well as by developing *esprit de corps* and the command capacity of its officers at all levels. The IAF, furthermore, continues to upgrade its proficiency in the handling of aircraft, weapons systems, electronics, and technology.

In short, the IAF is the strategic arm of Zahal (IDF), with the primary role of deterring the enemy during peacetime and subduing it in war.

---

*As given in *The Israel Air Force, 1983,* an official publication of the IDF.

Appendix II
Israeli Defense Force (Zahal)

More than 11 percent of the population of Israel—well over one-half of all Israeli men and a significant number of Israeli women—are active-duty members of the defense forces.

Manpower in the Israeli Defense Force consists of career service-members *(sherut qevah)* and those men and women who are fulfilling their term of compulsory service *(sherut hovah)*. Military service is compulsory for both men and women when they reach the age of 18. Women must serve between 18 and 24 months of active duty, while men must serve between 24 and 42 months of active service. In addition, every conscript must enter a reserve unit upon completion of active duty and continue to train for one day a month plus one month a year, until age 39 for women and 55 for men.

The nation's naval and air forces are not separate services. They are known as Cheyl Ha Yam (Sea Corps) and Cheyl Ha Avir (Air Corps) as part of the Israeli Defense Force.

The ground forces are made up of about 140,000 men and women—20,000 career soldiers and 120,000 conscripts. This highly mechanized force is backed up by an estimated 250,000 men and women serving in reserve units.

The sea force is the smallest unit of the nation's defense forces, consisting of about 5,000 men, 1,000 of whom are conscripts.

The air force is composed of approximately 21,000 men, of whom 19,000 are career professionals and some 2,000 are conscripts.

These regular forces are supported by the Noar Halutzi Lohem (Pioneer Fighting Youth), an organization that combines military service with agriculture training and has established outposts in farming towns and villages along the nation's borders.

Law enforcement is carried out by a national police force of approximately 17,000 men and women.

Appendix III
Uniforms and Insignia

When the War of Independence broke out, the primary concern was the acquisition of aircraft. As has been detailed earlier, Israeli purchasing teams were busy all over the world trying to buy combat aircraft—in many cases even non-combat aircraft were acquired. In this way the polyglot Israeli Air Service grew, with surplus World War II aircraft from the U.S., Great Britain, Czechoslovakia, Sweden, Italy, and elsewhere. These were the colorful Messerschmitts, Spitfires, and Mustangs that bore the blue, six-pointed star (the Mogen David) in a white circle.

By the same token, with the exception of Dan Tolkovsky, Ezer Weizman, and Aharon Remez, the fledgling air service was made up predominantly of foreigners. Here, too, the Air Service depended on "surplus" World War II pilots from the USAAF, the USN, the RAF, the RCAF, the RAAF, and the RSAAF. These American, British, Canadian, Australian, and South African pilots were for the most part Jewish, but many were not. They brought with them their own flying gear and uniforms. This made them a diversified and motley group, but their skills and tradition of victory remain with the IAF today.

As the Service progressed and the IAF was created as a separate fighting service, some sort of order and discipline was instilled—a matter easier said than done—but by the end of 1948, with more aircraft coming in, the forces were divided into a few squadrons. Among them, the 101st Squadron became famous, not only for its exploits, but also because of its members, several of them internationally renowned. At first, as the rest of the IDF installed a rank insignia scheme, the IAF decided to keep its own version of rank insignia and designation, which had a marked similarity to the familiar RAF system. Shoulder rings of blue-gray on a dark blue background were worn by officers, arm straps of white on blue by other ranks. Progressing from a single ring for a pilot officer, the highest rank at the time was equivalent to an RAF air commodore, this being the IAF commander. Pilot wings, originating in 1948 and still in service, are two cloth wings centered by a shield with a dark blue six-pointed Star of David, the emblem of the IAF. RAF-style battledress of darker and lighter blue-gray was later supplied but seldom worn. Instead, the tropical khaki shorts and blouses were preferred by the foreign volunteers who made up the majority of the IAF aircrews. B-17 bomber crews used to wear colored USN baseball caps. Officially, blue-colored berets with a metal, winged-shaped cap badge*was authorized; not many of the airmen wore these, preferring their own style or no headgear at all. Some years later, when former RAF Flight Lietenant Dan Tolkovsky took over and most of the foreign volunteers had gone

---

*This metal cap badge was exactly the same design as the embroidered pilots' wings worn over the left breast pocket.

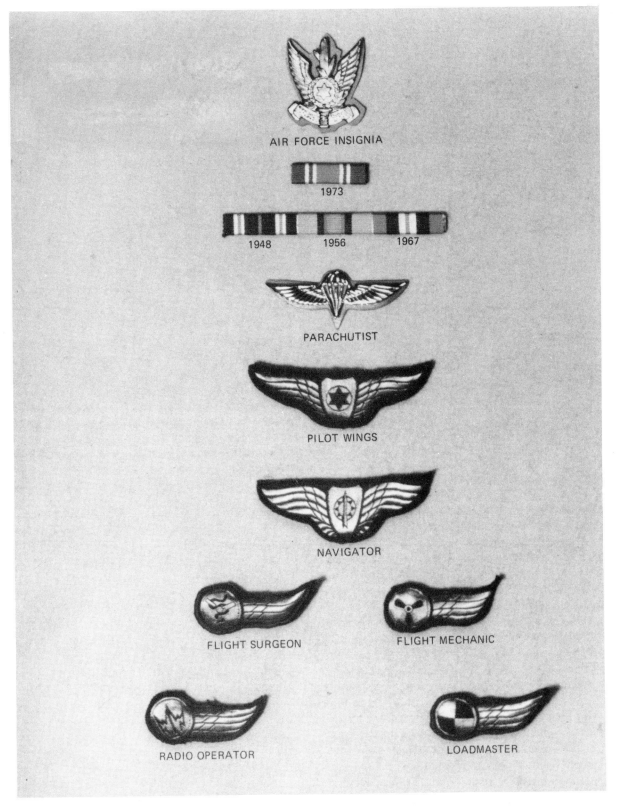

Air Force Wings and Campaign Ribbons.

OT HAMOFET

Medal for Distinguished and Out-standing Service in Action.

OT HAOZ

Israel's Second Highest Award for Courage on the field of battle.

OT HAGVURA

Medal of Supreme Bravery, Israel's Highest Award for Bravery in the field of battle.

home, discipline and service regulations were at last enforced.

The official uniform became, for most of the year, a light khaki uniform of trousers and blouse, rank insignia and designation being standard IDF. Officers, however, wore silver on a blue backcloth sleeve on their shoulder straps. Pilots' wings were unchanged, but other aircrews were allotted special double wings with aircrew trades on the center shield instead of the blue star. Blue berets became standard for other ranks, whereas officers wore a field-service cap with or without a black center band over the peak. The new IAF cap badge—a winged Star of David centered over a sword with scrolls below—became standard for all ranks on berets worn RAF-style. Later, shoulder straps with colored insignia for air units or support commands, as well as IAF HQ, were authorized to be worn on the shoulder strap or on RAF-type

battledress below the left shoulder patch.

Dress uniform is not usually worn, but for ceremonial occasions a gabardine-cloth blue-gray—formerly the RAF service dress uniform with cloth belt—was issued, to be worn with a light blue or white shirt and black tie. This was later modified to the USAF-style service uniform, but lacking the belt. Winter uniforms are usually worn with open collar, rarely with black tie.

Flight clothing has undergone many changes since 1948, when flight helmets originating from worldwide sources became fashionable, together with goggles and "Mae Wests." Some pilots painted colorful crests and drawings on their flight coveralls, according to their taste and imagination. Later some order was achieved, but only the jet era brought modern flight clothing into the IAF. From the older, dome-shaped pilot's helmet used in the Six-Day War, the IAF has now progressed to the modern, most up-to-date flight clothing and visored helmets and the rest of the special supersonic equipment used in ultra-modern combat aircraft.

Ground crews wear IDF fatigues on duty and sport colored baseball caps for the various ground duties. IAF women soldiers wear the usual IDF uniforms, but have a distinctive blue boat-shaped cap and waist belt of the same color.

Since the days of the colorful individuals who served in it 30 years ago, the IAF has become a top professional service, highly disciplined both in the air and on the ground. Its appearance immaculate, it remains, without doubt, the best-dressed service in the IDF.

Appendix IV
IAF Commanders

YEHOSHUA ESHEL (Nov. 1947–May 1948)—Eshel was the first commander of the preindependence Air Service, a division of the Haganah, which was established on November 10, 1947. Born in 1900 in Poland, Eshel served with the Jewish battalions in the British Army during World War I. Later he became a member of the Haganah. He died in 1966. (He was not a relative of coauthor David Eshel.)

ISRAEL AMIR (SABLODOVSKI) (May 1948)—Born in Poland in 1903, Amir was a Haganah member with the rank of lieutenant colonel. He became the first commander of the IAF upon its establishment, a position he held for only two weeks. Later he became chief of ordnance at the Ministry of Defense.

AHARON REMEZ (May 1948–Dec. 1950)—A Sabra born in Israel in 1919, he was the son of a leading personality of the Jewish Yishuv. He joined the British RAF in 1942 and, following training in Canada, became a fighter pilot. He served in a U.K.-based fighter squadron flying Supermarine Spitfires and later Hawker Tempests. Remez commanded the IAF during the 1948–49 War of Independence.

SHLOMO SHAMIR (Dec. 1950–Aug. 1951)—Born in Russia in 1915, Shamir was a member of the Haganah. He was active in the prewar armament industry and became a civilian pilot in 1940. He served as a major in the British Army during World War II. Shamir commanded an IDF infantry brigade during the 1948–49 War of Independence. Later he commanded the fledgling Israeli Navy. An excellent organizer, he undertook to reorganize the IAF but, due to illness, relinquished his command after a short time.

HAIM LASKOV (Aug. 1951–June 1953)—Born in Russia in 1919, Laskov lived and was educated in Haifa. A member of the Haganah, he joined the British Army, in which he attained the rank of major in the Jewish Brigade fighting in Italy. He commanded an Israeli Brigade during the War of Independence and was a leading commander in the Sinai campaign. He was promoted to general in charge of training before taking command of the IAF. A strict disciplinarian, he reorganized the force and its infrastructure. In 1958 he became chief of staff of the IDF. Laskov was a much-decorated officer.

DAN TOLKOVSKY (June 1953–July 1958)—Born in Israel in 1921, he joined the RAF in 1942 during World War II. Following flight training in South Africa, Tolkowski became a fighter pilot. He reached the rank of flight lieutenant, serving in the Middle East, Greece, and southern Europe. During his tenure as commander, the IAF converted to its first jets and fought the Sinai campaign.

AHARON REMEZ

Commander in Chief
IAF: 1948–50

Flight Sergeant
RAF: 1942–45

HAIM LASKOV

Commander in Chief
IAF: 1951–53

EZER WEIZMAN (1958–1966)—Weizman was born in Haifa in 1924, a nephew of the first president of Israel. During World War II he joined the RAF at the age of 18. He became a fighter pilot and served in the Far East, flying Spitfires. In the War of Independence he served as a Messerschmitt pilot and later flew Spitfires again. Weizman took part in the battle with the RAF above the Negev. Under his command the IAF developed into the first-class fighting force it is today, received its first supersonic Mirages and trained for its mission in the Six-Day War. Later Weizman served as chief of operations to the chief of staff during the Six-Day War, and became minister of defense in the first administration of Prime Minister Begin.

MORDECHAI HOD (1966–1973)—Born at Kibutz Degania in 1926, he joined the British

Army in World War II, serving as a driver in the Royal Army Service Corps. As a Palmach member he took part in a pilots' course in Italy in 1947. Later Hod was assigned to the Czech flight training course where he flew Messerschmitt Bf-109s (AVIA 210s). He took part in the long-range ferry flights of Spitfires to Israel in 1948. After the War of Independence he trained on jets in Britain. Commander of a Mustang squadron, he also led an Ouragan squadron into battle, escorting the paradrop at Mitla Pass during the Sinai campaign. He commanded the IAF in its lightning strike on June 5, 1967 (the Six-Day War). Under his command the IAF changed over from French aircraft to American Skyhawks and Phantoms.

BENJAMIN PELED (1973–1977)—A third-generation Israeli, Peled was born in Tel

DAN TOLKOVSKY

Commander in Chief
IAF: 1953–58

Flight Lieutenant
RAF: 1942–47

EZER WEIZMAN

Commander in Chief
IAF: 1958–66

Sergeant Pilot
RAF: 1942–45

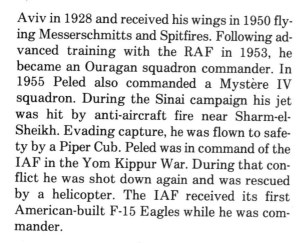

Aviv in 1928 and received his wings in 1950 flying Messerschmitts and Spitfires. Following advanced training with the RAF in 1953, he became an Ouragan squadron commander. In 1955 Peled also commanded a Mystère IV squadron. During the Sinai campaign his jet was hit by anti-aircraft fire near Sharm-el-Sheikh. Evading capture, he was flown to safety by a Piper Cub. Peled was in command of the IAF in the Yom Kippur War. During that conflict he was shot down again and was rescued by a helicopter. The IAF received its first American-built F-15 Eagles while he was commander.

DAVID IVRY (1977–1982)—Ivry was born in Tel Aviv in 1934. He joined the IAF when he was 18 and learned to fly in Spitfires. He flew Ouragan jets in combat during the 1956 war. Next he advanced to Super Mystères and later to Mirages. He flew the latter in the Six-Day

War. Commanding a combat wing in 1973, he became chief of operations during the Yom Kippur War. Under his command the IAF received its F-16 Falcon fighters and Grumman Hawkeye EAW (electronic airborne warning) aircraft. He also supervised the difficult withdrawal from the Sinai air bases, under the Camp David Agreement and the build-up in the Negev. Gen. Ivry also had command of the IAF during Operation Peace for Galilee, the incursion into Lebanon in pursuit of the PLO terrorists.

AMOS LAPIDOT (Dec. 1982–   )—Brig. Gen. Amos Lapidot assumed command of the IAF while the Israeli Defense Force was still in Lebanon, following Operation Peace for Galilee. He had been in charge of the Lavie (Lion) aircraft project, the new strike plane being manufactured by the Israel Aircraft Industries to replace the American-built A-4 Skyhawk.

MORDECHAI HOD

Commander in Chief
IAF: 1966–1973

BENJAMIN PELED

Commander in Chief
IAF: 1973–1977

DAVID IVRY

Commander in Chief
IAF: 1977–1982

Appendix V
Air Bases

Although it is an extremely tiny country (and there are those who would have it even smaller by making it give up more of its territory to the Arab countries), Israel has a number of air bases that dot the countryside. In most cases, however, they are well hidden, well protected, and under tight security. The casual traveler would not be aware that he was passing in the vicinity of an Israeli air base unless, of course, a flight of F-16s or F-15s happened to be taking off or roaring in low for a landing.

These air bases were either taken over from the RAF when British forces left Palestine, built by the IAF, captured from Arab adversaries, or built by the United States to replace airfields in the Sinai turned over to Egypt according to the Camp David Agreement. Recently, Israel turned over one of these captured bases to Egypt together with four of their own IAF-built fields, including Etzion and Eitam, under the terms of the treaty of peace with their neighbor to the south. As part of that same treaty, the United States is building air bases in the Negev to replace those presented to the Egyptians by Israel. In addition to the airfields built in the Negev at Ovda and Matred (Ramon) are new bases at Nevetim and Mashabim. These take the place of the air bases in the Sinai (Refidim, Atour, Santa Katorina, and others) turned over to Egypt.

Hence, air bases range from Mahanayim in the north, near the Lebanese and Syrian borders, to the new American-built fields in the Negev to the south. Other bases in the south are at Haifa, Ramat David, Herzlia, Ben Gurion/Sde Dov/Tel Nof, Lod, Hatzor, Hatzerim, Sedom, and Ramon. Following are brief descriptions of some of these Israeli bases.

Ramat David AFB

Built by the RAF in 1942, this northernmost combat air base operated as a bomber base, flying Baltimores and later accommodating the 208th and Thirty-second Squadrons, attacked in 1948 by Egyptian Spitfires. Taken over by the IAF following the establishment of the State of Israel, the base has become one of its major airfields, from which countless operations have been mounted in the country's 33 years of existence.

Tel Nof AFB

This base, known during its RAF days as Aqir, was used at the time as the training base for the Sixth Airborne Division Paratroop School. During the War of Independence the IAF flew many supply and combat missions from this base, located only minutes from Tel Aviv. For a time it housed the IAF Flight School without interrupting its function as an operational base, which it fulfills to this day. Tel Nof also includes a logistical center for newly introduced aircraft.

Hatzor AFB

Formerly RAF Qastina, from where Halifax bombers were flown, it was abandoned by the British in the 1940s and taken over by the Israeli Defense Force during the fighting in

1948. It was soon refurbished and provided an operational field for the IAF. The Sinai campaign in 1956 saw many Mosquitos and Mustangs using Hatzor for their home. Hatzor is still one of the major IAF air bases in service.

Hatzerim AFB
This fairly new air base near Beersheva, unlike several other bases, was built entirely to IAF specifications. It is the current home of the IAF Flight School, as well as of several combat formations; the latter have seen much action in Sinai and the Canal front.

Eitam AFB
One of the two air bases in Sinai constructed entirely by Israel in the light of its experiences in recent wars, this base on the Mediterranean coastline has been evacuated, in accordance with the peace treaty signed with Egypt.

Etzion AFB
This base, too, was specially constructed in the Sinai by Israel. Located northwest of Eilat, it was also evacuated and turned over to Egypt.

Negev Air Bases
Two new air bases, Ovda and Ramon (Matred), were constructed by American engineering personnel. The site for a third has been selected at Malhata, east of Beersheva.

Ophir (Sharm-el-Sheikh) AFB
Israel's southernmost air base, located at the tip of the Sinai Peninsula, was one of the first to be hit during the Yom Kippur War. The field was attacked by eight Egyptian MiGs—a complete surprise move—but seven of them were shot down by IAF Phantoms scrambled to intercept during the attack.

Ben Gurion AB
Located near Ben Gurion International Airport, this base houses transport squadrons and light aircraft such as Westwind and Arava.

Sde Dov AB
This field, on the northern outskirts of Tel Aviv, was the IAF's first operational airfield in 1948, flying supply missions to the cutoff Negev and Jerusalem fronts. Liaison aircraft and light transport helicopters are now stationed here.

Refidim AFB
Now evacuated, this was a major operational air base in the Sinai. Formerly an Egyptian fighter base named Bir Gafgafa, it was captured by Israel for the first time during the 1956 Sinai campaign while still under construction, and was destroyed before the enforced evacuation at the close of that year. During the 11 years preceding the Six-Day War, Bir Gafgafa was rebuilt and modernized by the Egyptian Air

IAF AIR BASE STRUCTURE

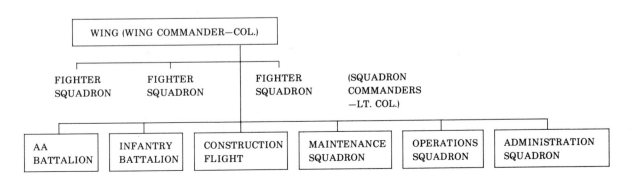

Force. One of the first fields to be hit by the IAF on June 5, 1967, it was captured relatively intact by Maj. Gen. Israel Tal's armored division and soon became an operational IAF base, flying Mirages. Later extensively enlarged, it became a forward operations base during the 1968–70 War of Attrition. Despite damage by the Egyptian Air Force during the Yom Kippur War, it remained in operation during and after the war, until evacuated as part of the peace process under the Camp David Agreement.

All IAF intercept squadrons of each specific base take part in the base intercept alert duty roster for the defense of their own base as well as of the airspace assigned to it. Each base is capable of mounting all forms of attack, and bases are connected to the IAF command and control center.

The various administrative functions ensure swift maintenance and proper treatment of all aircraft and equipment on base. Each base is capable of being adequately defended by its own aircraft and AA. In addition, ABC defense exists on all bases. A permanent transport schedule connects all IAF bases. Each base is capable of operating even after being hit hard. They feature modern designs of structure, shelters, and fast damage-repair programs.

Appendix VI
The Aircraft, Friend and Foe
(1947–1983)

Following are some facts and data on the principal aircraft employed by both the Israeli Air Force and the air arms of the opposing Arab forces from 1947 through 1983. Some of the aircraft served on both sides and on occasion fought against each other. Such examples include the Supermarine Spitfire and the Douglas C-47 Dakota in the War of Independence. Another is the Mirage, which was the backbone of the IAF in the Six-Day War but also flew with the Egyptian Air Force in the Yom Kippur War (a gift from Libya). A particularly bizarre combination was the Messerschmitt BF-109 (Avia S199), the former German Nazi Luftwaffe fighter-plane, flown by the Jewish pilots of the IAF.

During the Israeli War of Independence most of the aircraft flown by the Israelis and their Arab adversaries were surplus USAAF and RAF planes of World War II vintage. This situation lasted until the Sinai campaign, at which time the Israelis were armed with new jet fighters from France, and the Arabs had modern British and Soviet jets. In the Six-Day War the IAF was armed predominantly with French aircraft, and the Arab air forces, with one exception, had planes supplied by the USSR. The Jordanians flew British Hawker Hunters. Six years later, after Gen. Charles de Gaulle's France had suddenly switched allegiance from Israel to the Arabs and cut off the IAF's sup-

ply of aircraft and spare parts, the Israeli Air Force met the onslaught of the combined Arab forces with U.S.-built F-4 Phantoms, and A-4 Skyhawks. In that Yom Kippur War they acquitted themselves well against the Soviet MiGs and Sukhois, but suffered heavy casualties from the Russian surface-to-air missiles.

Although most of the aircraft described and depicted in this book are fighter aircraft, one transport plane is worthy of note, the American-built Lockheed C-130 Hercules. This medium airlift transport was invaluable at Entebbe Airport in an anti-terrorist action that will live in the annals of air rescue, conveying 103 hostages to freedom. Another noteworthy aircraft that is not a fighter is the Fouga-Magister, a French-designed, Israeli-built trainer that was used for combat missions in the Six-Day War.

In the 1982 Operation Peace for Galilee it was the American-built, Israeli-flown General Dynamics F-16 Fighting Falcons and McDonnell Douglas F-15 Eagles that delivered an astounding defeat to the Syrian Air Force with their Russian-built MiG-21s and MiG-23s—and their SAM batteries as well. The F-16s and F-15s were controlled from the air and vectored into battle by the U.S.-manufactured Grumman E2C Hawkeye. The home-built Israeli Kfirs also acquitted themselves well, along with the older F-4 Phantoms. In this operation the American-built Hughes Defender helicopters saw action for the· first time. Just one year earlier, on June 7, 1981, the F-15s and F-16s had first seen combat in the IAF precision attack that crippled the Iraqi nuclear reactor near Baghdad.

The aircraft listed below are organized under the heading of the conflict in which they appeared in the greatest numbers or in which they played their most important part. For example, while the C-47 Dakota and P-51 Mustang saw action in the War of Independence, they played their biggest roles in the Sinai campaign. By the same token, the F-15 and F-16 fighters enjoyed

great success in the long-distance strike on the Osirak nuclear reactor and their performance above Lebanon in the Operation Peace for Galilee is unparalleled in the history of aerial combat. The three-view drawings provided are limited to fixed-wing aircraft. However, this is in no way intended to diminish the part played by such great helicopters as the Bell 47, the Huey Cobra and Jet Ranger, the Hughes Defender, the Aerospatiale Gazelle, the Sikorsky S-58 and S-65, the Sud Aviation Alouette and Super Frelon, the Mi-24 Hind, and others. Some are covered elsewhere in this book.

WAR OF INDEPENDENCE, 1948

Messerschmitt Bf-109 (Avia S199)
Wingspan: 32 ft $6\frac{1}{2}$ in (9.92 m)

Length: 29 ft $10\frac{1}{4}$ in (9.1 m)

Engine: Junkers Jumo Ju 211F/1,350 hp
Speed: 366 mph (590 km/h)
Armament: 2 20-mm cannons, 2 12.7-mm machine guns

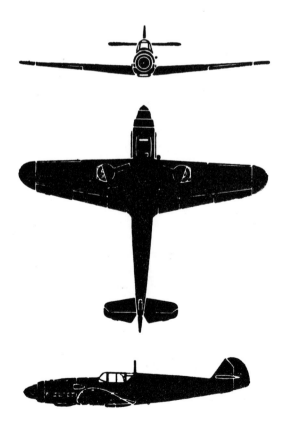

Supermarine Spitfire
Wingspan: 40 ft 2 in (12.24 m)
Length: 31 ft 4 in (9.55 m)
Engine: Rolls Royce Merlin 64 Vee/1,710 hp
Speed: 408 mph at 25,000 ft (658 km/h at
      7,620 m)
Armament: 2 20-mm cannons and 2 .303-caliber
       (7.7-mm) machine guns

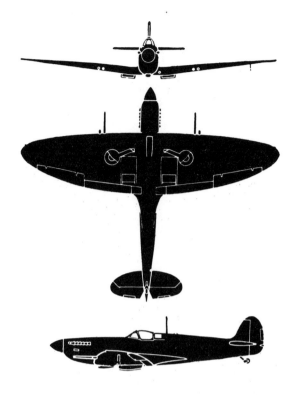

Bristol Beaufighter
Wingspan: 57 ft 10 in (17.63 m)
Length: 41 ft 8 in (12.7 m)
Engines: 2 Rolls Royce Merlin XX/1,280 hp
      each
Speed: 312 mph (502 km/h)
Armament: 4 20-mm cannons, 6 .303-caliber
       (7.7-mm) machine guns, bombs

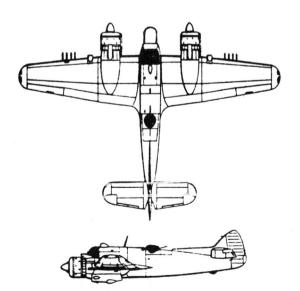

Boeing B-17 Fortress
Wingspan: 103 ft 9 in (31.6 m)
Length: 74 ft 9 in (22.8 m)
Engines: 4 Wright R-1820-97/1,200 hp each
Speed: 287 mph (462 km/h)
Armament: 13 .50-caliber (12.7-mm) machine
                 guns, bombs

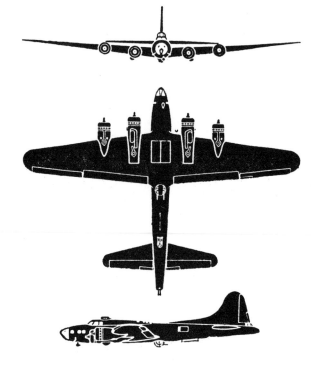

Lockheed C-121 Constellation
Wingspan: 123 ft (37.49 m)
Length: 95 ft $1\frac{1}{4}$ in (28.99 m)
Engines: 4 Wright R-3350 air-cooled
                 radial/2,200 hp each
Speed: 330 mph (531 km/h)
Armament: None; transport (also used as
                 bomber)

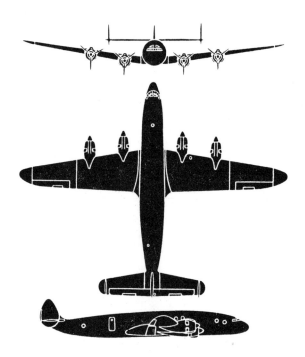

Hawker Hurricane
Wingspan: 40 ft (12.19 m)
Length: 32 ft $2\frac{1}{4}$ in (9.81 m)
Engine: Rolls Royce Merlin XX Vee/1,300 hp
Speed: 330 mph at 18,000 ft (532 km/h at
 5,486 m)
Armament: 8–12 machine guns or 4 20-mm
 cannons

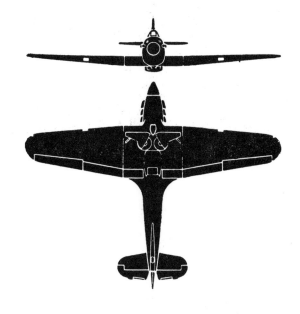

Hawker Sea Fury
Wingspan: 38 ft 5 in (11.71 m)
Length: 34 ft 8 in (10.57 m)
Engine: Bristol Centaurus, radial/2,470 hp
Speed: 448 mph (722 km/h)
Armament: 4 20-mm cannons, 12 3-in (1.2-cm)
 rockets, 2 500-pound (227-kg)
 bombs

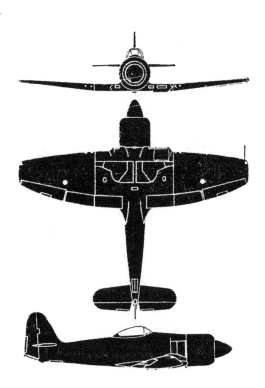

North American P-51 Mustang
Wingspan: 37 ft 0.5 in (11.29 m)
Length: 32 ft $3\frac{1}{4}$ in (9.83 m)
Engine: Rolls Royce Merlin V-1650/1,495 hp
Speed: 437 mph (703 km/h)
Armament: 6 .50-caliber (12.7-mm) machine
            guns

DeHavilland Mosquito
Wingspan: 54 ft 2 in (16.5 m)
Length: 40 ft 6 in (12.34 m)
Engines: 2 Rolls Royce Merlin/1,230 hp each
Speed: 380 mph (613 km/h)
Armament: 4 20-mm cannons, 4 .303-caliber
            (7.7-mm) machine guns, bombs

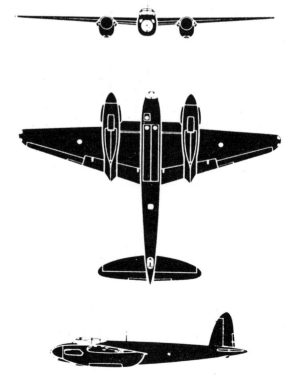

Dassault M.D. 450 Ouragan
Wingspan: 39 ft 11 in (12.17 m)
Length: 35 ft $2\frac{3}{4}$ in (10.74 m)
Engine: Hispano-Suiza Nene/5,000-lb (2,268-kg)
          thrust
Speed: 584 mph (940 km/h)
Armament: 4 20-mm cannons, rockets

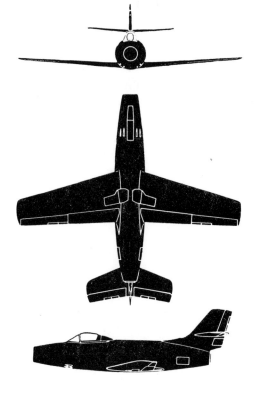

Gloster Meteor
Wingspan: 37 ft 2 in (11.33 m)
Length: 44 ft 7 in (13.59 m)
Engine: Rolls Royce Derwent 8/3,500-lb
          (1,588-kg) thrust
Speed: 592 mph (955 km/h)
Armament: 4 20-mm cannons

Dassault M.D. 452 Mystère
Wingspan: 38 ft 6 in (11.73 m)
Length: 35 ft (10.67m)
Engine: Hispano-Suiza Tay/6,270-lb (2,884-kg)
         thrust
Armament: 4 20-mm or 30-mm cannons, 16
           rockets

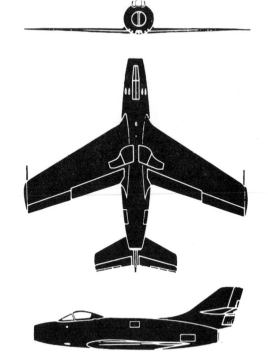

Douglas C-47 Dakota
Wingspan: 95 ft (28.96 m)
Length: 64 ft $5\frac{1}{2}$ in (19.65 m)
Engines: 2 Pratt & Whitney R-1830-92/1,200
          hp each
Speed: 229 mph (369 km/h)
Armament: None; transport (used by Egyp-
           tians as bombers)

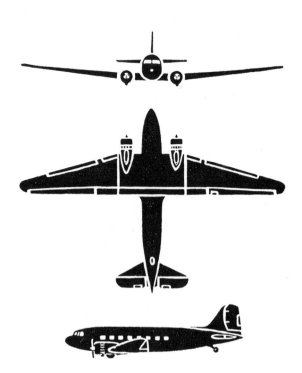

Mikoyan/Gurevich MiG-15 (Falcon and Fagot)
Wingspan: 32 ft 2 in (9.8 m)
Length: 32 ft 8 in (9.96 m)
Engine: VK-1/6,000-lb (2,722-kg) thrust
Speed: 661 mph (1,067 km/h)
Armament: 1 37-mm cannon or 2 23-mm
cannons

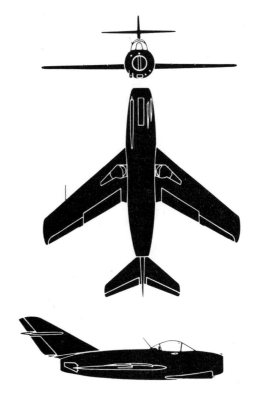

DeHavilland Vampire
Wingspan: 38 ft (11.58 m)
Length: 30 ft 9 in (9.37 m)
Engine: DeHavilland Goblin 3 turbojet/3,500-lb
(1,588-kg) thrust
Speed: 548 mph (884 km/h)
Armament: 4 20-mm cannons, bombs or
rockets

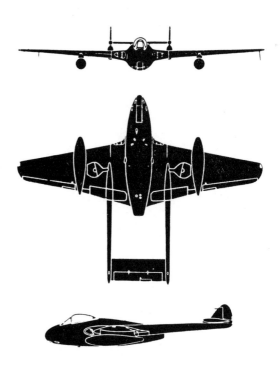

SIX-DAY WAR

Dassault Mirage III
Wingspan: 26 ft $11\frac{1}{2}$ in (8.22 m)
Length: 50 ft $10\frac{1}{4}$ in (15.5m)
Engine: Snecma Atar 9B single-shaft turbo-
          jet/13,225-lb (5,999-kg) thrust
Speed: 863 mph (1,390 km/h)
Armament: 2 30-mm cannons, bombs

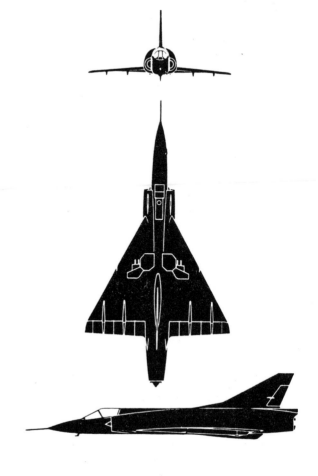

SNCASO Vautour
Wingspan: 49 ft 7 in (15.11 m)
Length: 54 ft 1 in (16.48 m)
Engines: 2 SNECMA Atar 101-3/7,716-lb
          (3,500-kg) thrust each
Speed: 685 mph (1,105 km/h)
Armament: 4 30-mm cannons, bombs

Fouga-Magister
Wingspan: 39 ft 10 in (12.15 m)
Length: 33 ft (10.06 m)
Engines: 2 Turboméca Marboré IIA turbo-
        jets/880-lb (399-kg) thrust each
Speed: 444 mph (715 km/h)
Armament: 2 7.62-mm guns, bombs, air-to-
        surface missiles, or rockets

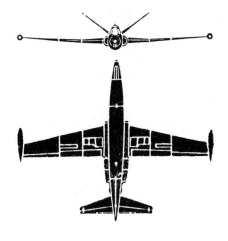

Hawker Hunter
Wingspan: 33 ft 6 in (10.21 m)
Length: 42 ft (12.8 m)
Engine: Rolls-Royce Avon/6,500-lb (2,948-kg)
        thrust
Speed: 736 mph (1,187 km/h)
Armament: 4 30-mm cannons

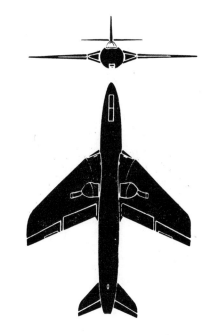

Mikoyan/Gurevich MiG-17 (Fresco)
Wingspan: 34 ft (10.36 m)
Length: 36 ft 3 in (11.05 m)
Engine: Klimov VK-1 single-shaft centrifugal
              turbojet/5,952-lb (2,700-kg) thrust
Speed: 710 mph (1,145 km/h)
Armament: 1 37-mm cannon, 3 23-mm cannons,
              bombs, and air-to-air rockets

Mikoyan/Gurevich MiG-19 (Farmer)
Wingspan: 29 ft $6\frac{1}{2}$ in (9 m)
Length: 42 ft $11\frac{1}{4}$ in (13.09 m)
Engines: 2 Mikuliu AM-5 single-shaft after-
              burning turbojets/6,700-lb (1,484 km/h
              at 6,096 m) each
Speed: 920 mph at 20,000 ft
Armament: Rockets, cannon

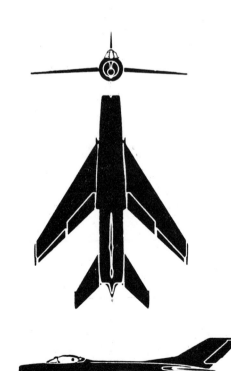

Sukhoi SU-7 Fitter
Wingspan: 29 ft $3\frac{1}{2}$ in (8.93 m)
Length: 50 ft (15 m)
Engine: Lyulka AL-7F turbojet/15,430-lb
    (6,999-kg) thrust (22,050 [10,002] with
    afterburner)
Speed: 1,055 mph (1,700 km/h)
Armament: 2 30-mm cannons plus additional
    weapons in wing pylons

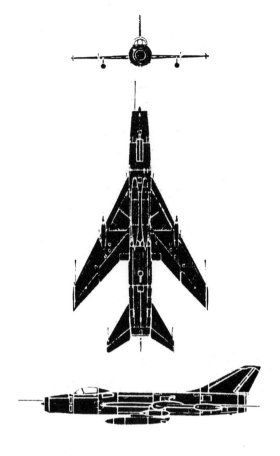

Ilyushin Il-28 "Beagle"
Wingspan: 68 ft (20.73 m)
Length: 62 ft (18.9 m)
Engines: 2 VK-1 turbojet/6,000-lb (2,722-kg)
    thrust each
Speed: 580 mph (935 km/h)
Armament: 4 23-mm cannons and bombs

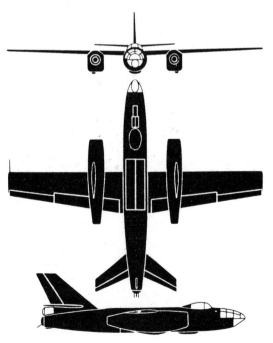

Tupolev Tu-16 "Badger"
Wingspan: 110 ft (33.53 m)
Length: 120 ft (36.58 m)
Engines: 2 Mikulin AM-3M turbojets 20,950-lb
        (9,503-kg) thrust each
Speed: 590 mph (952 km/h)
Armament: 7 23-mm cannons and 9 tons (9.9
        metric tons) of bombs, or 2 Kennel
        air-to-surface missiles, or 1 Kipper
        ASM

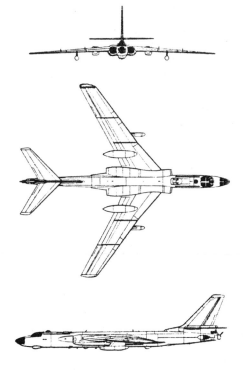

YOM KIPPUR WAR, 1973

McDonnell Douglas A-4 Skyhawk
Wingspan: 27 ft 6 in (8.38 m)
Length: 40 ft (12.2 m)
Engine: Wright J65-16A single-shaft turbo-
        jet/7,700-lb (3,493-kg) thrust
Speed: 675 mph (1,089 km/h)
Armament: Bombs, rockets, 2 20-mm cannons

McDonnell Douglas F-4 Phantom II
Wingspan: 38 ft 5 in (11.71 m)
Length: 58 ft 3 in (17.75 m)
Engines: 2 General Electric J79-8 turbojets
with afterburner/17,000-lb (7,711-kg)
thrust each
Speed: 1,600 mph (2,581 km/h)
Armament: 6–8 air-to-air rockets and a 20-mm
Gatling gun

Mikoyan/Gurevich MiG-21 (Fishbed)
Wingspan: 23 ft 5$\frac{1}{2}$ in (7.15 m)
Length: 46 ft 11 in (14.16 m)
Engine: Turmansky single-shaft turbojet with
afterburner/11,240-lb (5,098-kg) thrust
Speed: 1,285 mph (2,073 km/h)
Armament: Rockets

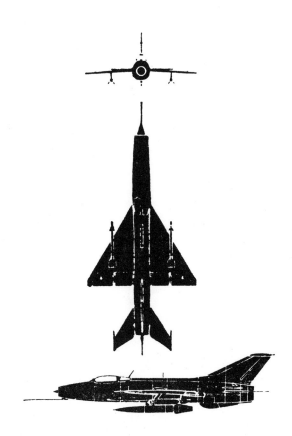

RESCUE AT ENTEBBE, 1976

Lockheed C-130 Hercules
Wingspan: 132 ft 7 in (40.41 m)
Length: 97 ft 8$\frac{1}{2}$ in (29.78 m)
Engines: 4 Allison T56-A-78 turboprops/
          4,050 hp each
Speed: 382 mph (616 km/h)
Armament: None, transport

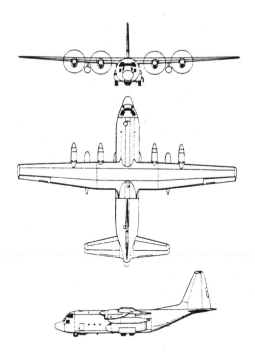

THE IRAQI NUCLEAR REACTOR, 1981

McDonnell Douglas F-15 Eagle
Wingspan: 42 ft 9$\frac{3}{4}$ in (13.05 m)
Length: 63 ft 9$\frac{3}{4}$ in (19.45 m)
Engine: Pratt & Whitney F100-100 two-shaft
          turbofans/14,871-lb (6,745-kg) thrust
          (23,810-lb [10,800-kg] with afterburner)
          each (2)
Speed: 1,650 mph (2,661 km/h)
Armament: 1 20-mm multibarrel cannon, 8 air-
          to-air rockets, and more

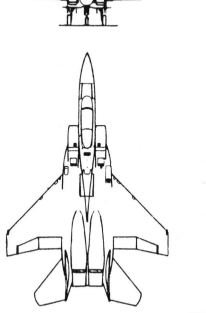

General Dynamics F-16 Falcon
Wingspan: 32 ft 10 in (10.01 m)
Length: 46 ft 6 in (14.17 m)
Engine: Pratt & Whitney F100-PW-100 two-
shaft afterburning turbofan/24,000-lb
(10,886-kg) thrust
Speed: 1,300 mph (2,097 km/h)
Armament: 1 20-mm multibarrel cannon, 2 air-
to-air rockets, and more

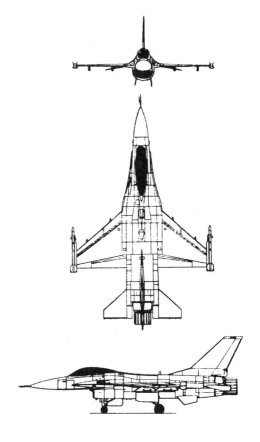

OPERATION PEACE FOR GALILEE

Israel Aircraft Industries Kfir C2
Wingspan: 27 ft (8.23 m)
Length: 51 ft 4 in (15.65 m)
Engine: General Electric J79-J1E/17,860-lb
(8,101-kg) thrust
Speed: Mach 2
Armament: 2 30-mm cannons, 2 Shafrir
missiles, bombs and rockets

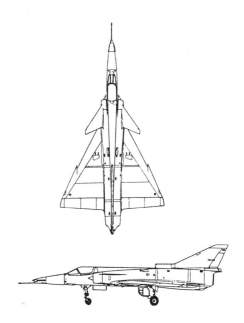

Grumman E-2C Hawkeye
Wingspan: 80 ft 7 in (24.56 m)
Length: 57 ft 7 in (17.55 m)
Engines: 2 Allison T56-A-425 turboprops/4,910
          hp each
Speed: 374 mph (602 km/h)
Armament: None; early-warning aircraft, radar,
electronic countermeasures, etc.

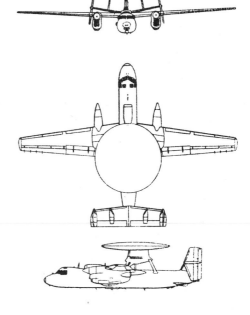

Mikoyan/Gurevich MiG-23 Flogger
Wingspan: 47 ft 3 in (14.4 m)
Length: 53 ft (16.15 m)
Engine: Turmansky R-29B/17,640-lb (8,001-kg)
          thrust (25,350-lb [11,499-kg] with after-
          burner)
Speed: 1,520 mph (2,443 km/h)
Armament: 1 23-mm twin-barrel guns, air-to-air
          missiles

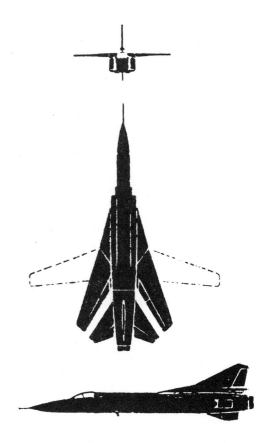

THE FUTURE

Israel Aircraft Industries Lavie
Wingspan: approx. 26 ft (8 m)
Length: approx. 50 ft (15 m)
Engine: Pratt & Whitney 1120/20,600-lb
(9,344-kg) thrust with maximum after-
burner
Speed: approx. 1,350 mph (2,170 km/h)
Armament: data not available at this time

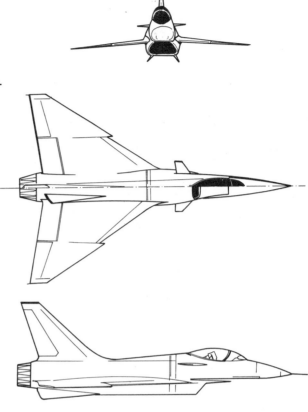

THE PRINCIPAL COMBAT HELICOPTERS OVER LEBANON, 1982

Syrian Air Force

Aerospatiale Gazelle (French-built)

Armed with 4–6 Euromissile *Hot* ATGW with
4000-meter range, the SA-342 Gazelle is cur-
rently the French Army's standard anti-tank
helicopter. Powered by Turbomeca Asta 1 OU
XIV turboshaft with 858 hp, it is also armed
with two pods of 36-mm rockets and two for-
ward-firing miniguns. The Gazelle is part of
Syria's 150-strong combat helicopter force, of
which over 60 have anti-tank roles, with more
to come. In action for the first time, the Gazelle,
an extremely powerful tank-killer, was used in
unison with the Syrian commando units in the
Bekaa Valley and central axis, although the
techniques used were unimaginative and resulted in little success. Several Gazelles were
brought down by Israeli ground air action, some
taken almost intact.

Mi-24 Hind D (Soviet-built)

The Mi-24 Hind D, the most powerful helicopter in the world today, is armed with four advanced *Swatter* ATGMS, a multibarrel
Gatling-type quick-fire gun, four pods for 32
57-mm rockets each. The Hind is the first Soviet
helicopter with an integral weapon system and
retractable landing gear. In action over Afghan-
istan, Iraq, and Iran, it was also used by the

The Soviet Hind D attack helicopter used by the Syrian Air Force during the war in Lebanon.

Syrians in Lebanon. Although a formidable opponent, Israeli tanks and aircraft knocked down a number of Hinds. A new type, the Hind F, is reportedly armed with a more powerful twin-barrel gun.

Israeli Air Force

Hughes 5000MD Defender (U.S.-built)
A recent addition to the IDF, this small, agile, and powerful anti-tank helicopter came through its first combat action in Lebanon with great success. Armed with four Hughes *Tow* missiles (4000-meter range), the Defender's quiet approach proved a great asset in mountain warfare. Operated with skill and originality by highly trained pilots, it destroyed large numbers of Syrian tanks hiding behind boulders otherwise inaccessible to direct fire. The Defender operated well integrated in the ground formation, but also tied in extremely well with fixed-wing aircraft flying close-support missions. The combined effort resulted in the destruction of many Syrian and PLO targets.

Bell AH-1S Huey Cobra (U.S.-built)
The other IAF anti-tank helicopter, the Bell AH-IS Huey Cobra, was also extremely successful over Lebanon, where its variety of powerful armament came into action. It is a much improved descendant of the U.S. Army Huey Cobra attack gunship of the Vietnam War.

The Bell Huey Cobra was acquired by the IAF after the Yom Kippur War demonstrated the need for a gunship that could be used against tanks and armored infantry.

SURFACE-TO-AIR MISSILES (SAMs) IN THE ARAB-ISRAELI WARS

Arab SAMs (Soviet-built)

For the most part the surface-to-air missiles employed by the Arab forces have been supplied by the Soviet Union. One exception is the United States *Hawk* and its new, up-to-date version, known as the *Improved Hawk* or *I-Hawk*.

In addition to serving with the Israeli Air Force, the *Hawk* can be found in the armed forces of Jordan, Egypt, Saudi Arabia, Morocco, Kuwait, and Iran. Also, several of the North African Arab countries, including Libya, Morocco, and Egypt, are armed with *Crotale,* a French SAM.

In the Yom Kippur War, for example, the committed Arab forces had 1,280 SAM launchers as opposed to 75 Israeli SAM launchers.

SA-2 *Guideline*

Introduced in 1957, this radio commanded missile system covers an altitude of 28 km. Its 130-kg HE warhead is effective at high altitude.

The *Guideline* has seen more action than any other SAM worldwide. Modified, it received the *Fan Song F* radar system in 1968. SAM-2 batteries were destroyed by the IAF in Lebanon.

SA-3 *Goa*

Coming into service in 1964, the *Goa* fires a Mach 3.5, 60-kg HE warhead to 12.5 km altitude, complementing the *Guideline* at low- and medium-altitude layers. Still extensively used by the Soviet air defense in Russia, it operates colocated *Squat Eye* and *Flat Face* radar systems for low-altitude coverage.

SA-5 *Gammon*

First deployed in the USSR in 1963, *Gammon* is a long-range interceptor missile designed to counter the threat of high-performance aircraft. It is effective at medium to high altitudes (30,000 meters), has a long slant range of 300 kilometers, and a maximum speed greater than Mach 3.5. The Russians supplied the SA-5 to Syria at the close of Operation Peace for Galilee, after the PLO forces had been expelled from Lebanon. The stationing of these two-stage solid-propellant SAMs in Syria raised a protest from the United States in early 1983, since the long range and high altitude of these missiles could threaten any aircraft flying over Lebanon and Israel. The principal cities of Tel Aviv, Haifa, Jaffa, and Jerusalem are well within the missile's effective range if positioned in the south of Syria. Obviously a threat of this nature does not contribute to peace; it readily invites a preemptive strike. The latest reports show two operational SA-5 batteries, one placed 12 kilometers south of Damascus and the other near Homs. Each is manned by a Soviet crew of 500 to 600 men. The Russians have threatened to intercede if the IAF attacked the SA-5s.

SA-6 *Gainful*

Fielded in 1967, this became the foremost and deadliest aircraft-killer in the Yom Kippur War. Designed to defeat low-flying aircraft, thus filling a crucial gap in Soviet tactical air defense, it is highly effective between 30 and 18,000 meters. Fully mobile, the *Gainful* launches three missiles with 80-kg HE warheads from a tracked launcher. Cooperating with a tracked *Straight Flush* radar vehicle, similar to the ZSU-23-4, the SA-6 was the main target for the IAF attack in the Bekaa Valley on June 9, 1982.

SA-7 *Grail (Strela)*

Operational since 1966, with a modified version in 1972. It is a man-portable IR homing light anti-aircraft missile, similar to the U.S. *Redeye* concept. Overall weight is 33 lb., minimum altitude 135 ft. (advanced version), maximum 5,000 ft. It was used by the PLO in very large quantities in Lebanon, but only one IAF Skyhawk was hit. The Soviet SA-9 *Gaskin* was developed on this design.

SA-8 *Gecko*

One of the latest Soviet designs in mobile air defense systems is the *Gecko*, first seen in 1974. The wheeled quadruple SA-8 launcher and its multipurpose *Roll* radar mounted on the six-wheeled amphibious vehicle form the first integrated tactical SAM effective at 145 ft. to a 32,800 ft. altitude. Able to fire two missiles simultaneously, it came into action for the first time in Lebanon, and three systems were destroyed by the IAF.

SA-9 *Gaskin*

Also introduced in 1974, this wheeled BRDM-2 mount fires four missiles in two launching containers. The single-stage IR missile is effective on heat-homing targets, i.e., aircraft heading away from the launcher. Its minimum altitude is 65 ft. to a maximum of 16,400 ft. It usually ties in with ZSU-23-4 anti-aircraft artillery defense systems. The *Gaskin* was first introduced to Lebanon by a Libyan contingent and some were destroyed in May 1981 by the IAF. During the Lebanon war, an SA-9 was destroyed by the IAF on the Damascus–Beirut road.

Israeli SAMs (U.S.-built)

Hawk and *Improved Hawk*

Its name is the acronym for its description—*Homing All-the-Way-Killer*. The American-built *Hawk* surface-to-air missile was integrated into the U.S. air defense system in 1959. Five years later it entered Israeli service. An Israeli *Hawk* claimed its first victory in the

The American Hawk SAM is used by several Arab armed forces as well as by the IAF.

Mideast when an attacking Egyptian MiG-21 was shot down on May 24, 1969, from an altitude of 6,700 meters. The *Improved Hawk* is an all-weather, low- to medium-altitude ground-to-air missile system. The improved version, first fielded by the U.S. Army in FY 73, provided advances in fire control, range, lethality, reliability, and effectiveness against jamming over the basic version.

The *I-Hawk* basic element, the firing battery, has two acquisition radars (one to detect medium-altitude targets and another for low altitude), a radar to give range information, a Battery Control Central (housing tactical displays and controls), a data processor, and two or three firing platoons. Each platoon has a tracking radar and three launchers with three ready missiles per launcher.

Hawk uses a high-reliability missile with a high-explosive, proximity-fused warhead that needs only to pass near the target aircraft to destroy it. The system is being kept up to date through a series of planned product improvements. *I-Hawk* resembles the SA-6. Though it is less mobile than the Soviet missile, it has a greater range and altitude.

Appendix VII
Israel—Some Facts and Figures

Official Name: State of Israel

Area: 7,850 square miles (20,325 square kilometers)

Capital: Israel proclaimed Jerusalem (400,000) its capital in 1950; the U.S., like most other countries, maintains its embassy in Tel Aviv. Population figure includes East Jerusalem, which Israel occupied in 1967

Other Major Cities: Greater Tel Aviv (1,158,000); Haifa (534,000)

Type of Government: Parliamentary democracy (the only one in the Middle East)

Population: 3,800,000. Jewish: 85 percent; Arab: 15 percent

Languages: Hebrew, Arabic, English

Literacy Rate: Jewish: 90 percent; Arab: 65 percent

Religions: Judaism, Islam, Christianity, Druse

Per Capita Income: $3,800

Currency: Israeli shekel (IS) which is divided into 100 agorot (sometimes referred to as a grush.) There are coins of 1, 5, and 10 agorot and half-a-shekel; banknotes are IS 1, 5, 10, and 50.

Flag: White field on which is centered a blue six-pointed Star of David bordered above and below by blue horizontal stripes (design based on Jewish prayer shawl)

The State of Israel is an area of 7,850 square miles (20,325 square kilometers) located on the eastern end of the Mediterranean Sea at the meeting point of Asia Minor and Africa. It stretches 260 miles (420 kilometers) from top to bottom.

It is bordered on the west by the Mediterranean, on the north by Lebanon, on the northeast by Syria, on the east by Jordan, and on the south by Egypt.

192

Within the compact country are four distinct regions:

The coastal plain that borders the Mediterranean—the nation has 120 miles of sandy beaches along the sea—and stretches from the Lebanese border to Gaza. This is a fertile, humid region, densely populated, and the location of much of the nation's agriculture.

The central hill region, with mountains nearly 1,200 meters high. To the north are the hills of Galilee; to the south, the Samarian and Judean mountains.

The Jordan Rift Valley, in which is located Lake Tiberias.

The Negev Desert, which comprises some 60 percent of Israel's total area and joins up with the Sinai Desert at the Egyptian border.

Israel, in general, has a Mediterranean climate characterized by a long, hot, dry summer and a short, cool, rainy winter.

In the Negev, there are two seasons: a short, sometimes comfortable spring, and a very hot nine-month summer.

Appendix VIII

A Brief History of Israel

The Middle East is an area rich in history. The birthplace of many civilizations and peoples whose thoughts have influenced others throughout the world, the Middle East is also the area where three of the world's great religions—Judaism, Christianity, and Islam—were founded. But the Middle East has also been an arena of violence from the days of its earliest recorded history up to the present time.

Some of the area's nations have histories dating back more than 4,000 years, while others came on the world scene only as creations of the twentieth century, when foreign domination finally ended.

One of the peoples who have claimed a part of the land as their own for 40 centuries are the Jews, since what is now part of the State of Israel was once the ancient land of Canaan where Judaic tribes first accepted a single, all-powerful God—Yahweh (Jehovah).

This is the land that was promised to Abraham and his descendants according to the Old Testament, the Jews' Book of Books.

King David sat on the throne of Israel. He was followed in the tenth century B.C. by Solomon, who brought ancient Israel to new heights and made it the commercial and intellectual center of the Middle East.

For unknown reasons the kingdom gradually lost its vitality and became easy prey for other tribes. The ancient Kingdom of Israel was conquered by the Assyrians, then by the Babylonians. Under their harsh rule, Jewish leaders were exiled, the people made slaves, and their temples destroyed.

Their belief in their religion was so strong, though, that wherever the Jews went they kept it alive.

Rome next conquered the region. Roman rule of the land they called Palestine was not harsh at first, but when a fanatical Jewish sect known as the Zealots revolted, Jerusalem and the Temple were destroyed. Rather than surrender, the last Zealot survivors died by their own hand at the mountain fortress of Masada. Fewer than 900 Zealots including women, children, and old men, held out for two years against an entire Roman Legion plus reinforcements. When the Roman governor issued laws that repressed their religion even further, Jews revolted again in the Bar Kokhba War of A.D. 132. Later they were forbidden to enter Jerusalem except on the one day of the year when they were allowed to mourn at the remaining fragment of the Temple, its western wall, which became known as the Wailing Wall. (It is called the Western Wall by the Israelis today.)

Jews were dispersed (the Diaspora) throughout the Roman Empire. Some settled in the colonies along the North African coastline, others crossed the strait to settle in Spain, while still others made their way into what is now France and Italy. Wherever they went, they were persecuted, as were the followers of a new religion, Christianity.

As Rome's power waned, some Jews returned

to Palestine, but for the most part the land was taken over by Arabs. By the time the Turkish Ottoman Empire spread across the face of the Middle East in the fourteenth century, Islam had become a firmly established religion for the majority of the people living in Palestine. There were Jewish communities scattered in among the Arab villages; they flourished there as they did elsewhere in the Ottoman Empire.

However, wherever Jews were, they held hope of returning to the land of Israel—the "promised land."

It was not until the founding of the Zionist movement at the end of the 19th century that practical steps were taken toward securing international aid for large-scale Jewish resettlement in Palestine.

In November 1917 a letter that became known as the Balfour Declaration was issued by the British government. The letter stated that the government favored "the establishment in Palestine of a National Home for the Jewish people . . . it being clearly understood that nothing shall be done which may prejudice the civil and religious rights of existing non-Jewish communities in Palestine. . . ."

At the end of World War I Great Britain was given a mandate over Palestine by the League of Nations, which called upon it to aid in the establishment of a Jewish national homeland there.

Following this policy the British permitted the immigration of Jewish families into Palestine in the 1920s, a flow that increased sharply in the 1930s due to Hitler's persecution of German Jews. Palestinian Arabs who had lived on and farmed the land for centuries became increasingly concerned. Their concern led to attacks on Jewish settlements and counterattacks by Jewish guerilla groups. At times the British units in Palestine became targets. At best a very uneasy truce—one frequently broken—existed in the area at the end of the World War II.

Great Britain, unable to find an acceptable solution to the Palestine problem, finally referred the matter to the United Nations in 1947. After months of investigation and testimony the UN adopted a partition plan in November of that year. It called for dividing Palestine into a Jewish state and an Arab state and for establishing Jerusalem as an international city

under United Nations administration.

This plan appealed to no one, however, although the Jewish Agency reluctantly endorsed it, and violence continued. As the end of the British Mandate approached, both sides were prepared for war.

On May 14, 1948, as the last British soldier departed, the State of Israel was proclaimed.

Armed forces from neighboring Arab nations immediately entered Palestine and engaged in open warfare with the defense forces of the new state. After heavy fighting a truce was negotiated under UN auspices, and in 1949 four separate armistice agreements were entered into between Israel and its neighboring states, Egypt, Jordan, Lebanon, and Syria. These agreements only stopped the immediate fighting. Since peace treaties were never signed, the de facto borders of the new state were those of the armistice lines.

Unfortunately, violence continued on both sides. In October 1956, as British and French armed forces mounted operations against Egypt in the Suez Canal area, Israel took advantage of the confusion to invade the Gaza area and the Sinai in order to end an Egyptian arms buildup and terrorist attacks originating from the area.

Once again the UN stepped in to bring peace to the area. The international organization also set up the United Nations Emergency Force (UNEF) in an effort to keep Egyptian and Israeli forces separated in Gaza and the Sinai.

The peace that followed was an uneasy one. Open warfare broke out again in June 1967 between Egyptian and Syrian forces and Israel after the Egyptian leader insisted that the UN forces be removed. At the end of six days of fighting a cease-fire was again obtained by the UN. By this time, however, Israel had occupied all of the Sinai, the Gaza Strip, the Golan (Kuneitra) area of Syria, and the West Bank of the Jordan River, including the eastern sector of Jerusalem, an area that had been occupied since 1948 by Jordan.

Sporadic fighting continued. In early 1969 the UN was again called in to bring a halt to warfare. On October 6, 1973, Syrian forces attacked Israeli positions in the Golan area while Egyptian forces attacked along the Suez Canal. The UN, aided by the diplomacy of the United States, negotiated a cease-fire. This time the way seemed open for productive negotiations.

Suffering and damages had been high on all sides, but one of the greatest tragedies of the years of fighting in the area was the estimated 1.7 million Palestinian Arabs who were now refugees from their homeland and living in camps in adjoining Arab countries.

The efforts of the United States, the United Nations, and other countries to bring about peace in the Middle East were based on the UN Security Council's Resolution 242, which was adopted in November 1967 and was reaffirmed in a later resolution.

Resolution 242 calls for, among other things:

- withdrawal of all Israeli forces from territories occupied in 1967
- the end of all fighting by all parties.
- respect for, and acknowledgment of, the sovereignty, territorial integrity, and political independence of every state in the area
- the right of all peoples in the area to live in peace within secure and recognized boundaries.

The UN resolutions also affirm the need for freedom of navigation for all ships through international waterways in the area and a just settlement of the Palestinian refugee problem.

With the UN resolutions as a cornerstone, the United States has actively pursued efforts to aid Israel and its Arab neighbors negotiate a resolution of their conflict.

The process has not been an easy one. It was not until the Geneva Peace Conference in December 1973 that Arabs and Israelis met face to face to discuss peace. Egyptian-Israeli agreement on disengagement of forces was subsequently achieved as a result of the efforts of the U.S. Israeli forces pulled back from the Suez

Canal in March 1974, permitting Egypt to assume control of both banks of that waterway. Further U.S. efforts led to a Syrian-Israeli disengagement agreement in May 1974. This was followed in 1975 by an Egyptian-Israeli agreement leading to further withdrawal of Israeli forces in the Sinai, limiting the number of units along the new line, and setting up of U.S.-manned observation stations in the Sinai.

One of the most dramatic breakthroughs in the search for peace in the Middle East was the visit by Egypt's president to Israel in November 1977. By this unprecedented official and public act, Egypt became the first Arab state to recognize Israel's right to exist as a state. It also set up the basis for direct talks between the two countries. These led to the Camp David Agreement of 1978, in which Egypt and Israel agreed on a framework for a negotiated peace between them, for a resolution of the Palestinian problem in all its aspects, and for an eventual negotiated peace between Israel and all its Arab neighbors.

After further talks in which the U.S. played a major role, a peace treaty between Israel and Egypt was signed on March 26, 1979, in Washington, D.C., and ratified by the two countries on April 25. Among the accomplishments of the treaty are the recognition for the first time of an international boundary for the State of Israel, Israel's agreement to withdraw fully from the Sinai, the establishment of the diplomatic relations between the two countries, and the right of free passage for Israeli ships through the Suez Canal.

Negotiations on other phases of the Middle East peace, particularly the question of autonomous self-government and eventual final status of the West Bank and Gaza Strip, have continued with U.S. participation since the signing of the treaty.

Appendix IX

A Chronology of Highlights from Biblical Times to the Present

B.C.
1750*   Abraham settles in Canaan
1700–1600   The Israelites migrate from
             Canaan to Egypt
1280   Exodus of Israelites from
             Egypt led by Moses
1280–1250   Israelites wander in Sinai
             Desert; Moses given Ten
             Commandments
1250–1200   Conquest of Canaan
1150–1000   Philistines rise to power
1020–1000   Saul
1000–961   David
961–922   Solomon
922   Division of the realm into the
             Kingdoms of Judah and Israel
722   Samaria falls; kingdom no
             longer divided
621   Deuteronomy
586   Fall of Jerusalem; destruction
             of Temple; Nebuchadnezzar;
             Exile of Jews to Babylon;
             Diaspora—Jews scattered to
             other countries from Palestine
538   Cyrus of Persia conquers

Babylon, grants permission
for Jews to return to
Jerusalem
520–515   Rebuilding of Temple
490   Battle of Marathon
336–323   Alexander the Great
167   Maccabean revolt, leading to
             Jewish independence from the
             Greeks and Syrians
63   Pompey captures Jerusalem;
             beginning of Roman
             overlordship
37–4   Herod the Great

A.D.
c. 0   Birth of Jesus Christ
29   John the Baptist executed
26–36   Pontius Pilate
c. 33   Jesus is crucified
70   Jerusalem destroyed by Titus
70–72   960 Jewish men, women, and
             children hold out at Masada
             for two years against a vastly
             superior military force, the
             entire Tenth Roman Legion
             plus auxiliaries
116   Jews rise up against Trajan
132–135   Bar Kochba Rebellion crushed

---

*This date and some of the others in the B.C. era are approximate.

197

	by Hadrian; start of Great Diaspora		Germany (father of Emancipation; also father of Felix Mendelssohn); published first periodical in Hebrew language
bef. 300	Settlement in Spain		
311–337	Constantine the Great; becomes a Christian in 312		
321	First documentary proofs of Jewish settlement having been established earlier within the Roman Empire (in Germany)	1700	French Jews begin to resettle
		1776	American Revolution; Declaration of Independence
		1791	Jews declared full citizens in France following the French Revolution
622	Hegira, Muhammad's flight; spread of Islam	1812	Prussian Jews emancipated
711	Moslems invade Spain	1815	Battle of Waterloo
732	Battle of Tours; the Franks halt the advance of the Moslems into western Europe	1825–1855	Czar of Russia Nicholas I; severe oppressions
		1848	Immigration of German Jews to U.S.
768–814	Charlemagne; Jews serve at his court	1870	French Jews establish agricultural school near Jaffa, Palestine
1066	Battle of Hastings; Normans conquer Britain		
1206–1227	Genghis Khan conquers much of Asia and eastern Europe	1878	Founding of first agricultural settlement in Palestine
1096	First Crusade; immigration begins to Poland and Russia	1881–1882	Pogroms in Poland and Russia, a continuation of murders and theft; May Laws against Jews; mass migration of Russian Jews to America begins; third and largest wave of Jewish immigration to the U.S.
1215	Magna Carta		
1290	Jews expelled from England		
1348–1349	Black Death; Jews in Germany falsely accused of poisoning wells; immigration to Poland and Russia to escape persecution in Germany		
		1882	First Russian farm settlers arrive in Palestine
1492	Inquisition causes expulsion from Spain; Spanish Inquisition; settlement in Turkey (Palestine), Holland; Moslems driven out of Spain; Columbus discovers America	1883	Baron Edmond de Rothschild supports Jewish agriculture in Palestine
		1860–1904	Theodore Herzl (founder of Zionism)
1519–1522	Magellan circumnavigates the globe	1891	Jews expelled from Moscow
		1894–1895	Dreyfus affair in France; Emile Zola's *J'Accuse* leads to complete vindication of Jewish officer in French Army
1648–1655	Chmielnicky massacres of Jews in Russia and Poland; mass murders		
1654	First Jewish settlement in America	1901	Jewish National Fund established to purchase land in Palestine
1655	First synagogue in U.S.; first stream of immigration (Sefardim)	1903	Wright brothers make first flight in a powered airplane
1656	Oliver Cromwell invites Jews to return to England; Puritan Revolution	1907	First Jewish defense units in Palestine organized
1729–1786	Moses Mendelssohn in	1909	Hashomer established as settlement guards

1910	Establish first kibbutz (Degania)
1914–1918	World War I; Zion Mule Corps in action at Gallipoli; airplanes engage in aerial combat for first time
1916	David Ben-Gurion sails for America after expulsion from Palestine; Chaim Weizman, Nobel Prize laureate, assumes leadership of Zionist movement in England
1917	Balfour Declaration promises Palestine as a homeland for the Jews; U.S. enters war; Jabotinsky joins British Army; Jewish Battalions of Royal Fusiliers organized in Britain, Canada, and Egypt; Gen. Allenby's troops advance into Judea
1919	Brutal pogroms against Jews in the Ukraine
1920	Haganah replaces Hashomer as defense force; Britain given Palestine Mandate and France the Syrian Mandate; France separates Lebanon from Syria and expels Feisal; Sir Herbert Samuel, a British Jew, appointed first high commissioner of Palestine
1921	Britain separates Transjordan including Judea and Samaria, parts of biblical Israel— today's West Bank from Palestine and names Abdullah king; his brother, Feisal, named king of Iraq
1922	British Colonial Secretary Winston Churchill excludes Transjordan from the Jewish National Home policy; new villages established in reclaimed Jezreel Valley
1924	Economic crisis and resultant anti-Jewish laws encourage new migration from Poland
1927	Lindbergh makes first nonstop flight across the Atlantic
1932	Since the end of the war 95,000 Jews emigrated from England to Palestine; the following year immigration to Israel was swelled by 30,000 more German Jews escaping from Hitler
1933–1945	Adolph Hitler, Nazi German dictator; the systematic murder of six million European Jews
1939–1945	World War II; Jewish troops serve in all Allied armies, navies, and air forces; Jewish Brigade in British Army; 26,000 Palestinian Jews in military service
1934	Immigration continues to rise by 42,000 more, although now being limited; *Velos* first illegal immigrant ship
1939	Haganah members imprisoned for marksmanship training
1940	British laws restrict Jews from purchasing land in Palestine
1941	Palmach units of Haganah join British in invasion of Syria
1945	Arab League established
1946	Jewish leaders arrested in Palestine, Haganah goes on the offensive; Irgun Zvai Leumi, under leadership of Menachem Begin, blows up King David Hotel; Jewish refugees interned in Cyprus as illegal immigrants
1947	Refugee ship *Exodus* denied entry to Palestine; Sherut Avir (Air Service) established
1948	British Mandate ends; David Ben-Gurion proclaims State of Israel and heads provisional government; the new nation is invaded by combined Arab armies; start of War of Independence; new state recognized by U.S. and USSR. Establishment of Israeli Defense Force (Zahal) and the Israeli Air Force (Cheyl Ha Avir)

1949	Chaim Weizmann elected and sworn in as first president of the State of Israel; UN admits Israel as 59th member
1956	Suez campaign; Israel, with French and British allies, invades Egypt to break the blockade of the Gulf of Aqaba and the Egyptian seizure of the Suez Canal
1967	The Six-Day War; the IAF's "finest hour"
1969–1970	War of Attrition; first Israeli contact with Soviet SAMs
1973	Yom Kippur War; Arab-employed Soviet surface-to-air missiles take serious toll on IAF; both sides are resupplied by massive airlift from major allies
1976	IAF's impossible rescue at Entebbe, Uganda
1981	The Cheyl Ha Avir neutralizes Iraqi nuclear reactor in Baghdad
1982	Operation Peace for Galilee, the invasion of Lebanon in pursuit of PLO terrorists, Israel's sixth major war since 1948; the IAF achieves one of its greatest victories, shooting down 85 Syrian MiGs and destroying 23 SAM batteries without the loss of a solitary Israeli aircraft in air-to-air combat.

Appendix X
Religions of Israel

In addition to being a melting pot for Jews from around the world, Israel is also a nation of different religions.

Jerusalem, for example, is a city sacred to Jews, Christians, and Moslems. This is the city where the stones of the Western Wall of the Temple are visited annually by tens of thousands of Jews. It also holds the Church of the Holy Sepulchre, the awe-inspiring destination for Christians who live in or visit the country. And this is the third holiest city in the world to Moslems, who make their pilgrimage to the Dome of the Rock mosque.

The major religions among the citizens of Israel are Judaism, Islam, and Christianity.

JUDAISM

An estimated 16 million people practice this religion, one of the oldest in the world. It is the predominant religion in Israel. In fact, Judaism is more than a religion; it is a way of life. Six Jewish holidays are celebrated as national holidays in Israel, and certain Jewish religious laws are part of the national law of the country.

Judaism bases its creed on the experiences of Jews for the past 4,000 years, beginning with Abraham, and was the first religion to teach belief in one God.

Judaism has its basis in two works—the Old Testament's *Pentateuch*, the first five books of the Bible, known as the *Torah* in the Hebrew language; and the *Talmud*, a collection of centuries-old teachings and interpretations that have been handed down from generation to generation. The *Torah* contains the legends of its own origin. According to these beliefs, God gave the Ten Commandments and the *Torah* to Moses on Mount Sinai as the Jews camped in the wilderness after being freed from Egyptian bondage.

The original Ten Commandments were added to until the laws covered every aspect of a believer's life. The *Talmud* is, in effect, an extension to the Ten Commandments designed to meet conditions that Jews faced in later times.

There is no central religious leader in Judaism. Each congregation governs itself; rabbis are laymen, not priests.

Generally speaking, Judaism can be separated into Orthodox Judaism, Conservative Judaism, and Reform Judaism.

In some Jewish communities the Sabbath is strictly observed. No manual work is permitted, meals are cooked ahead of the day, and Jewish families leave their homes only to go to the synagogue. Individuals driving cars into these communities during the Sabbath observance have been attacked with stones.

ISLAM

Islam, derived from the Arabic word *aslama*—submission—is the second largest religion in the world, with more than 600 million followers. The religion was founded by Muhammad, who is revered as the last prophet of their one great God, Allah. The simplicity of the religion, which started in A.D. 610, appealed from the first to the desert dwellers in what is now Saudi Arabia. Muhammad received the contents of Islam's Holy Book, the *Qur'an* (Koran), from the Archangel Gabriel.

Within 100 years after the founder's death in 632, Islam had spread throughout the Middle East and into North Africa, Spain, and eastern Europe.

With the death of Muhammad, there occurred a religious split that continues to this day. Sunni Muslims believe that the leadership of Islam can pass to any individual according to merit, in much the same manner as the leadership of desert tribes is decided. Shia (Shiite) Muslims believe that only direct descendants of Muhammad through his daughter, Fatima, and her husband, Ali, should be leaders of Islam.

Whatever their sect, Muslims practice the five main duties required by the *Qur'an*, namely:

- reciting and believing in the Islamic creed that "There is no god but God, and Muhammad is His Prophet"
- praying five times a day
- giving of money to those less fortunate
- fasting during the holy month of Ramadan
- completing a pilgrimage to the holy city of Mecca during the follower's lifetime.

CHRISTIANITY

An estimated one billion persons are followers of the various denominations of Christianity.

This religion is based on the teachings of Jesus of Nazareth, who was born in Bethlehem. He was one of the early followers of John the Baptist, who preached of a new kind of life marked by repentance for past wrongdoings. Jesus took this message to the cities of Judea, where he faced not only ridicule from the people but persecution from the Roman soldiers.

His primary commandment was to believe in God and through this belief to take part in doing the work of God among fellow men. Jesus spoke to the common man and woman, often using parables to make his points and illustrate his teachings. He stressed the virtues of meekness and aid to the poor. To Jesus the Kingdom of God was the ultimate goal, and this Kingdom did not depend on a certain time or place.

The Christian religion is based on the belief that Jesus was the son of God, that He was born to save the world and was crucified for His teachings, but was resurrected and will return on the last day of the world to judge humanity.

The denominations of Christianity that have developed over the centuries since its founding can be generally categorized as:

- the Catholic Church, with its Roman, Alexandrian, Maronite, Antiochene, Chaldean, Armenian, and Byzantine rites
- the Protestant churches, which include Lutherans, Anglicans, Presbyterians, Baptists, and Methodists as major groups
- the Eastern Orthodox Church, which was formed after disputes with Rome as a result of the splitting of the Roman Empire

DRUSE

An estimated 300,000 followers of the Druse religion live in the Middle East. In Israel they number about 35,000 and are found mostly in villages in the Galilee and Carmel range. The Druse are forbidden to reveal the secret doctrines they follow; only the *uggal*—sages—can pass on the teachings of their God, *al-Hakim bi-Amr Allah*, the sixth caliph of the Fatimid dynasty of Egypt. The Druse religion is an offshoot of Islam. The Druse serve in the Israel Defense Force.

Index